Audrey Davids
1997

Audrey Davids
1997

English Song 1600–1675

Facsimiles of Twenty-six Manuscripts and an Edition of the Texts

Edited with Introductions by
Elise Bickford Jorgens
Western Michigan University

A Garland Series

Contents of the Set

1. **British Library Manuscripts, Part I**
   Add. Ms. 15117
   Egerton Ms. 2971
   Add. Ms. 24665 (Giles Earle's Songbook)
   Add. Ms. 29481, ff. 2–26v

2. **British Library Manuscripts, Part II**
   Add. Ms. 10337 ("Elizabeth Rogers hir Virginal Booke: Februarye ye 27, 1656"), ff. 20v–23, 26v–27, 35v–37, 41v, 46v–60
   Egerton Ms. 2013
   Add. Ms. 31432 (William Lawes's Autograph)

3. **British Library Manuscripts, Part III**
   Add. Ms. 53723 (Henry Lawes's Autograph)

4. **British Library Manuscripts, Part IV**
   Add. Ms. 11608
   Add. Ms. 32339 (John Gamble Songs)

5. **British Library Manuscripts, Part V**
   Add. Ms. 29396 (Songs in the Hand of Edward Lowe)

6. **Manuscripts at Oxford, Part I**
   Christ Church Ms. 439
   Tenbury 1018, ff. 7v–8, 10, 11v–12, 30v, 33–48
   Tenbury 1019
   Christ Church Ms. 87 ("Mrs. Elizabeth Davenant, her book," 1624)
   Bodleian Library Music School Ms. F. 575
   Bodleian Library Ms. Don.c.57

7. **Manuscripts at Oxford, Part II**
   Bodleian Library Ms. Mus. b.1

8. **Edinburgh University Library Manuscript**
   Ms. Dc.I.69 (Songs in the Hand of Edward Lowe)

9. **New York Public Library Manuscripts, Part I**
   Drexel Ms. 4041

10. **New York Public Library Manuscripts, Part II**
    Drexel Ms. 4257 (John Gamble, "His booke, amen 1659")

11. **Miscellaneous Manuscripts**
    Edinburgh, National Library of Scotland, Advocate's Library Ms. 5.2.14 (Leyden Manuscript)
    Cambridge, Trinity College Ms. R. 16. 29 (Songs by George Handford)
    London, Lambeth Palace Ms. 1041 (Songbook Belonging to "The Lady Ann Blount")
    New York, New York Public Library Drexel Ms. 4175 ("Ann Twice, Her Booke")

12. **The Texts of the Songs**

3

British Library Manuscripts, Part III

Add. Ms. 53723 (Henry Lawes's Autograph)

INTRODUCTION BY
Elise Bickford Jorgens

Garland Publishing, Inc.
New York & London 1986

Introduction copyright © 1986 by Elise Bickford Jorgens

Library of Congress Cataloging-in-Publication Data

Lawes, Henry, 1596–1662.
  [Songs. Selections]
  Add. ms. 53723 : Henry Lawes's autograph.

  (English song, 1600–1675 ; 3) (British Library manuscripts ; pt. 3)
   Songs for voice and continuo.
   English (principally) and Italian words.
   1. Songs with continuo. I. Jorgens, Elise Bickford.
II. British Library. Manuscript. Add. 53723.
III. Title. IV. Series. V. Series: British Library manuscripts ; pt. 3.
M2.E65 1986 pt. 3 [M1620]   86-752721
ISBN 0-8240-8233-8 (alk. paper)

Design by Jonathan Billing

The volumes in this series have been printed on acid-free, 250-year-life paper.

Printed in the United States of America

Introduction

London,
British Library,
Add. Ms. 53723

Henry Lawes's Autograph Manuscript is an impressive volume containing 325 songs in large folio format. Pamela J. Willetts, whose excellent catalogue and study is crucial to anyone working with the manuscript, speculates that Lawes began entering his songs in the volume before 1626, when he entered the Chapel Royal, and continued until sometime around 1652, when John Playford started publishing them. The placement of his songs for Milton's *Comus* (Nos. 74–78) and of several containing topical allusions to people and events through the 1630s and 40s supports a chronological ordering. The exceptions are the songs entered at the bottoms of pages not filled up by the original songs, often on staff lines drawn in by hand, which are probably later additions. *Every* song, whether in the original ordering or squeezed into an unused space, bears Henry Lawes's signature at its start.

This manuscript looks as if its principal contents were entered as fair copy upon completion of individual songs. Some corrections appear, but in general the copy is very clean. In some instances, however, Lawes has included new copies of songs with only slight alterations, typically in rhythmic placement of the text or in ornamentation. An interesting example is "Unto the soundles vaultes of Hell," which appears first on f. 8 and then again on f. 11, the tune identical except for a few rhythmic and ornamental details, but in a different clef. More significantly, the second copy has a new bass line that alters the harmony at a few key points (see, for example, the cadences of the first and sixth phrases). In another instance ("Feare not deere loue," ff. 102 and 114) the second copy is transposed to another key, perhaps for a student for whom the first did not lie well.

Details like these prove this a working manuscript as well as a repository for completed songs. The years 1622–51 saw a hiatus in the publication of secular solo song in England, although clearly their production continued to flourish. Given these conditions, a composer-teacher had to provide his own copies for immediate use as well as for posterity.

The contents of the volume include nearly all of Lawes's solo songs. Many of them appeared after 1651 in Playford's publications, in collections devoted exclusively to Lawes's songs and in miscellanies put together by Playford. But for some songs (the *Comus* songs, for instance) this is our only source. Furthermore, the near-complete nature of the collection allows us to view the variety of Lawes's output in this genre, from the many lighthearted (some, indeed, might say silly), tuneful airs, typically in triple meter, to the extended, highly dramatic, declamatory laments linking his work with that of the Italian monodists a generation earlier.

Lawes's oeuvre is especially notable for the poets and playwrights whose lyrics he set: Sidney, Spenser, Sandys, Carew, Harington, Herrick, Herbert, Jonson, Milton, Suckling, Beaumont, Fletcher, Cartwright, Davenant, Townsend, Waller, Strode, Shirley, Lovelace, and—one must add—Henry Hughes, for whose pastoral lyrics Lawes seems to have had a special fondness; all these and more make up the texts of this remarkably literary collection. Lawes is known to history more for his relationship with poets and his care in setting their words to music than for the music itself, and the manuscript's contents bear out that dimension of his renown.

Bibliography

General Chan, Mary. *Music in the Theatre of Ben Jonson*. Oxford, 1980.
Doughtie, Edward, ed. *Lyrics from English Airs, 1596–1622*. Cambridge, MA, 1970.
Ford, Wyn K. *Music in England before 1800: A Select Bibliography*. London, 1967.
Greer, David. "Songbooks, 1500–1660." *New Cambridge Bibliography of English Literature*. 5 Vols. Cambridge, 1969–77.
Hollander, John. *The Untuning of the Sky: Ideas of Music in English Poetry, 1500–1700*. Princeton, 1961.
Hughes-Hughes, Augustus. *Catalogue of Manuscript Music in the British Museum*. Vol. II, Secular Vocal Music. London, 1908.
Jones, Edward Huws. "'To sing and play the base-violl alone': The Bass Viol in English Seventeenth Century Song." *Lute Society Journal* (1975) 17–23.
Jorgens, Elise Bickford. *The Well-Tun'd Word: Musical Interpretations of English Poetry, 1597–1651*. Minneapolis, 1982.
North, Nigel. *Thoroughbass Accompaniment for the Lute, Archlute, and Theorbo*. London, forthcoming.
Schleiner, Louise. *The Living Lyre in English Verse from Elizabeth through the Restoration*. Columbia, MO, 1984.
Spink, Ian. *English Song, Dowland to Purcell*. New York, 1974.
———. "Sources of English Song, 1620–1660: A Survey." *Miscellanea Musicologica* (1966) 117–36.
Swanekamp, Joan, compiler. *English Ayres: A Selectively Annotated Bibliography and Discography*. Westport, CT, 1984.
Willetts, Pamela J. *Handlist of Music Manuscripts Acquired 1908–67: The British Museum*. London, 1970.

On British Library, Add. Ms. 53723 Applegate, Joan S. *The Henry Lawes Autograph Manuscript: B.M. Loan 35*. Ph.D. Dissertation, Univ. of Rochester, Eastman School of Music. 1966.
Emslie, McDonald. "Milton on Lawes: the Trinity MS Revisions" in *Music in English Renaissance Drama*, ed. John H. Long. Lexington, KY: 1969. Pp. 96–102.
Evans, C. "Cartwright's Debt to Lawes" in *Music in English Renaissance Drama*, ed. John H. Long. Lexington, KY: 1969. Pp. 103–16.
Evans, Willa McClung. "Henry Lawes and Charles Cotton." *Publications of the Modern Language Association* (1938) 724–29.
———. *Henry Lawes, Musician and Friend of Poets*. New York: Kraus Reprint, 1966. First printed 1941.
Hart, Eric Ford. "An Introduction to Henry Lawes." *Music and Letters* (1951) 217–25 and 328–44.
McGrady, R. J. "Henry Lawes and the Concept of 'Just Note and Accent.'" *Music and Letters* (1969) 86–102.
Willetts, Pamela J. *The Henry Lawes Manuscript*. London, 1969.

Contents

London, British Library, Add. Ms. 53723 (Henry Lawes's Autograph)

1. I Rise, & greive, I walke & se my sorrow	f. 3
2. My Lute, wthin thy Selfe, thy tunes enclose	f. 3v
3. Greife com away and doe not thou refuse	f. 4
4. Though my torment farr Exceedes	f. 4v
5. O y^t Joye soe soone should waste	f. 5
6. Ah loue! where is thy Abydinge	f. 5v
7. Speake, speake, at last replye	f. 5v
8. Or you, or I! Nature did wronge!	f. 6
9. Marke well this stone! it hydes a precious tresure!	f. 6v
10. Hard harted faire, if thou wilt not consent [another copy f. 19]	f. 6v
11. If I freely may discouer	f. 7
12. One wth Admiration tolde me	f. 7v
13. Unto the soundles vaultes of Hell below [another copy f. 11]	f. 8
14. Deere, thy face is Heau'n to me	f. 8
15. As on a daye Clorinda fayre was bathinge	f 8v
16. When I Adore you and you haue me in scorne	f. 9
17. Fye awaye fye what meane you by this	f. 9v
18. O let me groane one word into thyne Eare	f. 10
19. Sweet staye a whyle whye doe you Rise	f. 10v
20. Unto the Soundles vaults of hell below [see f. 8; some variants in both treble and bass]	f. 11
21. O sweet woodes, y^e delight of Sollitarines	f. 11v
22. Falce loue awaye, & all my sighes send back	f. 12
23. Thou by y^e pleasant springe shalt lye	f. 12
24. I loud [= loved] thee once I'le loue noe more	f. 12v
25. Disdaine me not sweet loue though I be Ould	f. 12v
26. Must I in my most Hopefull yeares, at once refraine	f. 13
27. Sweet Lady & sole mistres of my loue	f. 13v
28. Oh, Oh, where shall I lament	f. 14
29. Breake Hart in twayne, fayre Ronile may se [another copy f. 31]	f. 14v
30. Twixt hope & feare ye best affection Sits; A Dialogue	f. 15
31. Can soe much beautye Owne a Mynde	f. 15v
32. Transcendent beautye, thou y^t Art	f. 16
33. Since ev'rye man I com Amonge [bass incomplete]	f. 16v
34. More then most fayre [bass incomplete]	f. 17

ix

35. Sweet louely Nimphe, whose eyes doe moue me; A Dialogue	f. 17v
36. Woe is mee, woe is mee, y^t I from Israell	f. 18
37. Like to ye damaske Rose you see	f. 18v
38. Hard harted fayre if thou wilt not consent [see f. 6v; some variants in both treble and bass]	f. 19
39. Weep not my Deere, for I shall goe	f. 19v
40. Sleep Ould man let Sylence Charme thee	f. 20
41. Sweet I Am not Come too soone	f. 20v
42. Sorrow, in vayne, why doost thou seeke to Tempt	f. 21
43. Wherfore peepst thou Envious daye	f. 21v
44. Sweet doe not frowne on me though I must goe	f. 22
45. Sacred Flora Crowne this ffeild	f. 22v
46. Haue I watcht the winters Nyght	f. 23
47. Slyde Softe, yea Siluer floods	f. 23v
48. If my Mistris fyx her Eye	f. 24
49. Doe not delaye me though you haue the powre	f. 24v
50. Celia, thy sweet Angels face [another copy f. 65]	f. 25
51. Though you on seas in stormes haue bin	f. 25v
52. I haue praysd wth all my skill	f. 26
53. Rejoyce whyle in thy youth thou Art	f. 26v
54. What man would sojourne heer	f. 27
55. Harke how ye Nightingale displayes	f. 27v
56. Sweet death com vissit my sicke hart	f. 28
57. She is too Cruell, alas too Cruell	f. 28v
58. Seest thou those dyamonds wch she weares	f. 29
59. Ile tell you how ye rose	f. 29v
60. You are fayre, and louely too	f. 30
61. Be not proud, nor coye nor cruell	f. 30v
62. Breake Eart in twayne [see f. 14v; some variants]	f. 31
63. I prithee Sweet to me be kinde	f. 31v
64. Giue back my hart againe to me	f. 32
65. My sweetest Byrde that Art incaged heere	f. 32v
66. 'Tis Christmas now, 'tis Christmas now	f. 33
67. Why should Only man be tyde	f. 33v
68. Cease, sorrow cease, & doe noe More torment	f. 34
69. Hence vayne delights be gone	f. 34v
70. Though Cupid be a God, Alass hee's but a boye	f. 35
71. Cupid thou Art a sluggish boye	f. 35v
72. Deere leave thy home, and com wth me	f. 36
73. Beautyes haue yee seene a Toye	f. 36v

74. From ye Heau'ns, now I flye [bass incomplete]	f. 37
75. Sweet Eccho, sweetest Nimphe that liu'st vnseene	f. 37v
76. Sabrina, Sabrina fayre, listne where thou Art Sittinge	f. 38
77. Back shepperds Back	f. 38
78. Now my taske is smoothly done	f. 39
79. Out uppon it I haue lou'de	f. 39v
80. Com my Sweet whylst eu'rye strayne	f. 40
81. Com from the Dungeon to the Throne	f. 40v
82. Com heauye Soules, Oppressed wth ye weight of Crymes	f. 41
83. Staye, staye Ould Tyme, repose thy Restles winges	f. 41v
84. Whyther soe gladly and soe fast	f. 42
85. Bacchus, I-Accus, fill our braines	f. 42v
86. Goe Naked truth, and let thy bashfull teares	f. 43
87. Haue pittye Greife	f. 43v
88. Wooe then the Heauens	f. 43v
89. Cruell! but once againe	f. 44
90. Deere turne a waye thyne Eyes soe bright	f. 44v
91. O smoother me to death	f. 44v
92. Ould poets Hypocreene Admyre	f. 45
93. Wert thou yet fayrer then thou Art	f. 45v
94. Whyther Are all her falce Oathes blowne	f. 46
95. Death cannot yet Extinguish that entyre pure flame	f. 46v
96. What shall I doe I'ue lost my hart	f. 47
97. I am confirmde a woman can	f. 47v
98. See see how careles men are growne	f. 48
99. Cast a way those silkne clouds	f. 48v
100. Set to ye sun a Dyall yt doth pass	f. 49
101. Amoret, the Milkye waye	f. 49v
102. 'Tis but a frowne, I prithee let me dye	f. 50
103. Behold and listne whylst ye faire	f. 50v
104. Tell me not I my tyme Mispend	f. 51
105. Will you know my mistris face	f. 51v
106. Pale Inke, thou art not black Enough of hew	f. 52
107. Noe Noe faire Herritick	f. 52v
108. When thou faire Celia like the Setting Sunn	f. 53v
109. Thy beauty Israell	f. 54
110. Com O Com I brooke noe staye	f. 54v
111. Keep on yor veile & hyde yor Eye	f. 55
112. O Now the Certaine cause I know	f. 55v
113. Lou'ly Cloris though thyne Eyes	f. 56
114. Sure thou framed wert by Art	f. 56v

xi

115. Restles Streame thy self persuinge	f. 57
116. Com, com sad Turtle Mateles Moaninge	f. 57v
117. Faine would I Cloris (Ere I dye)	f. 58
118. Come Louers All to mee, and Cease yor Mourninge	f. 58v
119. Was it A forme, A Gate, a grace	f. 59
120. Staye, staye Aeneas, for thyne Owne sake staye	f. 59v
121. Admit thou darlinge of myne Eyes [treble only]	f. 60
122. Deerest doe not Now delaye me	f. 60v
123. Why stayes my floramell where Loue	f. 61
124. Sweet Morphe Lend a feelinge Eare	f. 61v
125. Once Venus Cheekes y^t shamde the Morne	f. 62
126. Ladyes, you y^t seeme soe Nice [treble only]	f. 62v
127. If you can finde a Hart Sweet Loue to kill	f. 63
128. I doe confess th'art smooth and faire	f. 63v
129. Tell me noe more tis Loue	f. 64
130. Ah, ah ye falce fatall tale I read	f. 64v
131. Celia, thy Sweet Angels face [see f. 25; variants in rhythm]	f. 65
132. Sleep, sleep Softe, you Colde clay Cindars	f. 65v
133. Deere throw y^t flattringe glass a way	f. 66
134. Greeue not deere Loue, all though we Often part	f. 66v
135. Hither we com into this world of woe	f. 67
136. Yes, yes, 'tis Cloris singes, 'tis she	f. 67v
137. What Meanes this Straungnes now of late	f. 68
138. Swift through ye yeildinge Ayre I glyde	f. 68v
139. Not that I wish my Misteris or more or less	f. 69
140. Would you know what's softe	f. 69v
141. Am I dispisde because you saye	f. 70
142. Her Eyes, wch all ye world but me	f. 70v
143. Sees not My Loue how Tyme resumes	f. 71
144. Cupid as he Laye amonge roses	f. 71v
145. One sylent Night of Late	f. 72
146. My Mistris blushde and ther wth all	f. 72v
147. Amarillis, by A springes (softe and soule Meltinge,) Murmeringes slept	f. 73
148. Goe, hunt the whyte Ermin	f. 73v
149. When thou art dead, and thinkst to com into Elizium	f. 74v
150. Bid me but liue ["to" amended to "but"]	f. 75
151. About the Sweet Bagg of a Bee	f. 75v
152. Heau'n & Beautye are aly'de	f. 76
153. Com louly Phillis, Since it thy will is	f. 76v

154. Farwell faire Sainct, May not ye Seas	f. 77
155. Amonge the Myrtles as I walk'de	
Also Thou shepperd, whose Intentiue Eye;	
A Second Dittye to the former Ayre	f. 78
156. The God of Loue my shepperd is	f. 78v
157. Venus Redres a wronge thats done	f. 79
158. Canst thou Loue me and yet doubt	f. 79v
159. When wee were parted	f. 80
160. Aske me why I send you heere	f. 80v
161. Com Cloris, Hye we to yᵉ Bowre	f. 81
162. Celia turnes away her Eyes	f. 81v
163. Cloris, since my death doth com from you	f. 82
164. Where shall my Troubled soule	f. 82v
165. A Louer Once I did Espye	f. 83v
166. Thou art soe faire, & younge wᵗʰall	f. 84
167. Till now I never did beleiue	f. 84v
168. Must we be devyded now	f. 85
169. Though my Bodye be restrain'd	f. 85v
170. Whyle I listne to thy voice	f. 86
171. Noe, she ne're lou'de, twas the excess of myne	f. 86v
172. Lately on yonder swellinge Bush	f. 87
173. It is not that I loue you less	f. 87v
174. Not Careinge to Oberue the wynde	f. 88v
175. Loue Chill wᵗʰ Colde & missinge in the skies	f. 89v
176. Our sighes are heard	f. 90
177. Phillis why should we delaye	f. 90v
178. I loue thee for thy ficklnes & great Inconstancye	f. 91
179. Loue thee, good faith not I	f. 91v
180. Saye, must wee part, Sweet mercies bless us both	f. 92
181. Those Curious locks soe Aptly twynde	f. 95
182. Hence vaine intruder haste awaye	f. 95v
183. Goe thou gentle whis'pringe winde	f. 96
184. Careles of loue & free from feares	f. 96v
185. I'le Gaze noe more on her bewitchinge face	f. 97
186. I burne, and cruell you (in vayne)	f. 97v
187. If the Quick spirrits in yoʳ Eye	f. 99
188. How ill doth he deserue a louers Name	f. 99v
189. All yᵉ workes of Nature are defectiue	f. 100
190. You that thinke Loue can convaye	f. 100v
191. Cloris, since first our Calme of peace was frighted	f. 101

xiii

192. Happye youth, that shalt posses	f. 101v
193. Feare not deere loue y^t Ile reveale [another copy, transposed, f. 114]	f. 102
194. Let fooles, great Cupids yoake disdaine	f. 102v
195. If when ye sun at Noone displayes	f. 103
196. When this flye Liu'de	f. 103v
197. Wonder not though I am blynde [treble only]	f. 104v
198. I prithee Loue take heed	f. 105
199. He y^t Loues a rosye cheeke [treble only]	f. 105v
200. Reade in these roses, ye sad stourye	f. 106v
201. Vnfolde thyne Armes & let me goe [another copy f. 122v]	f. 107
202. Ladyes fly from Loues smooth tale	f. 107v
203. Gaze not on thy beautyes pryde [continues on f. 108v]	f. 109
204. When on ye Alter of My Hand	f. 109v
205. When thou, poore Excomunicate	f. 110
206. I was foretolde yor Rebell sex	f. 110v
207. Delicate Beautye whye should you disdayne	f. 111
208. Harke, harke how my Celia [treble only]	f. 111v
209. Seeke not to know my Loue	f. 112v
210. Noe More blinde God	f. 113v
211. Feare not deere Loue [see f. 102; bass incomplete]	f. 114
212. Know Celia, since thou art soe proude	f. 114v
213. Giue me more Loue or more disdayne	f. 115
214. Staye Coward blood	f. 115v
215. That lov'lye spott	f. 116v
216. Poor Pensive I O're Chargde wth woe	f. 117v
217. Sweetly breathinge vernall Aire	f. 118
218. Wherfore doe thy Sad Numbers flow [treble only]	f. 118v
219. Looke sweetest Doris	f. 119v
220. Still Amathea thou art fayre	f. 120
221. Taught from yor Artfull straines my faire	f. 120v
222. In Celia's face a Question did arise	f. 121
223. Had I a Trumpet, and that Trumpet Fames	f. 121v
224. Unfolde thyne Armes & let me goe [see f. 107; slight rhythmic and ornamental variants]	f. 122v
225. Cloris farwell I now must goe	f. 123
226. Greedye Louer pause a whyle	f. 123v
227. Theseous! o theseus! heark! but yet in vaine; Ariadne deserted by Theseus sittinge uppon a Rock in ye Island Naxos. Thus Complaines [incomplete]	f. 124
228. Beautye Once blasted wth the ffrost of Age	f. 128

xiv

229. To loue thee w^{th}out flattrye were a sinn	f. 128v
230. I prithee send me back my hart	f. 129
231. Whye up soe earlye in ye world; to ye first Object y^t Euer gaue true content	f. 129v
232. Forgiue me loue, what haue I done?; A Recantation	f. 130
233. Com, Com thou gloryous Object of my Syght	f. 130v
234. To man that was i'th Eu'ninge made	f. 131v
235. They that never had the vse	f. 132
236. Though thou hast witt and beautye too	f. 132v
237. Ha! Posanes, by my loss of peace 'tis shee!	f. 133
238. Gaze not on Swans	f. 135
239. On a cleere morne as phoebus run his Race	f. 135v
240. In Loue! away, you doe me wronge	f. 136
241. O let me still, & sylent lye	f. 136v
242. Be not proud, cause faire and trymme	f. 137v
243. Noe, noe I never was in loue	f. 138
244. Fond woman thou mistakst thy marke	f. 138v
245. Let me alone, I'le loue noe more	f. 139
246. Imbre Lachrymarum Largo; An Eccho	f. 139v
247. As sad Amintor in A Meadow laye	f. 141
248. Oh, now I fynde tis nought but fate	f. 141v
249. Thrice happye is that Humble payre	f. 142
250. Stand still yee floods	f. 142v
251. When you the Sun-burnt Pilgrim see	f. 143
252. Tell mee yee wandringe Spirrits of ye Ayre	f. 144
253. Cloris now thou art fled awaye	f. 144v
254. The Chyldishe God of Loue did sweare	f. 145
255. Take heed bould Louer doe not Looke	f. 145v
256. Haue you eare Seene the Morninge Sunn	f. 146
257. Cloris when I to thee present	f. 146v
258. By all thy Gloryes willingly I goe	f. 147
259. My wandringe Thoughts haue Travelde Rounde	f. 147v
260. O del Sol piu Luccente, Echi non brama	f. 148
261. Lasso, perche mi fuggi	f. 148v
262. Amarantha sweet and Fayre	f. 149
263. What! wilt thou pyne, or fall awaye	f. 149v
264. If to be Absent, were to be, Awaye from thee	f. 150
265. See Cloris See how Nature bringes	f. 150v
266. See, see! my Cloris, my Cloris comes; Amintor Sittinge on a Rock Expectinge Cloris	f. 151
267. O I Am Sick, I am Sick to death	f. 152

xv

268. Take heed Fayre Cloris how you Tame	f. 153
269. Staye, staye, you Greedye Merchants staye	f. 153v
270. O Tell me Loue, O tell me Fate	f. 154
271. How happi'art thou & I	f. 154v
272. How Cruels Love when shees too kinde	f. 155
273. If thou dost Loue me as thou sayst	f. 155v
274. Goe little winged Archer & convay	f. 156
275. Beautye & Loue, once fell at Ods	f. 156v
276. Mourne, mourne wth me	f. 157
277. Cloris, when eare you doe Intend	f. 157v
278. When as Leander, (younge) was drownde	f. 158
279. Noe Falce, noe Faithles Lindamore	f. 158v
280. Now I greiue that I am well	f. 159
281. Begone, begone, thou perjurde man	f. 159v
282. On this Swellinge Banke	f. 160
283. Her Eyes the Glow-worme Lend thee	f. 160v
284. Let Longinge Louers sit and pyne	f. 161
285. How Coole and Temp'rate I am Growne	f. 161v
286. Com Cloris Leaue thy wand'ringe sheepe	f. 162
287. Harke! harke how Belona Thunders	f. 162v
288. Help! help! o help! devinitye of Loue; A Sea Storme	f. 163
289. Noe more of Loue, noe More of Hate [alternative melody f. 164v]	f. 165
290. How Longe shall I A Martyr be	f. 165v
291. Since Fate Commaunds me hence	f. 166
292. Blacke as thy Louely Eyes	f. 166v
293. Did I once Saye that thou wert fayre	f. 167
294. When shall I see my Captiue Hart	f. 167v
295. Goe Louely rose, tell her that wasts her tyme [treble only]	f. 168
296. Art thou in Loue? it cannot be	f. 168v
297. Let not thy Beautye make thee Proude	f. 169
298. O Fayre Astrea, whyther, whyther art thou gone	f. 169v
299. The Turtle is a simple byrde	f. 170
300. Noe, twas her Eyes, starrs haue noe Influence	f. 170v
301. When as black night, her vaile displayes; On the Lady Diana Sidney	f. 171
302. Harke, harke, methinkes I heer Loue saye	f. 171v
303. Little Loue serues my turne	f. 172
304. Those Heau'nly Rayes of thyne; On the Lady Anne Percy	f. 172v
305. Wher shall a man an Object finde	f. 173
306. Faine would I Loue	f. 173v

307. Goe younge man let my hart alone	f. 174
308. O Turne away those Cruell Eyes	f. 174v
309. Thou art heau'n Olimpia	f. 175
310. Noe More of teares; I'ue now noe More	f. 175v
311. Lagrimas que no pudieron	f. 176
312. Goe Fayre Inchantres, charme noe more	f. 176v
313. Ofte haue I swore I'de loue noe more	f. 177
314. How Sad's a Scorched Louers Fate [treble only]	f. 177v
315. Cloris yor selfe you soe Excell	f. 178
316. Treadinge the pathe to Nobler Ends [treble only]	f. 178v
317. Cruda Amarrilli, che col nome [treble only]	f. 179v
318. Since thou wilt goe fond hart	f. 180
319. Tis not thy well-mixed Red & Whyte	f. 181
320. Ladyes, whoe gilde ye glitteringe noone	f. 182
321. Alas poore Cupid art thou blynde	f. 182v
322. A willow Garland thou didst send	f. 183
323. When I adore thee, (sweet) & Implore thee; for ye Gittar	f. 183v
324. If I seek t'enjoy y^e fruit of my paine [text only]	f. 184
325. Art thou gone in haste; A Swaine persuing a Nimphe that flyes him &c. [treble only]	f. 184

xvii

HENRY LAWES Servant to his late Ma:^tie
in his publick and private Musick.
W.^r Faithorne fecit.

The Composers of English Church Music.

BY GEORGE S. OUTRAM, RECTOR OF REDMILE, NOTTS.

Henry Lawes.   Benjamin Rogers.

THERE were two composers of the name of Lawes, William and Henry, brothers, and both famous in their day. William drew the sword for Charles the First, and died in his cause before the walls of Chester. Being well known to the king he was much lamented by his royal master; and Fuller tells us how much he was respected and beloved by all who 'cast any looks towards virtue and honour.' Henry his brother, however, was more fortunate, being one of the three gentlemen of the Chapel Royal who survived the Civil Wars, and claimed their station after the Commonwealth had collapsed. He died, however, very soon after he had composed the Coronation Anthem for Charles the Second.

When troublous times came, Henry Lawes had to shift for himself, and this he effected by teaching ladies to sing. He had been educated by Signor Giovanni Coperario, and this fact was then a passport, as it might be now, to the favour of many persons. With a knowledge of English human nature that marks him as a shrewd man, a certain John Cooper had left England, and had returned from Italy no more John Cooper, but Signor Giovanni Coperario; and his new name had no doubt its potency, and justified Mr. Cooper's politic action.

His pupil, Henry Lawes, shone chiefly in secular music. 'He has but small claim upon our gratitude as a Church composer,' says Sir J. Hawkins. 'Though a servant of the Church, he has contributed but little to her stores.' Nevertheless, we cannot say what Lawes might have done, had not the great political whirlwind silenced all the cathedral choirs for so long a time. His chief productions for the use of the sanctuary seem to have been, *Choice Psalms put into Music for Three Voices, by Henry and William Lawes, Brothers, and Servants of His Majesty* (the last production of sacred music published during the life of Charles the First); certain tunes for Mr. Sandys' paraphrase of the Psalms, one of which used to be played by the chimes of St. Lawrence, Jewry, three times a-day; anthems in Dr. Tudway's collection; and some chants. Of these productions very little good is said by Dr. Burney:—'They have no felicity; no attempt at air; all the movements flow in one even tenor of mediocrity; and none of them enables us to account for the great reputation which these musicians so long enjoyed.'

The fame of Henry Lawes rests chiefly, as we have before observed, upon his setting of secular songs to music. The first poets of the age asked him to compose tunes for their songs. Waller has celebrated his skill in a line which thus runs,—

'Let words and sense be set by thee.'

But a greater than Waller, even John Milton himself, as we shall see, loved and valued Henry Lawes.

In 1633, on the king's return from Scotland, after ending the discontents of that kingdom, several grave and learned lawyers and men of note, as Selden and Edward Hyde (Lord Clarendon), and others, spent a very large sum upon 'an elegant piece of foolery' called a masque, which was got up for the king's enjoyment, and called *The Triumphs of Peace*. Lawes got 100*l.* for writing the music. This Whitehall frolic, however, is forgotten. Not so another masque, which was presented at Ludlow Castle, the seat of the Earl of Bridgewater.

One day the Earl's three children, Lord Brackley, Mr. Egerton, and Lady Alice Egerton, were passing through Hay Wood, in Herefordshire; Lord Brackley being only twelve years old, and Lady Alice a year his senior. The night came on ere they had threaded the darkling alleys of the forest, and Lady Alice was actually lost for some time. This incident furnished Milton with ideas which he wrought into one of the finest dramatic poems in existence. Henry Lawes composed melodies for the songs 'Sweet Echo,' 'Sabrina Fair,' &c.; and this celebrated *Masque of Comus* was acted at Ludlow Castle on Michaelmas Night, A.D. 1634, Lawes himself taking the part of 'the attendant spirit.' The great poet has immortalised the musician in one of his sonnets beginning,—

'Harry, whose tuneful and well-measured song,' &c.

And he also elsewhere eulogised Lawes; as, *e. g.*:—

'Who, with his soft pipes and smooth-dittied song,
Well knows to still the wild waves when they roar.'

Lawes may be content to bear the scant measure of praise accorded him by Dr. Burney, when so great a man as Milton has thus declared how great was his own delight caused by the musician's artful strains.

The subject of our memoir died October 21, 1662, and was buried in Westminster Abbey.

A Catalogue of the Songs
Contained in this Book Alphabeticall

A

A[h?] love, what is Page	6
As on a day Clorinda	12
Amour, & ye milky way	93
A[h?] wert thou darlinge of mine Eys	114
A[h?] ye fair fatall fair	123
Am I despis'd because you say	134
Amarillis by a Spring	140
About ye silent hours of a [?]	145
Amongst ye[?] myrtles	150
Ask me why I send you here	155
A thousand times I did [?]	161
At the works of nature	206
As sad Aminder in a meadow lay	288
Amarant la [?]	304
Art thou in town	355
	25
Break hart in twain	56
Be not proud nor coy, nor cruell	67
Beautys have no then stop	70
back shepherds back	79
Bacchus, Bacchus	95
behold and listen	144
bid me but live	262
beauty one blast	285
Be not proud cause fayr & trym	301
Be all thy glorys willingly I gone	319
Beauty & love one [?]	335
Be gon be gon thou perjur'd	28
Cloris! since first our [?]	27
Can you much beauty	46
celia thy sweet Angels face	63
can sorrow cease	65
cupid thou art a sluggish boy	74
[?]	75
come from ye Dungeon	76
come sleep gentle	82
cruell but once	85
cast away stroks upon clouds	103
come seek I took [?] stay	107
come sad thoughts	111
celia thy sweet Angels face	127
cupid as he lay Among roses	137

Cloris forbear now must you	252
Canst thou love me & yet doubt	153
Com Cloris hye we to ye down	155
Celia let not love	167
Cloris [?] my rivalls	158
Com thou glorious object	267
Cruelty of love	145
Cloris now thou art fled away	285
Cloris [?] to the present	...
Cloris when can you [?]	11
	45
Dare thy face's heaven to me	66
Do not delay me	83
Don't leave thy flock	87
Divine turn'd away	115
Death cann'd yet distinguish	126
Divines [?] not now delay me	2
Give throw that flattering glass	228
Disdain me not sweet love	350
Deliciah Beauty	
Did I once say	

E

[?]	349

F

Fye away fy	
False love away	
From ye Heavens now I fly	
Fair wood of Cloris	
Farewell fair Jamet	
Fear not dear love	
So give me love with love [?]	460
Fond women thou mistak'd	

Griefe come away	3		Joves force	
giue back my heart	59			
goe naked truth	80			
grieue not deere loue	127			
Go Heard of silly Groome	141			
goe you yonder whispering wynde	188			
gaze not on thy beauty's pride	224			
giue my mans loue or mony disdayne	236			
Goodye Loue pause a while	253			
gaze not on Swans	276			
you little winged Archer	318			
Go lovely Rose	352			
Help help, o help			Keep on yo vaile	104
Harke how Bellona	341		know Celia	235
How coole & temperate	339			
	337			
Hard hearted faire			Loue Chill is Cold	173
Have I watcht the winters night	34		let fooles great Cupids yoake	211
harke how the Nightingale	42		Ladyes flye from loue	227
honi vaine delights begon	50		looke homeward Doris	249
Have pitty griefe	64		Loue feare good faith not I	177
Hither wee come into this world	128		Lovely Cloris & rough her Eys	106
her Eyes with all the world	135		Let me alone she loue no more	281
heauen and beauty	146		Lasso, pichio	303
hence vaine intruder	187		Let Longing Louers	338
how ill doth he deserue	205		let Loue serue	360
happy youth	209		Let not thy beauty make y proud	357
he that loues a rosy cheeke	217			
harke how my Celia	229			
How posanes	272			
had I a Trumpet	249.250			
how you ever seen of morninge	298			
How happiar	315			
How cruell Loue	316			
Reiose and grieue	2		My life is in thy selfe	2
If lovely may discover	9		marke well this stone	8
Smile this once			must I in my most ioyfull	22
my mistris from her Eyes	44		more then most happy	30
I have praisd with all my skill	48		my sweetest bird	60
Ile tell you how ye rose	54		must wee be divided	164
I saw sweet beauty beside	58		my wandring thoughts	302
I am confirmed a woman	89		mournes with mee	320
If you can finde a heart				
I doe confess that proud	121			
It is not that I loue you less	169			
Loue this for thy fickleness	176			
gaze not more on her	200			
burne & consume you in vaine	201			
let the Queicke spirits	204			

Now my taske is	72
nor nor fain'd Horrible	99
nor she nor loud	167
not carvinge to Obscure y° wynd	171
now she burnes as well as J	202
no more blinde God	233
no nor J never was in Love, nor	282
	132
not that J wish my mistris	
nor Pale, nor Faithles	333
now J grieve, J am well	334
no More of Love	346

O that Joy° soe soone	v
or you or J, nature did wrong	7
one wth Admiration told me	10
: let me groane	15
o sweet woods	18
o wilt shall J lament	24
out uppon it J have lov'd	73
oude poete hipocrite admyr°	84
o now ye Certain cause J know	105
one vertues cheefe	118
one Sylent nyght of late	138
our Syghes are heard	174
o smoothe me to death	83
o let me still, & Sylent	279
on a cleare morne as phebus	271
o now J find tis nought but fate	289
o doll sol pu le sient	302
o J am sick	310
o tell my Love, o tell me fate	314
~~...~~	
~~...~~	
~~...~~	
on this swelling banke	336

P	
Pale Jnke	98
phillis why should	175
poor pindar	241

Rejoice whilst in thy youth	43
not by streame, thy selfe	108
rude in thy rocks	217

Speake, at last reply	6	the God of Love my shepard	151
Saire stay a while	16	thou art soveraigne & young	152
Sweet lady, & sole mistris	23	till now I nev'r did believe	163
Since every man I come amongst	29	though my body be restrained	165
Sleepe guild man	36	those curious locks	186
Sweet I am not come	37	that lovely spot	289
Sorrow in vaine	38	Theives, o theives	254
Sweet doe not frowne	40	to love thee w'thout flattery	263
Sacred flora	41	to man that was his running mad	269
Stopp softe your silver flood	43	they that never had y'one	270
Sweet Isaell come visit	51	taught from y'tilfull straines	247
She is too cruell	52	though thou hast witt &	275
Sweet thou those diamonds	53	though Cupid be a God	64
Sweet Ecchlo	69	thrice happy is that lovely page	290
Sabrina	70	Tell me ye wandring spirits	294
Stay guild Tyme	77	the clyderish god of Love	296
See how coyley misian	90		297
Set to y' Sun y' dyall	92	bade heed fayre Cloris how ye love	312
Sure thou freshed wert	107		
Stay showes	113	Unto ye soundles vaults of hell	11
Sweet Morphe	117	Venus redres a wrong	152
sleep soft, ye Cold	125	unfold thyne Armes	220
wilt thorow y' guiding ayre	131		
seeke not my love	136		
Seeke not to know my love	231	When I I done you	13
Stay love and blood	237	weep not my dear	85
sweetly doubling vernall ayre	242	wherfore prayest thou	39
tell Amathiea	246	why should only man be hyd	62
Stand still ye floods	295	whither soe gladly & soe fast	78
in my Cloris	304	wert thou yet fairer than thou art	85
Cloris see how nature brings	307	whybut are all her false oaths blown	86
stay ye greedy merchants	313	will you know my mistris face	97
must we part	178	when thou faire Celia lie'st	101
		was it a forme, a gate, a grace	112
		why stay's my floramell	116
		what meanes this strangnes	130
Though my torment bonds	4	would you know whats soft	133
	11	when thou art dead	143
twixt hope & feare	26	when wee were parted	154
	28	where shall my troubled soule	159
though you are fair	47	while I listen to thy voice	166
tis Christmas now	67	when this fly lived	215
	94	when on y' Altar at my hand	225
tell me not I my tyme	96	when thou poore Excommunicate	226
thy beauty jewell is hid	102	wherfore doe thy sad numbers flow	248
tell me now owne tis love	122	what man would sojourn her	49
		why up soe early in the wood	265
		work is mine	32
		whither the Sun burnt pilgrim fice	292

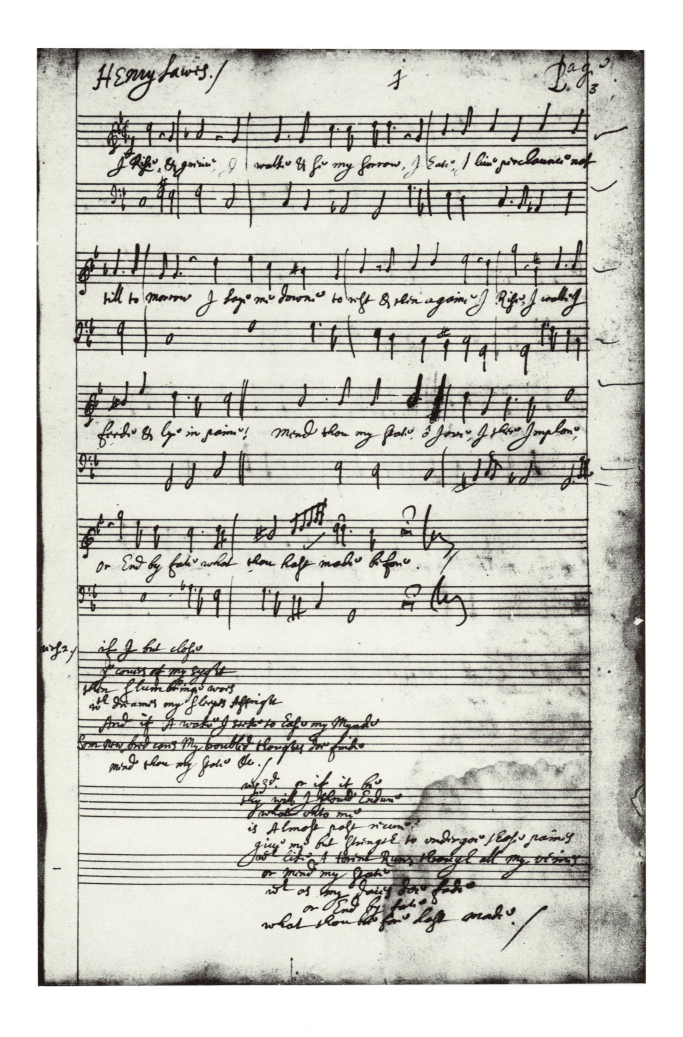

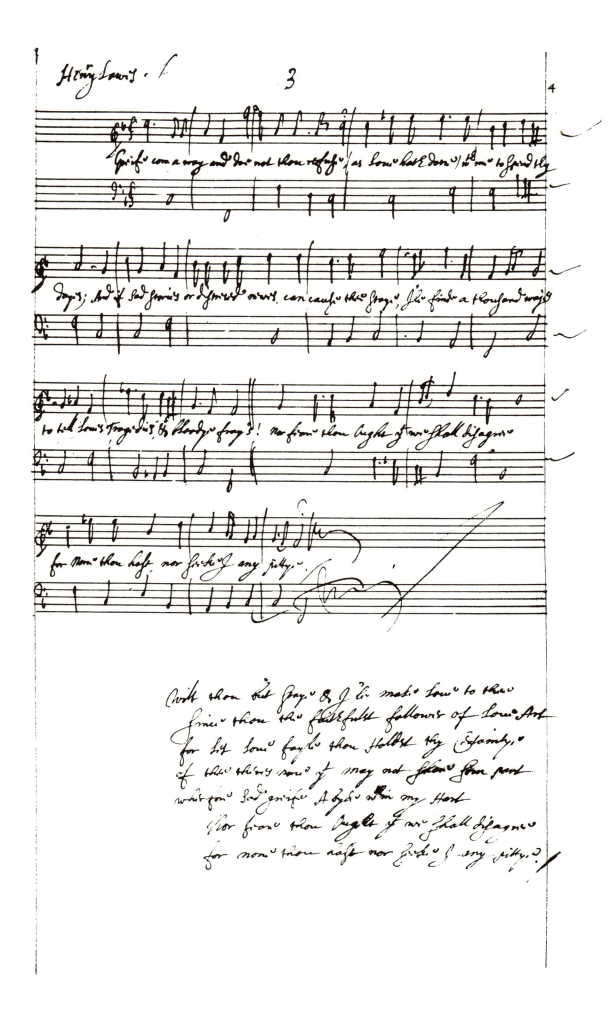

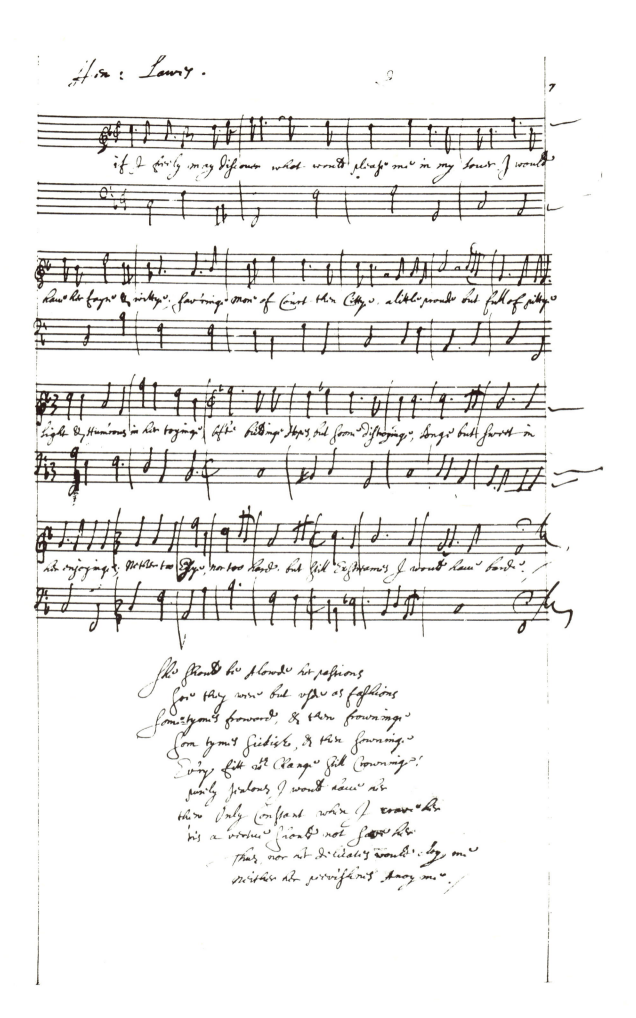

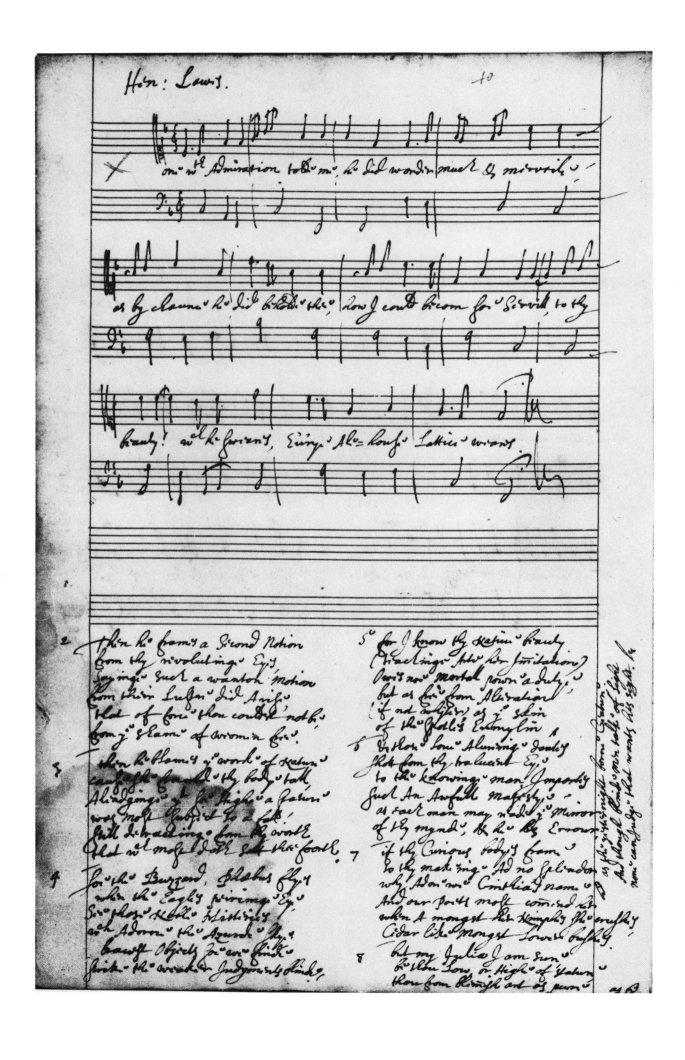

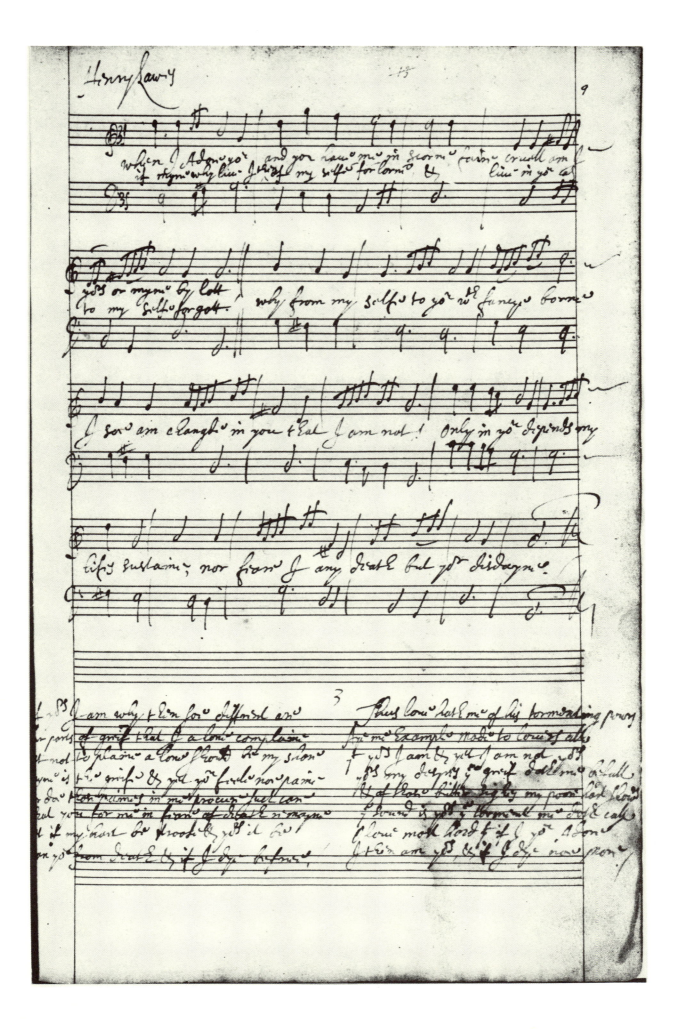

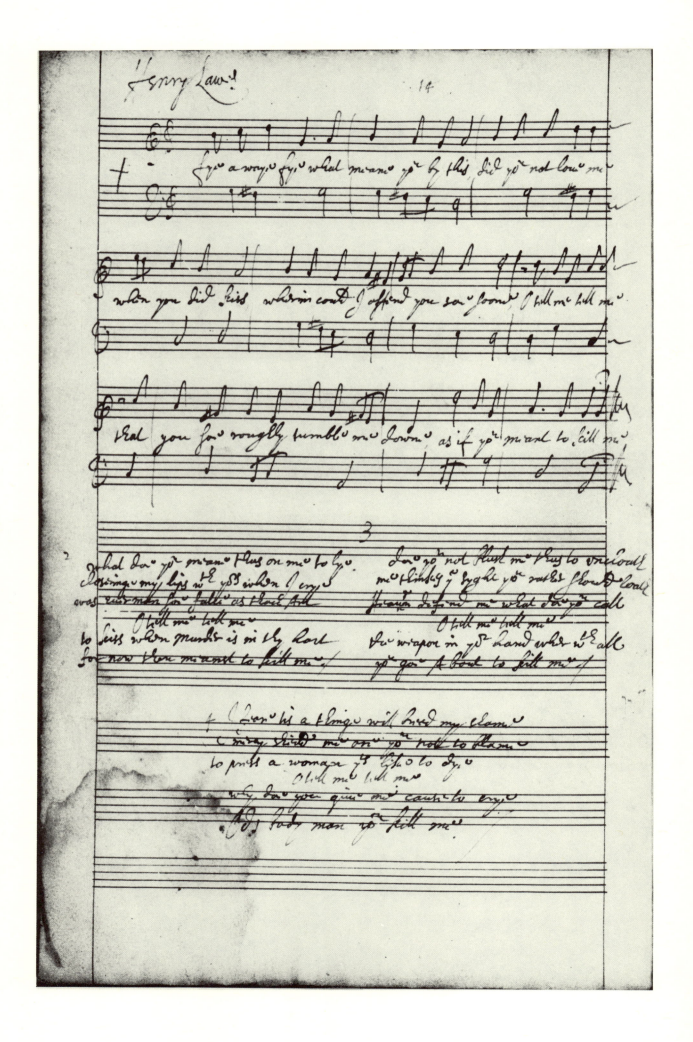

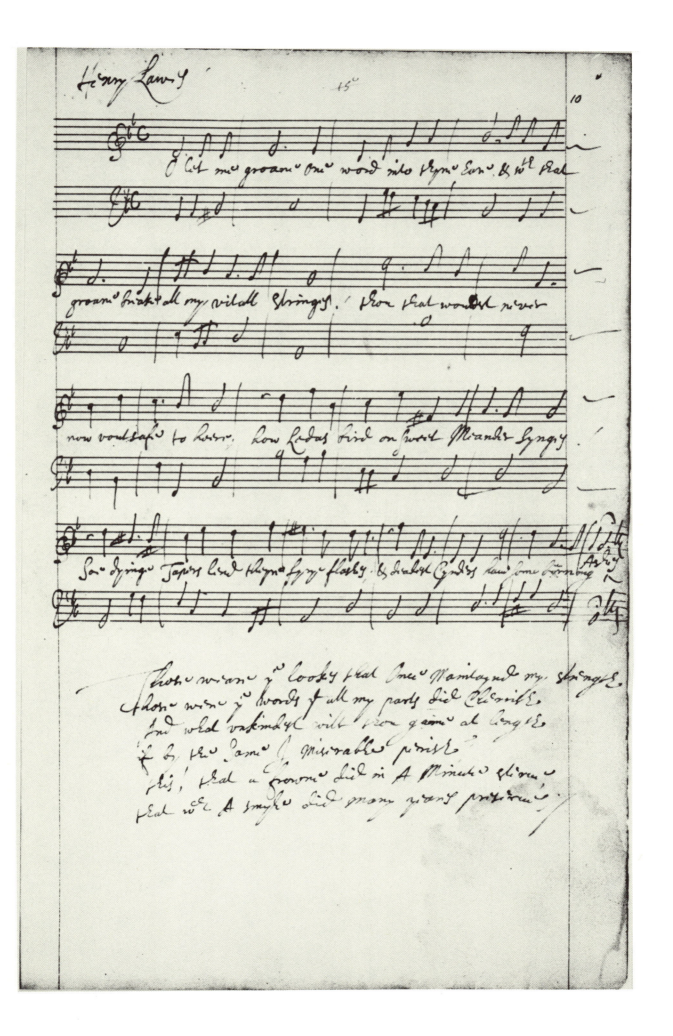

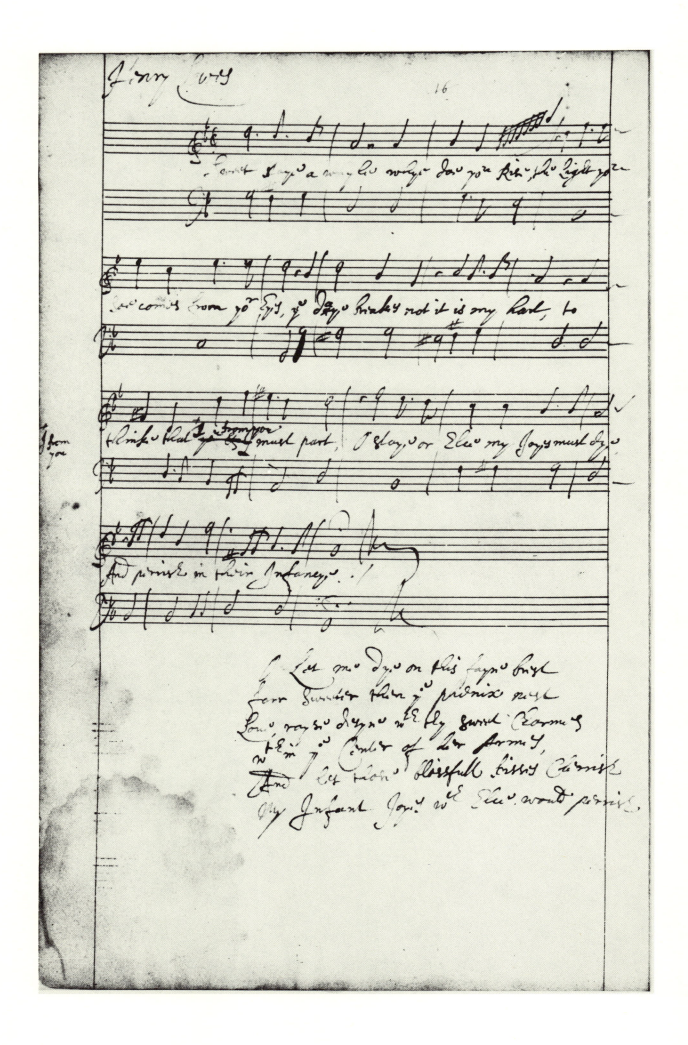

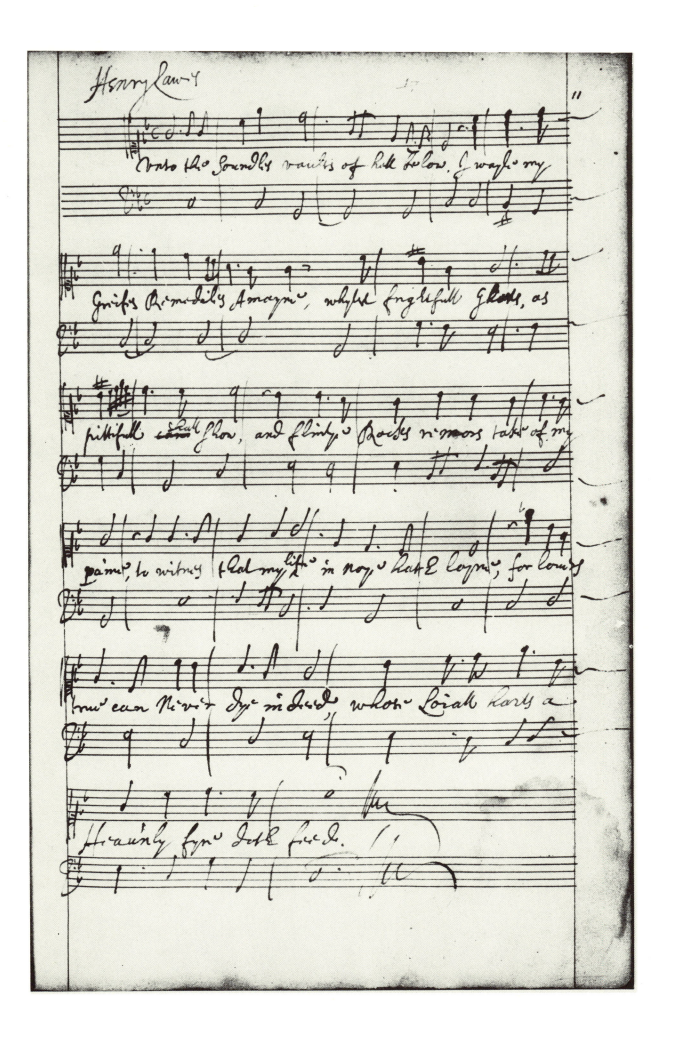

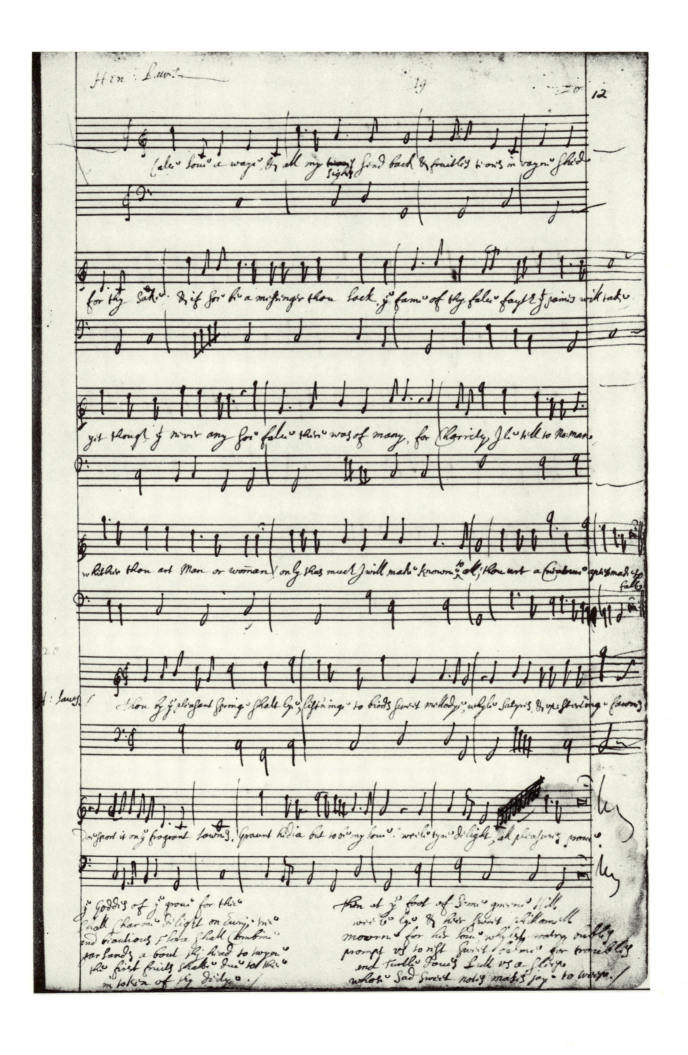

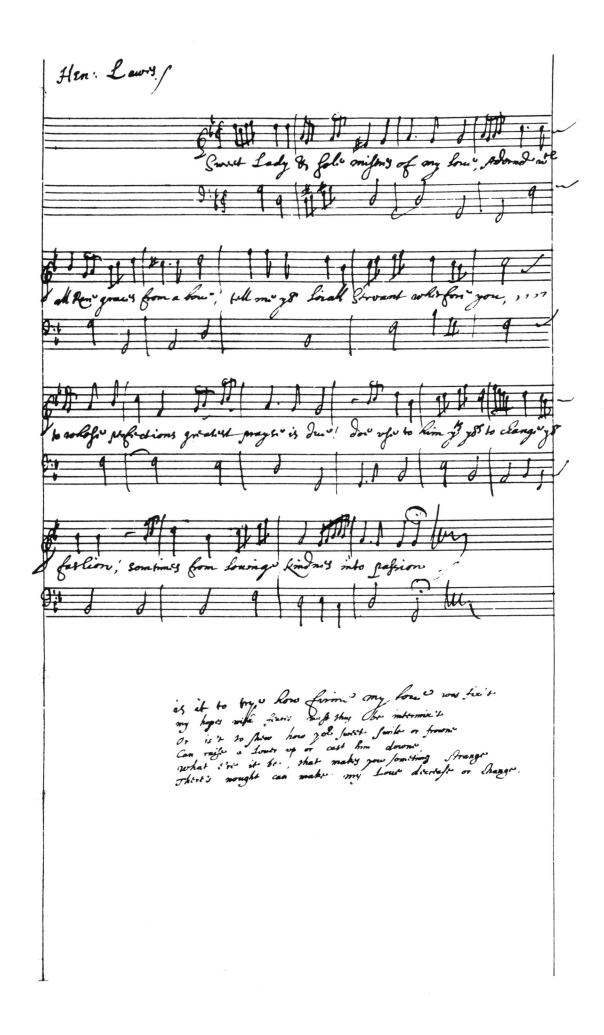

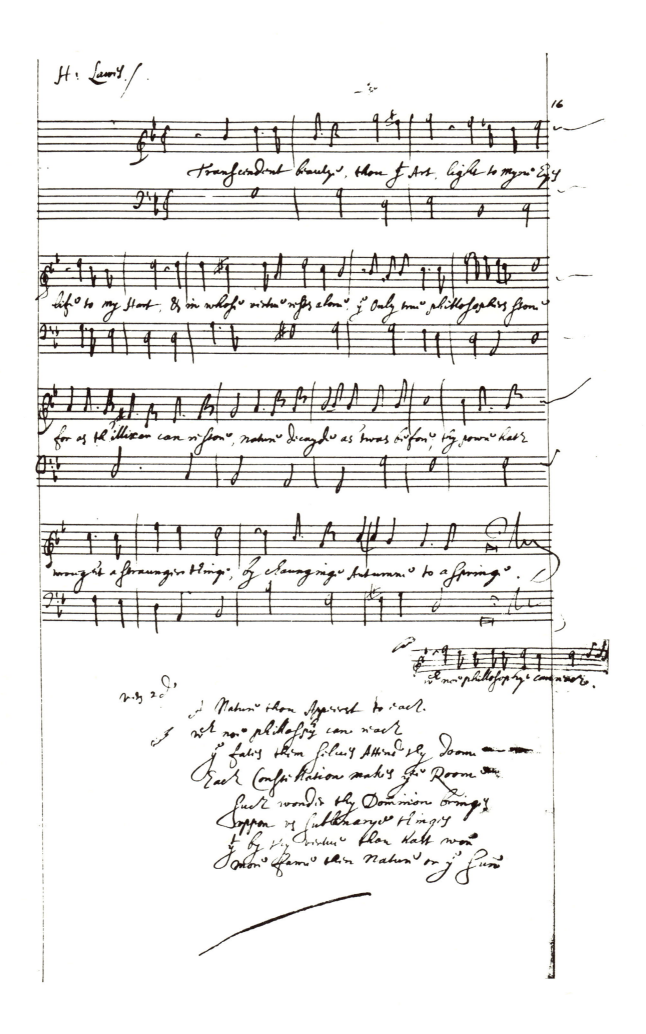

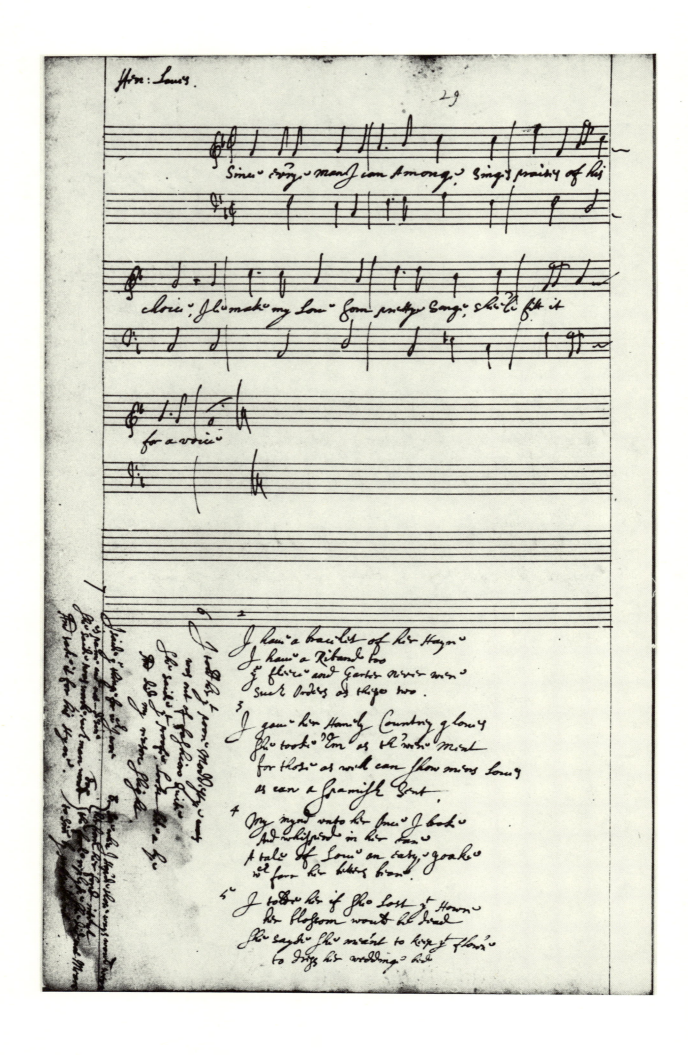

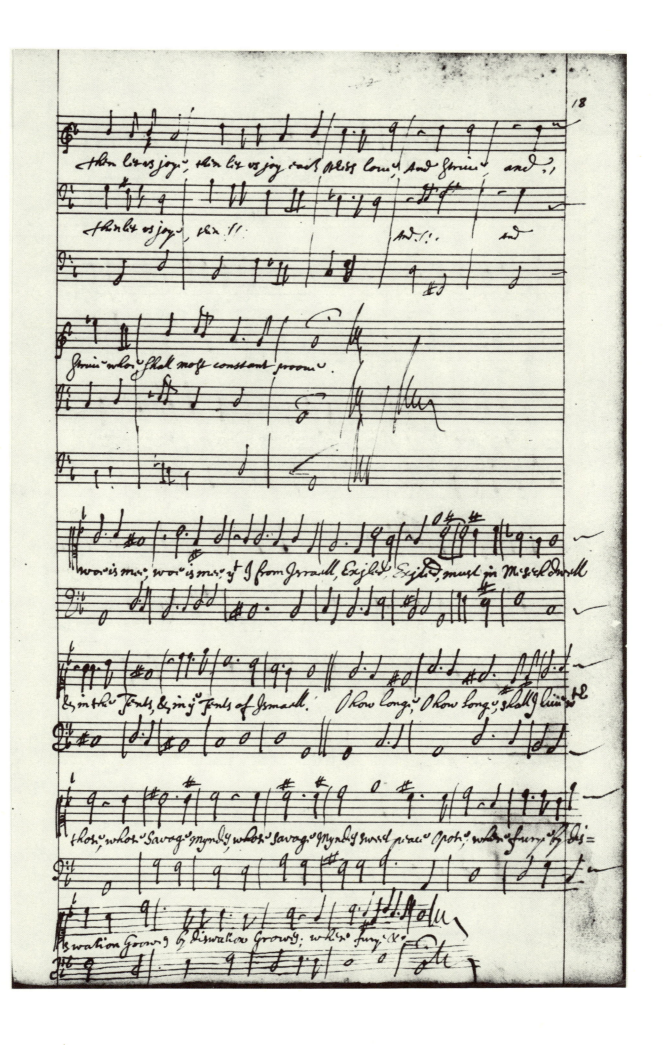

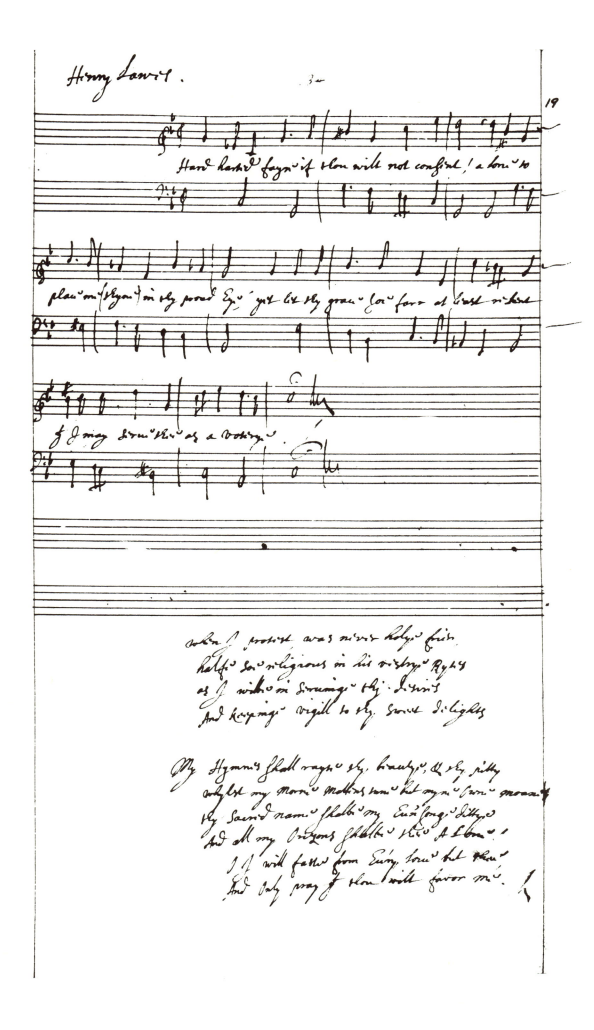

Henry Lawes

weep not my Deere, for I shall goe Loaden E-
-nough with myne Owne woes. Ad not thy heavinesse to
myne, since fate our pleasures must disjoyne.

why should our sorrowes Meet, if I
must goe & leave thy Company,
I wish not theirs, it shall relieve
my hart to thinke thou doest not grieve
yet grieve and weep, y͡t I may beare
Every sighe and Every teare.
Away w͡th me, you shall my hart & Eyes
discharged, Enjoy their rest.
And it shall glad my hart to see
thou wert thus Loath to part w͡th me.

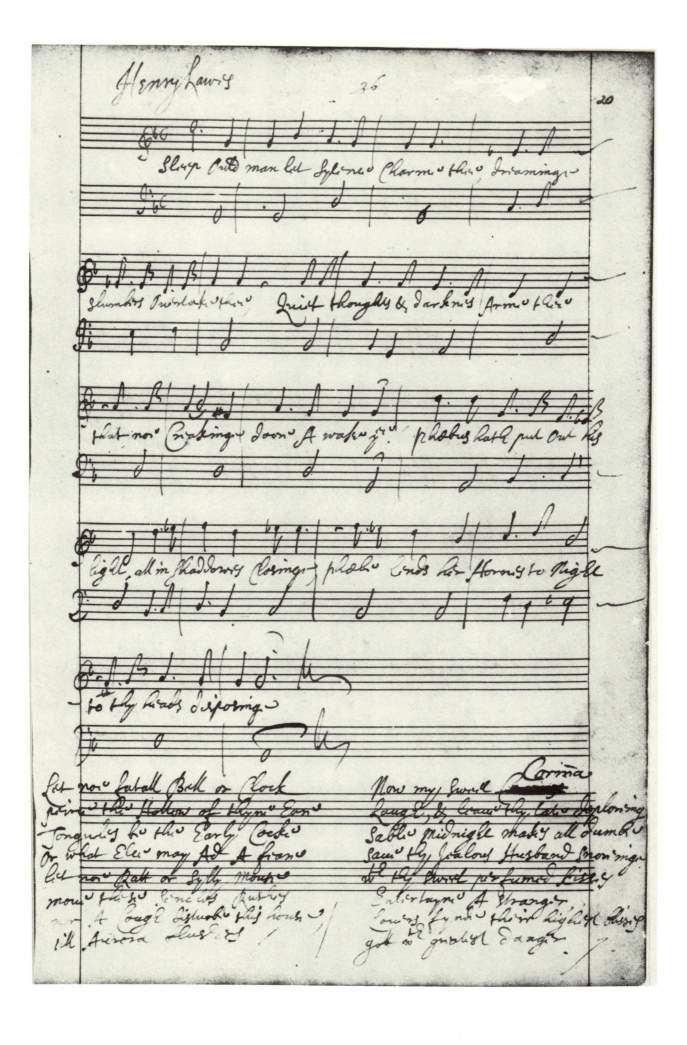

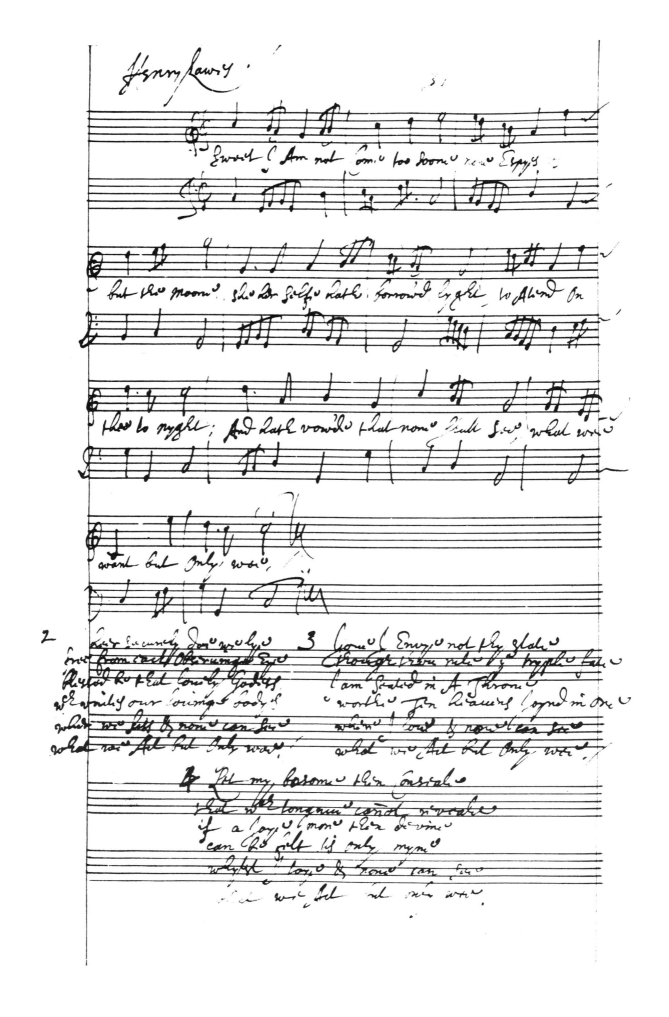

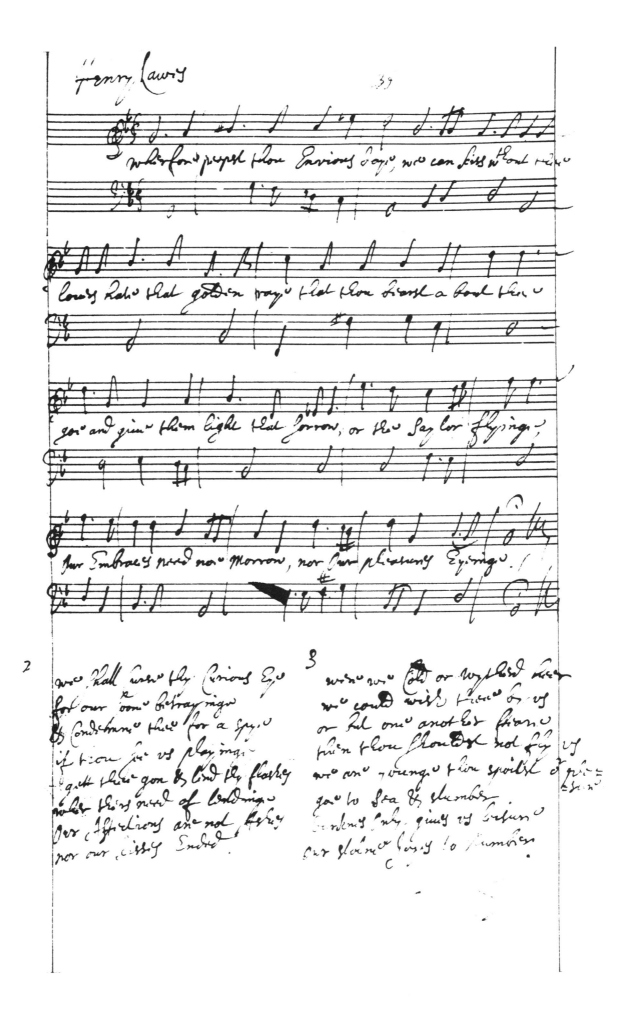

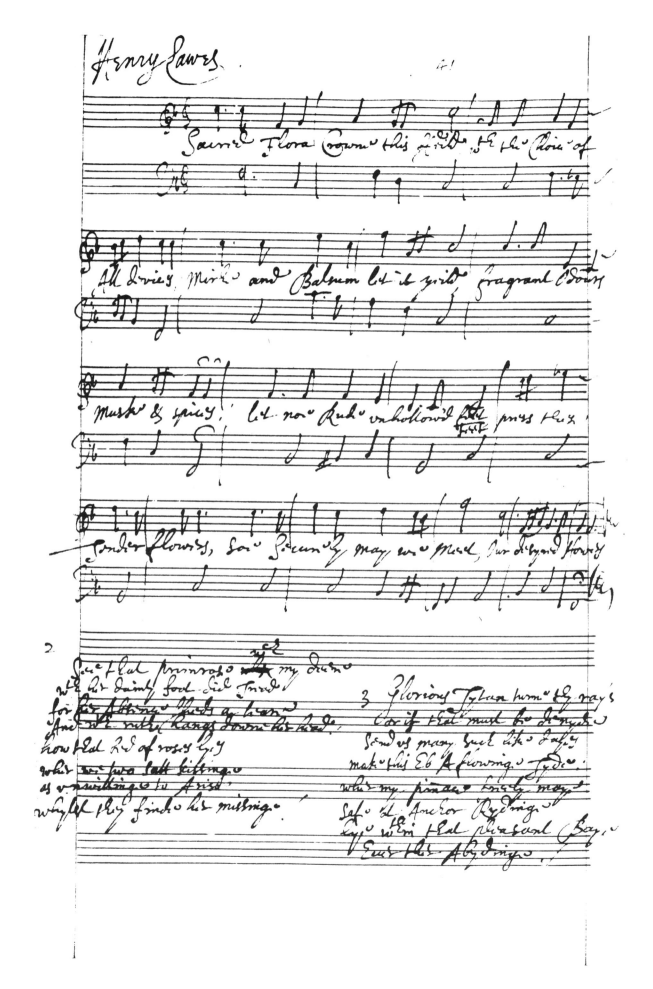

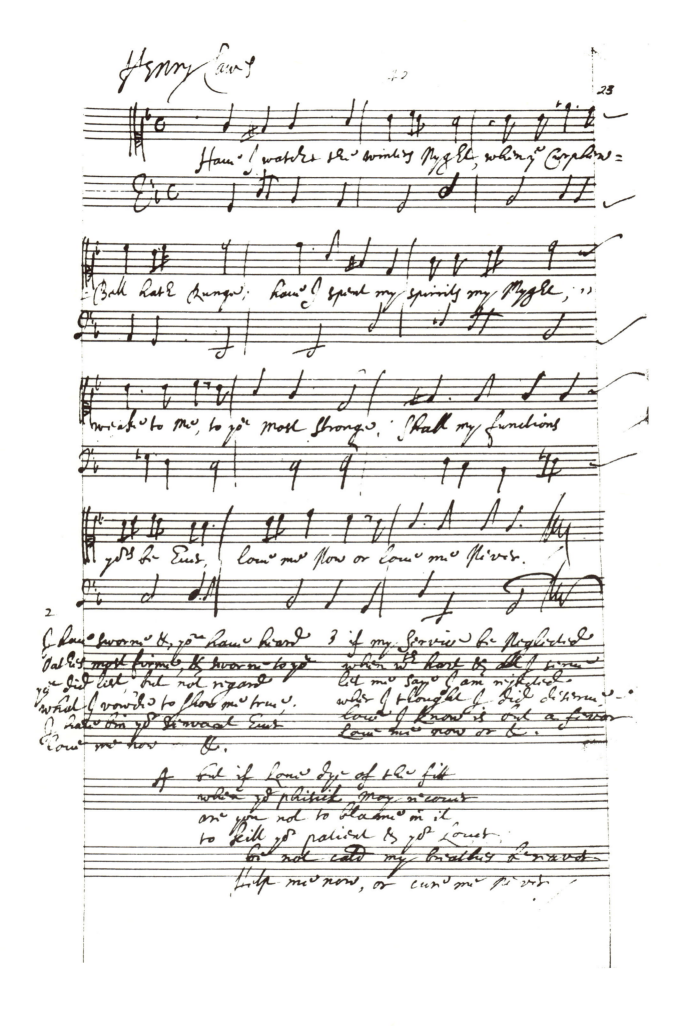

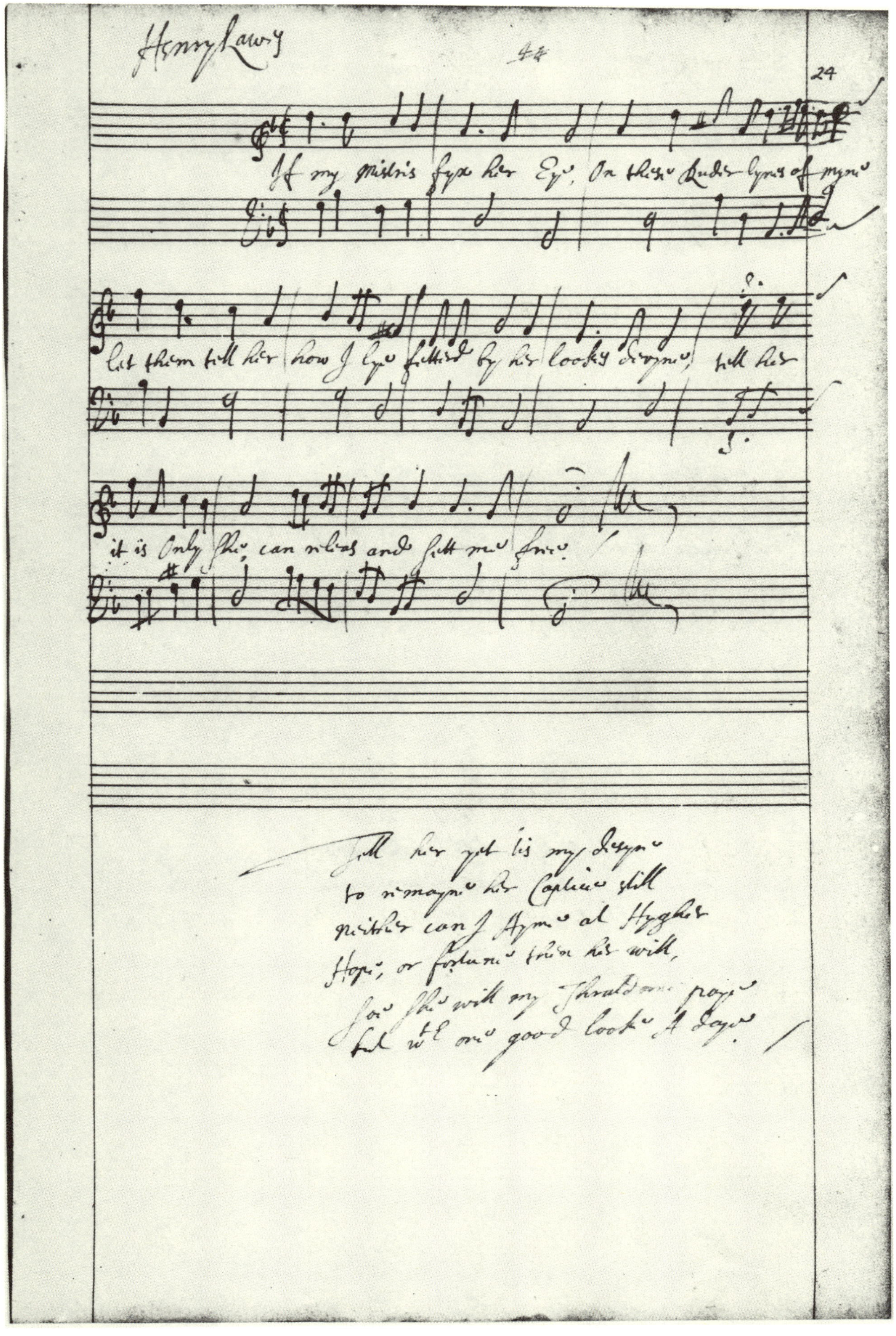

Henry Lawes

If my Mistris fixe her Eye, On these Rude lynes of myne
let them tell her how I lyve fettered by her lookes devyne, tell her
it is Only shee can release and sett mee free.

Tell her yet tis my Desyre
to remayne her Captive still
neither can I Ayme at Hygher
Hope, or fortune train his will,
for shee with my Thraldome payes
full well one good looke A daye.

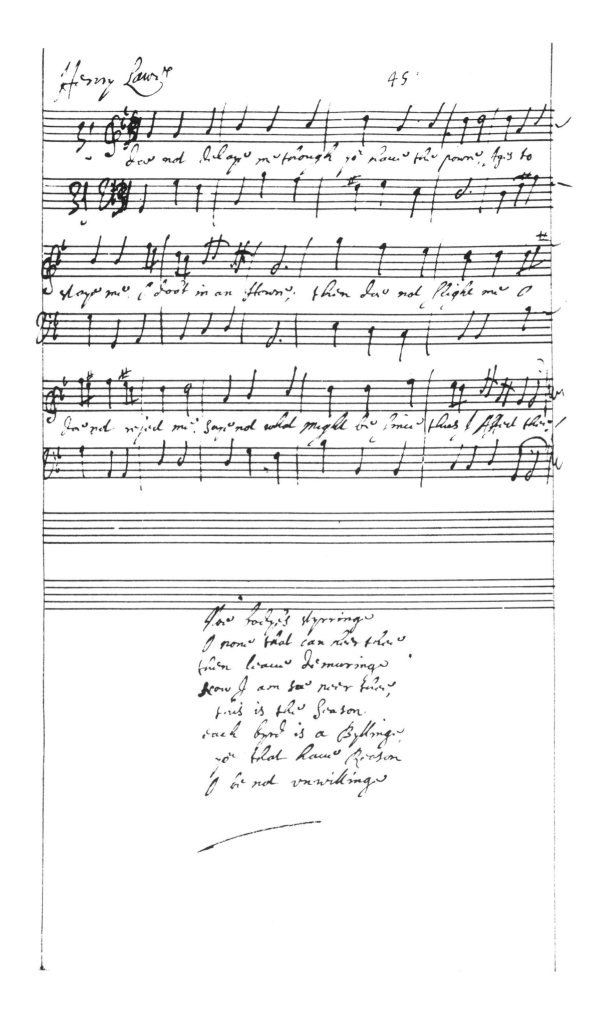

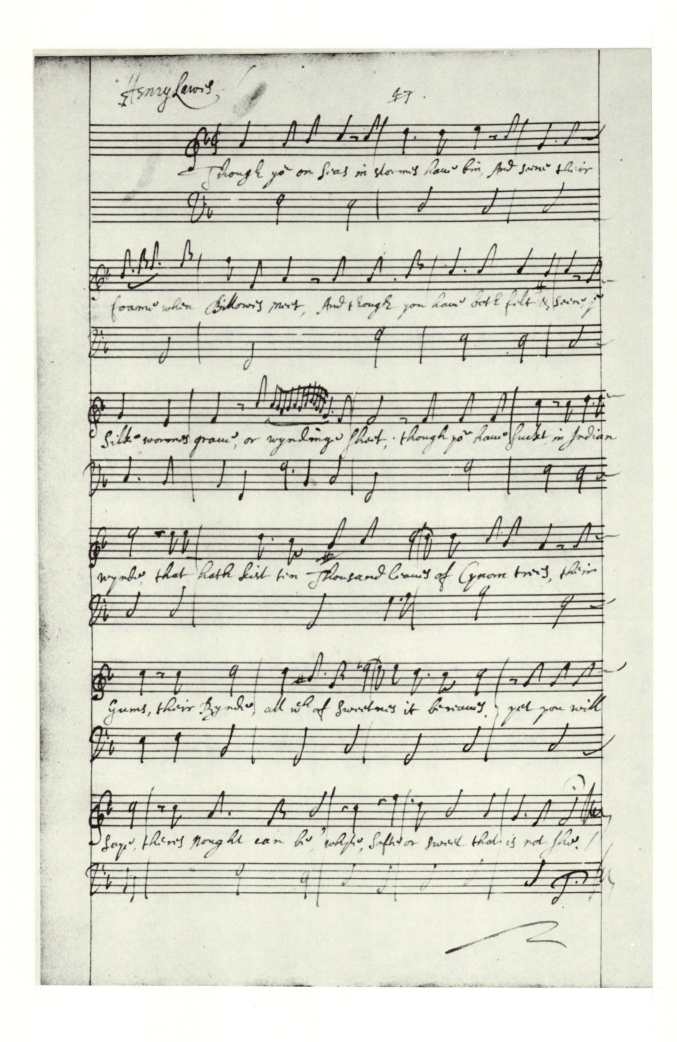

Henry Lawes

Hark how ye Nightingale displays ye Cahest pleasures of her
Throats, and dyes content if her poore Notes might Serue but as one
Step to raise A Trophy to yr beauties prayse.

The rose in which rich odours lye   Aurora weepes to See a light
The perfumed treasures of ye yeare   Outvye her splendor in yr eye
Doth blush to death when yu appear   The Sunn's ashamed to walke ye sky
And Martyr-like towards yu doth flye   And th' envious Moone growne pale for
To weare yr Cheekes fresh Liuory   vexes now to Reveile but ye night

The sawcy wynds w'th somewhat ease
(Seeminge to feele soft sense of bliss)
Steales through yr hayre yr lips to kiss,
Sow Riuals mee, w'ch now despayre
To touch yr lip, cheeke, eye, or hayre.

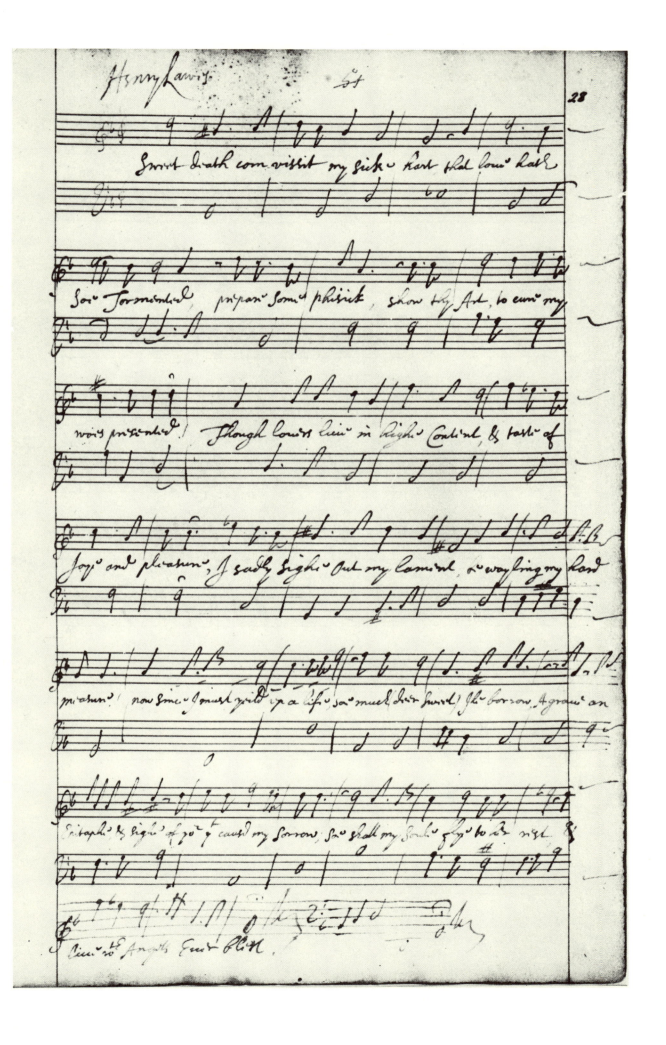

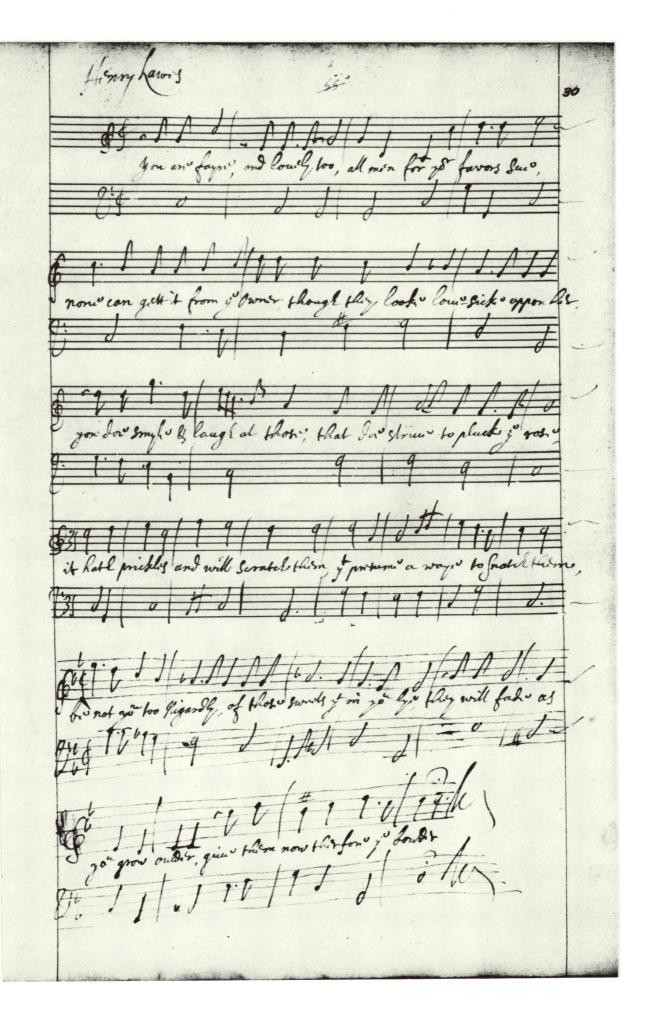

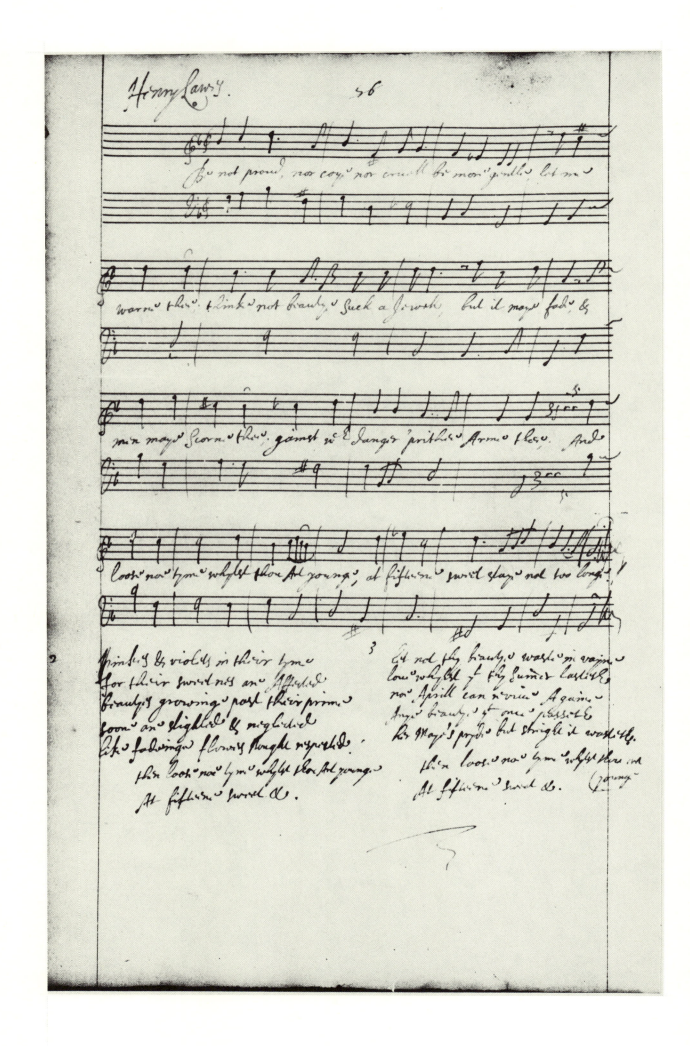

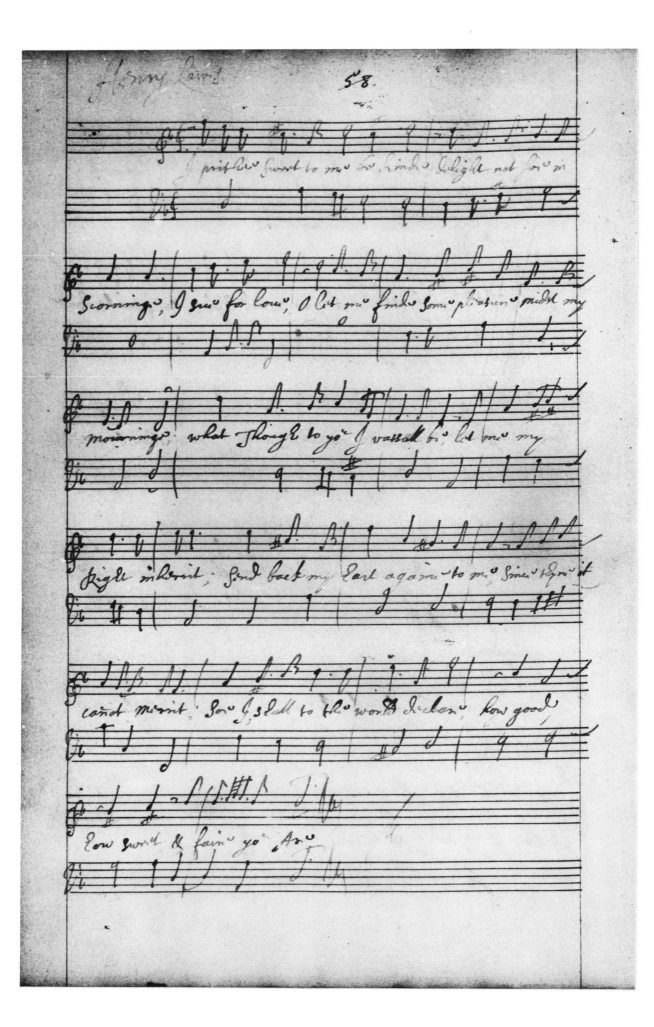

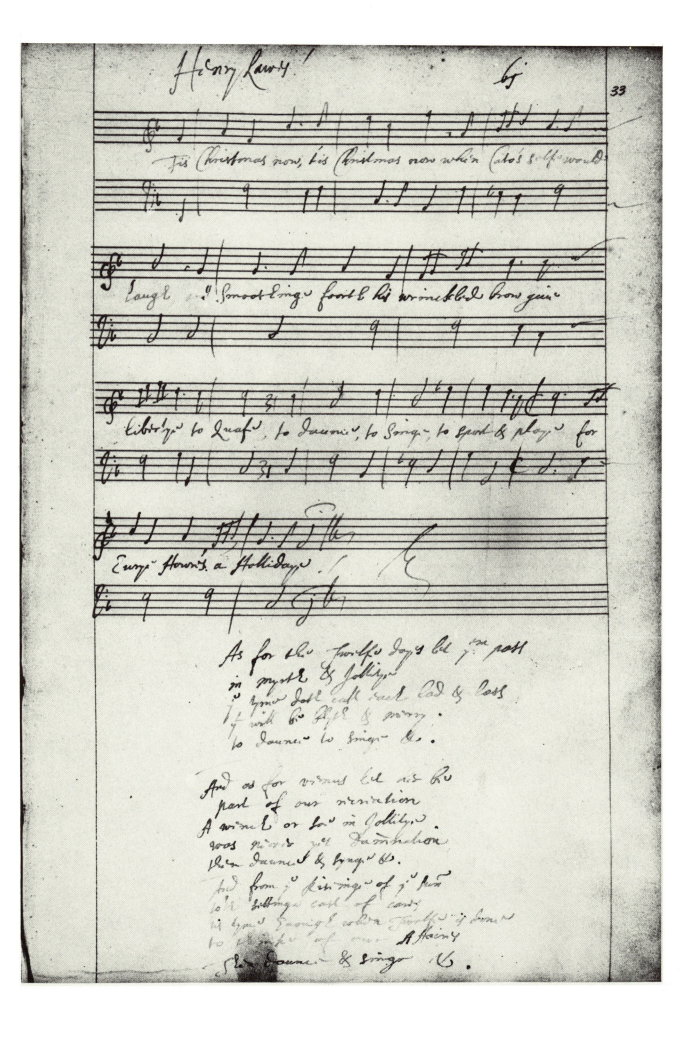

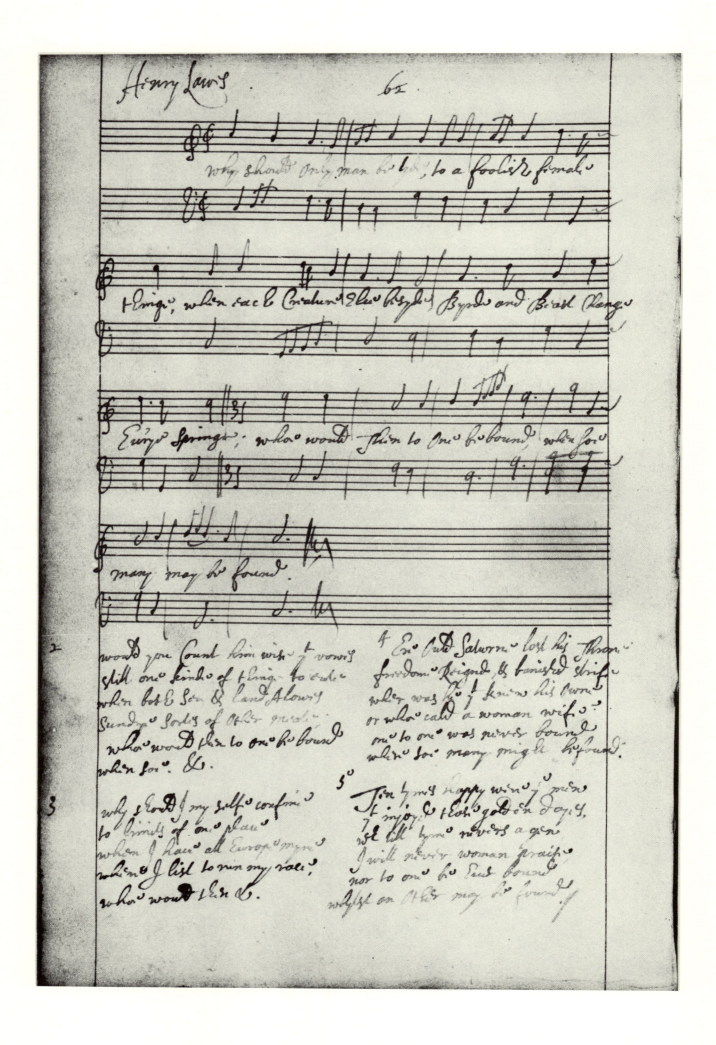

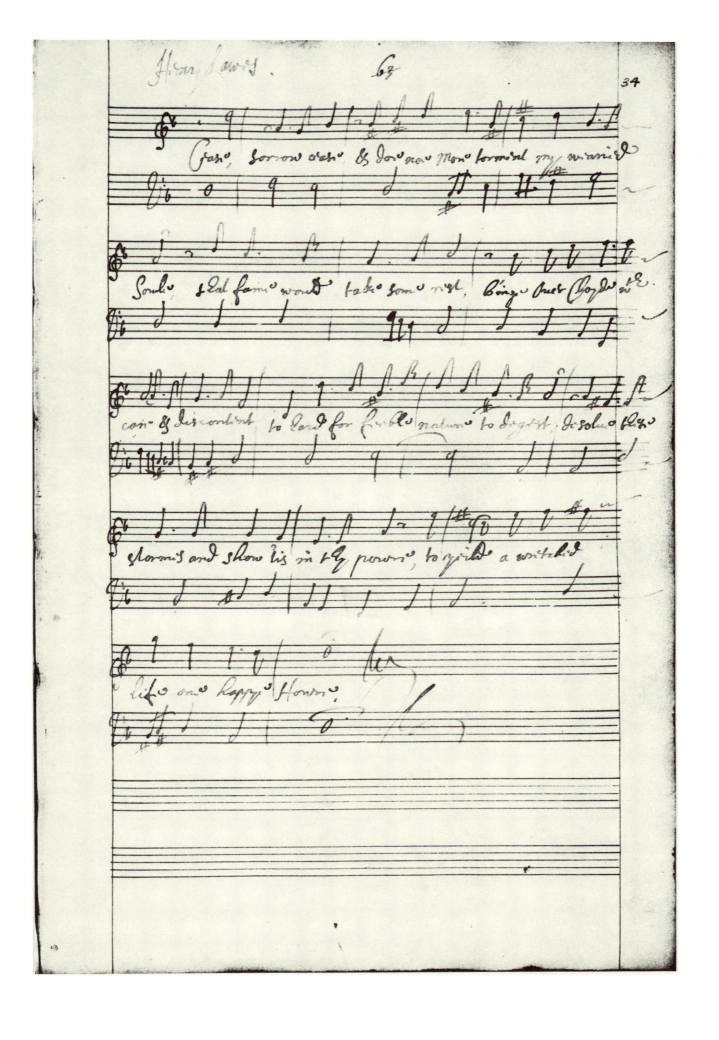

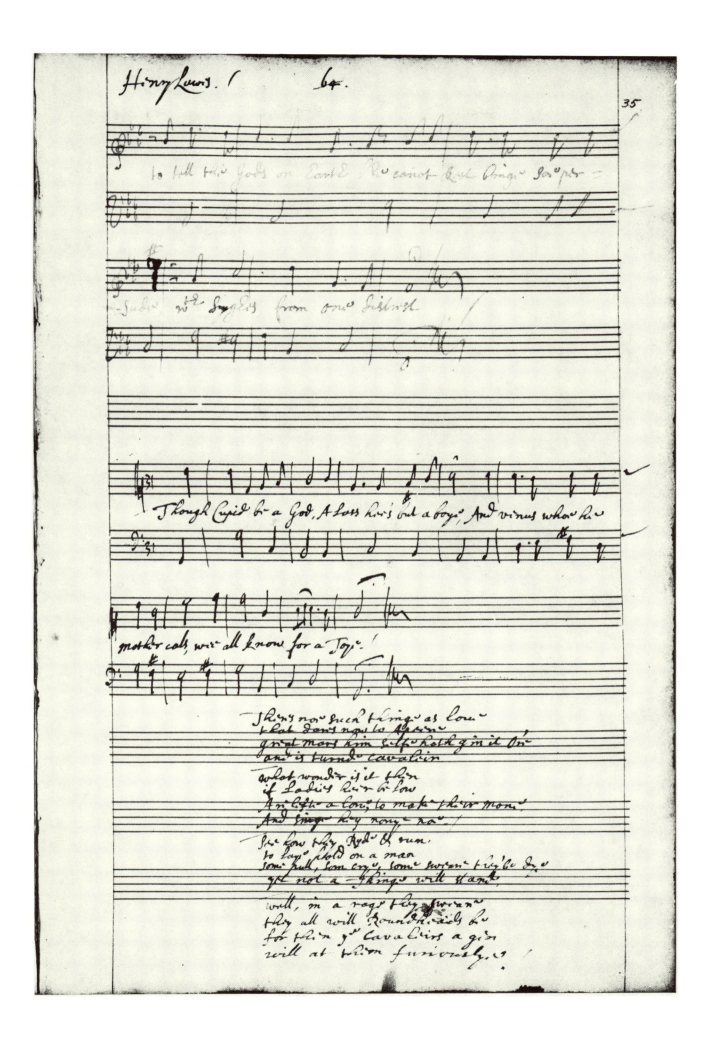

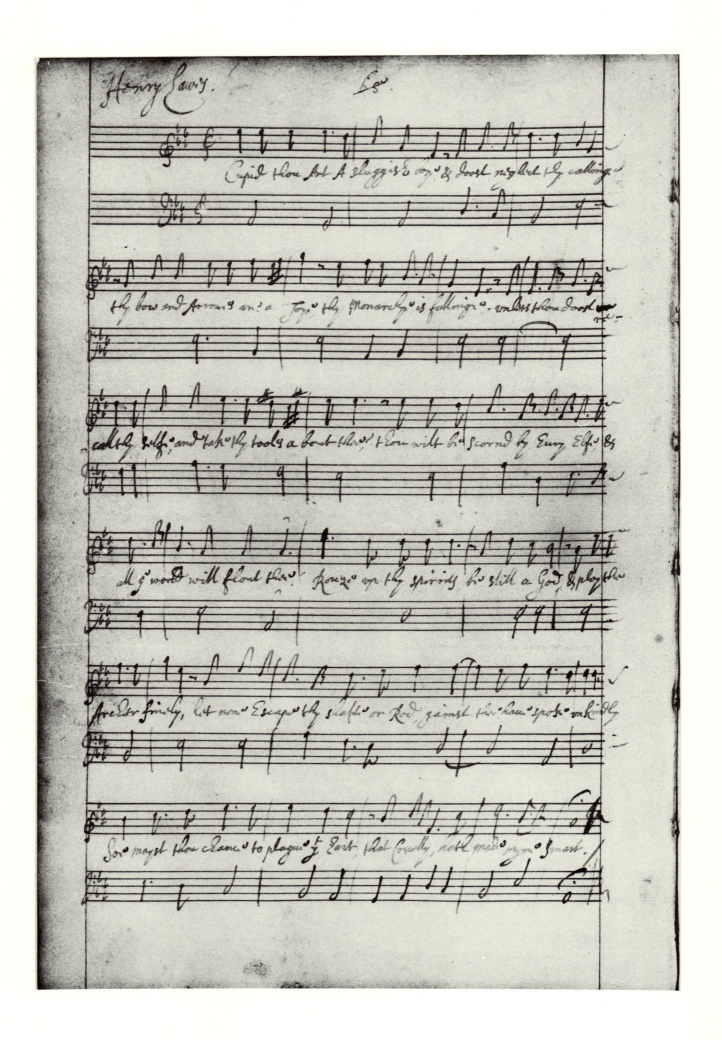

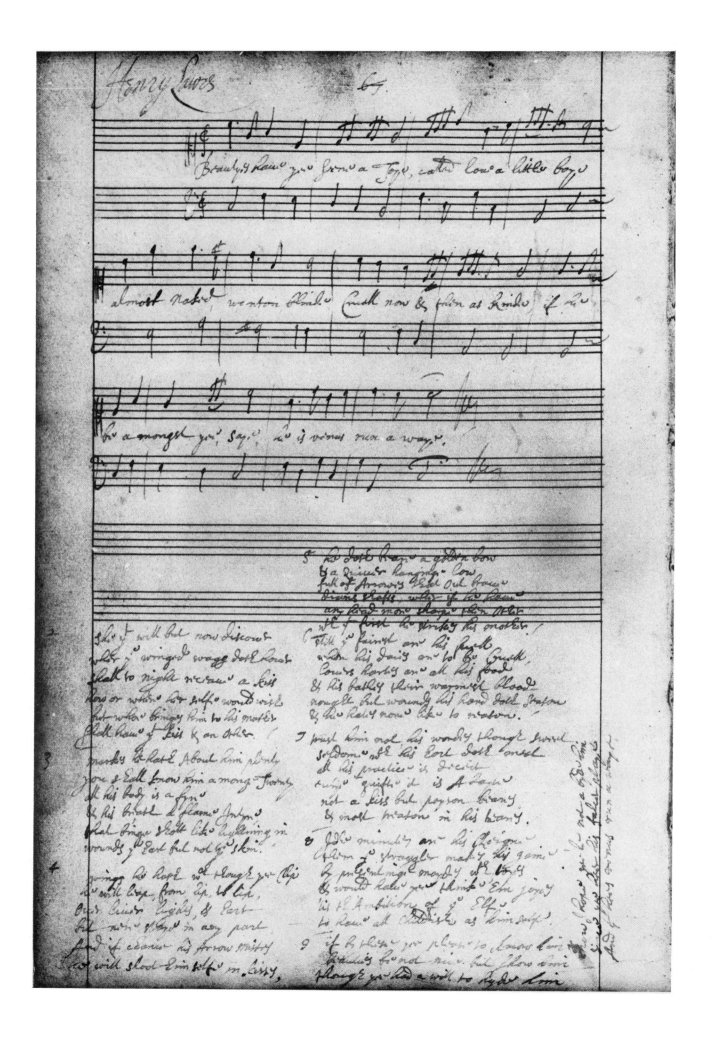

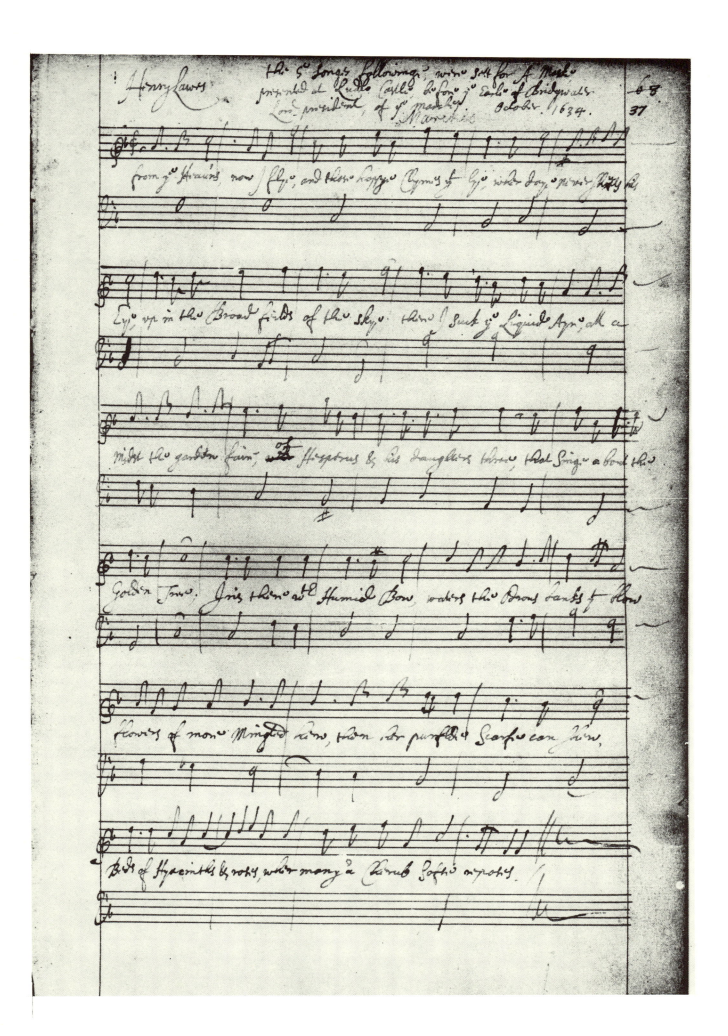

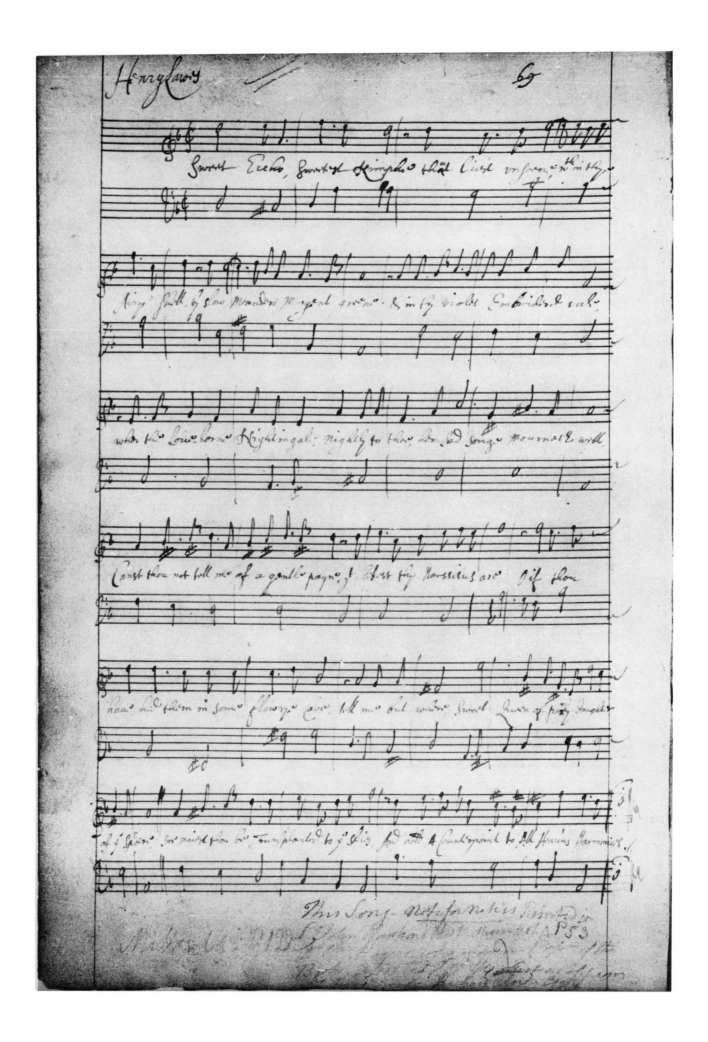

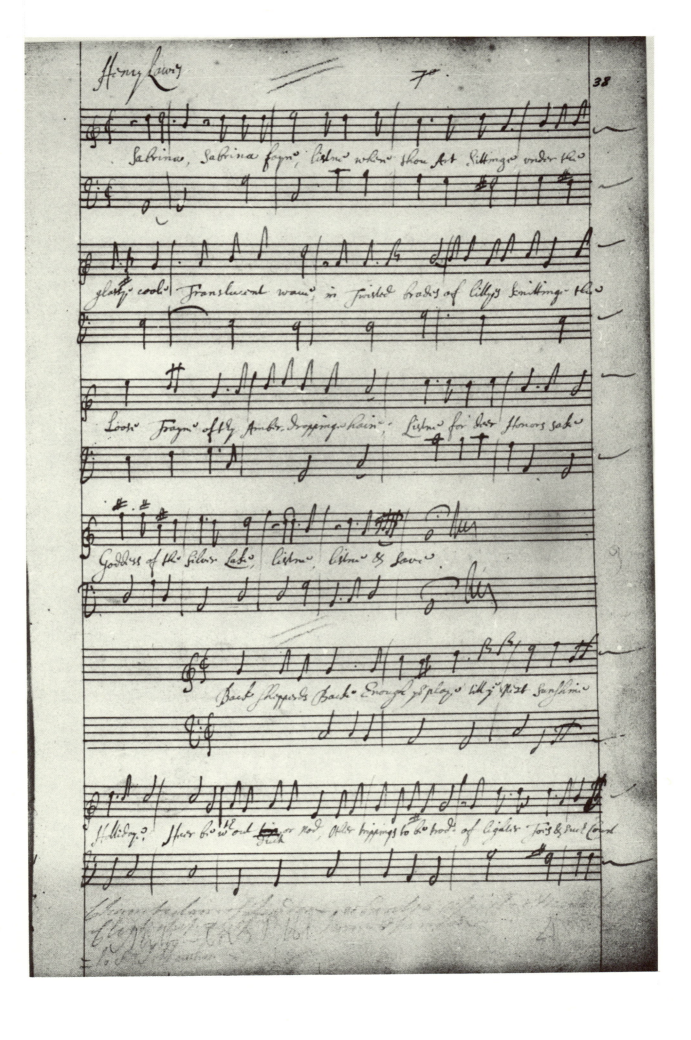

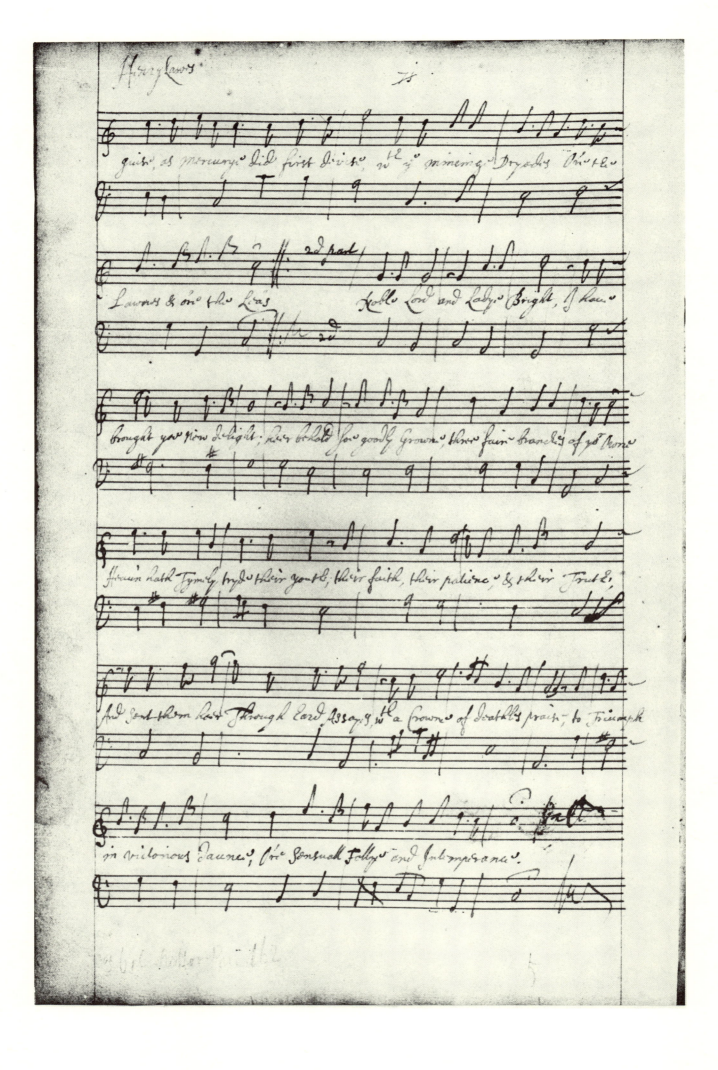

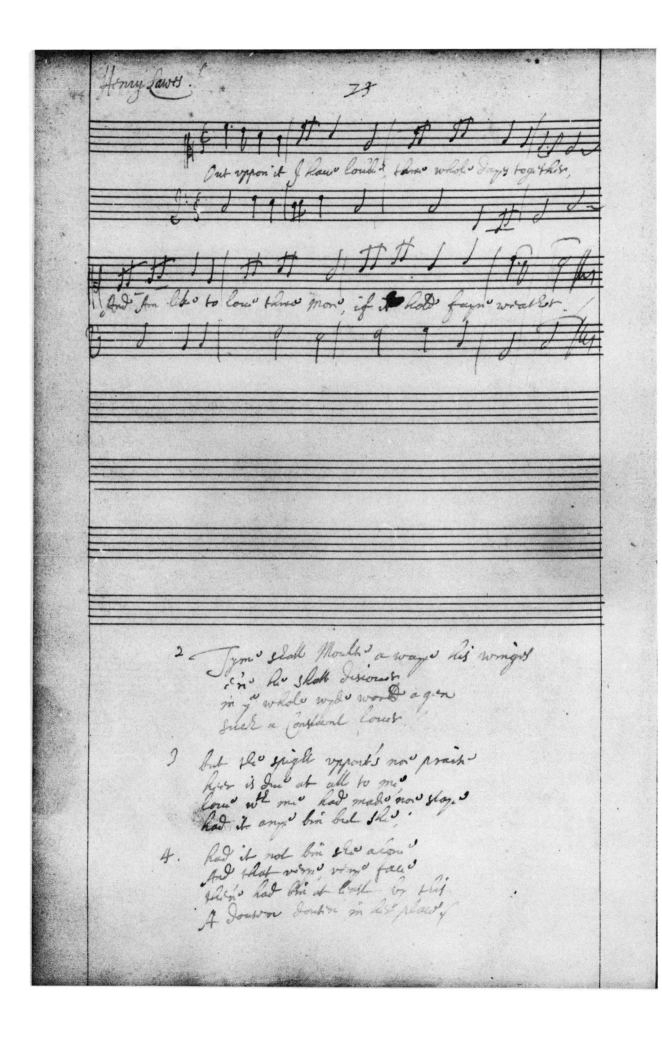

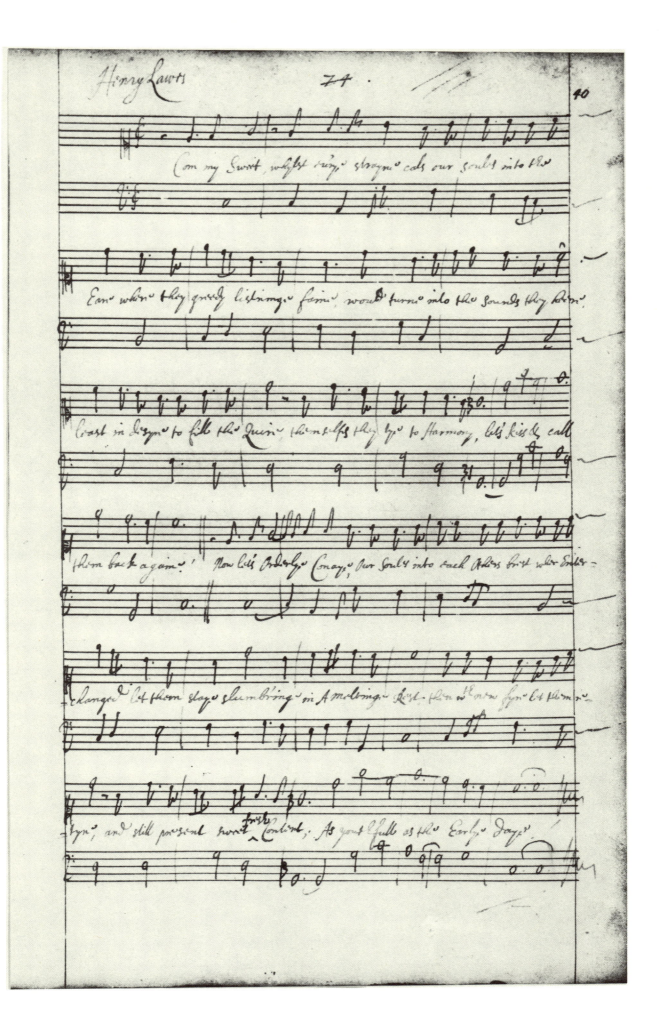

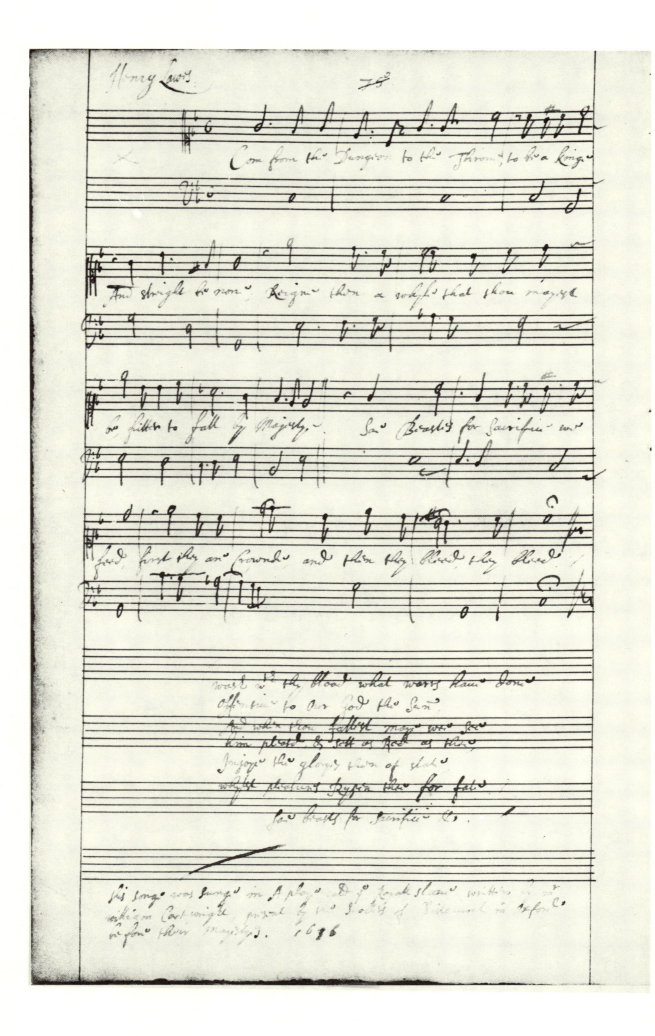

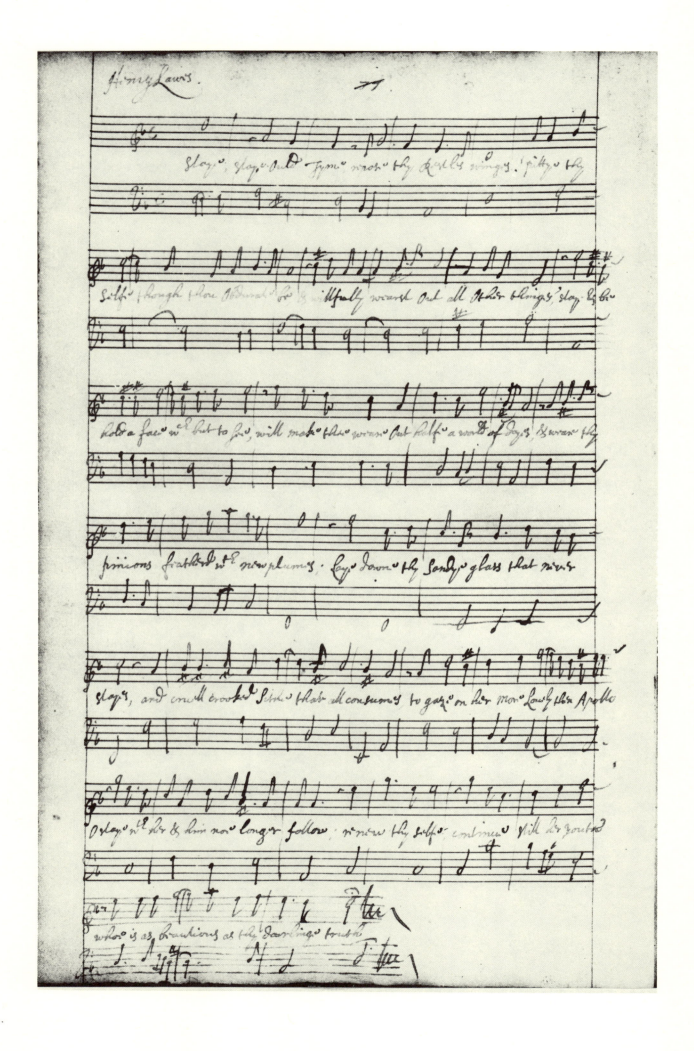

Henry Lawes — Cupid to y'e Knights Templars in a Maske at y'e middle Temple.

whystle soe gladly and soe fast, as if y'u knew all Dang'r past of a Combatt and of of warr, as y'u beleiv'd my Arrows were bound or when I shoot that Ev'ry wound I make is but a scarr, Arme now y'r brests w'th sheilds of steele, & plates of brass y't you shall feele, my mother taught me &c.

2
Arme now y'r brests w'th sheilds of steele
& plates of brass y't you shall feele
my Arrows are soe keene
Like lightening y't not hurts y'e skin
yet melts y'e solid parts w'th in
they'le wound although unseene.

3
my Mother taught me longe agoe
to Arme my shafts and draw my bow
when shee did Mars subdue
And now you must resigne to Love
y'e warlike shafts that shee may prove
showe Antick stamped true.

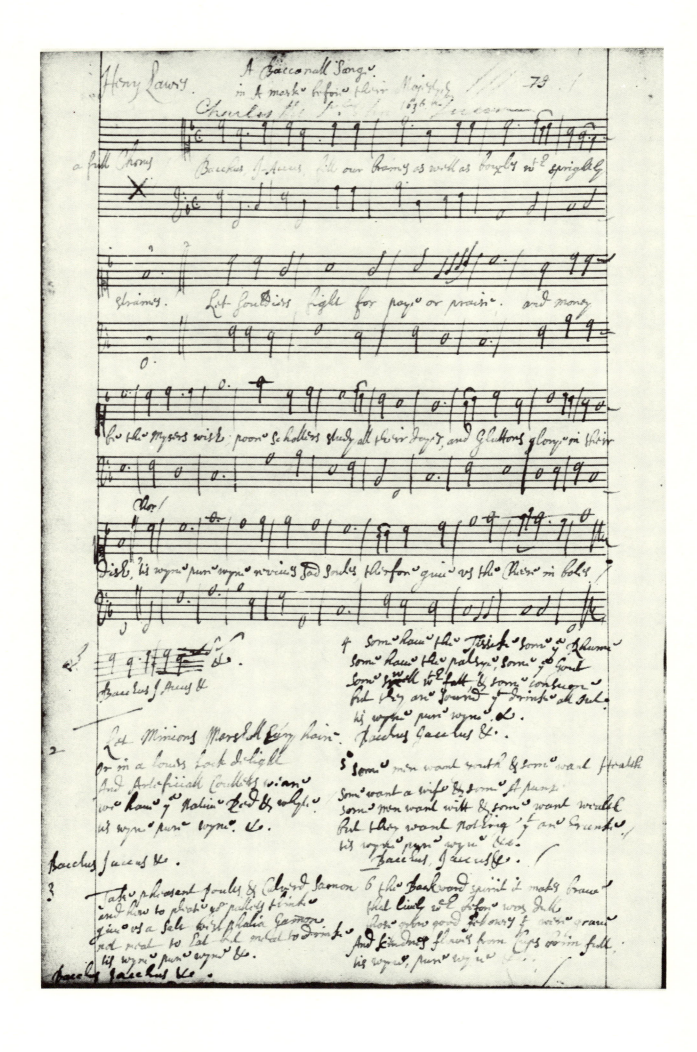

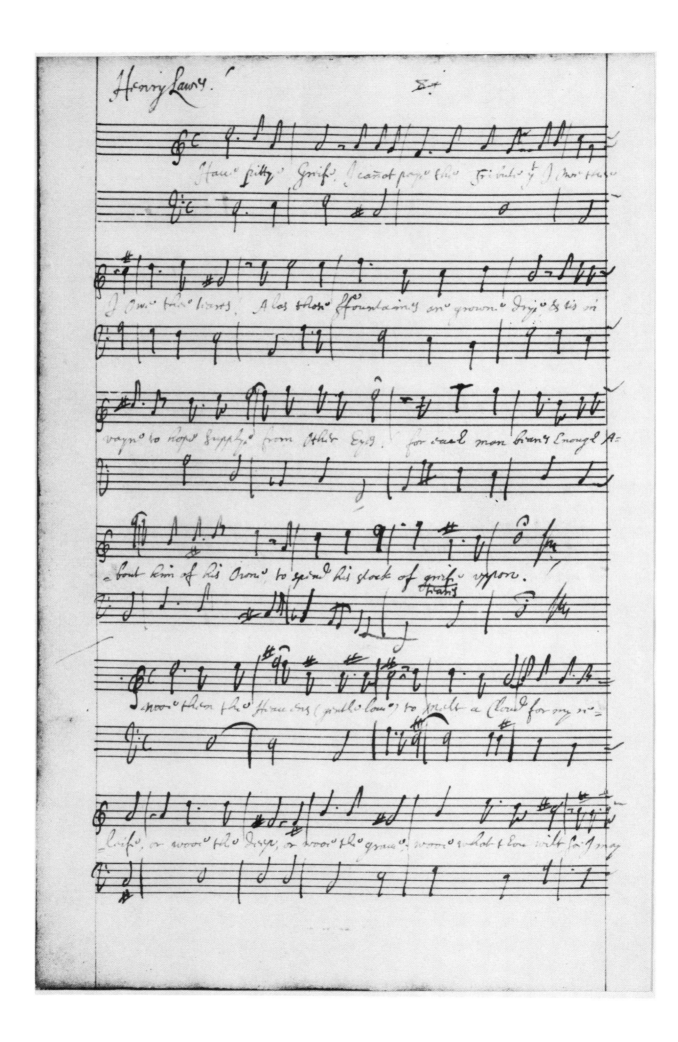

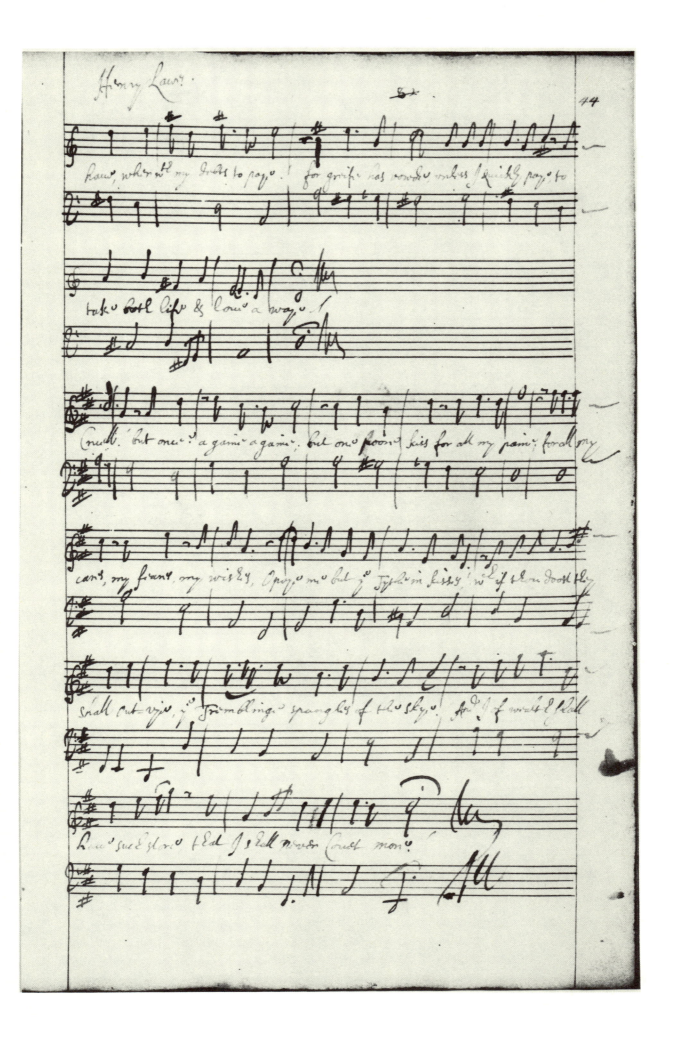

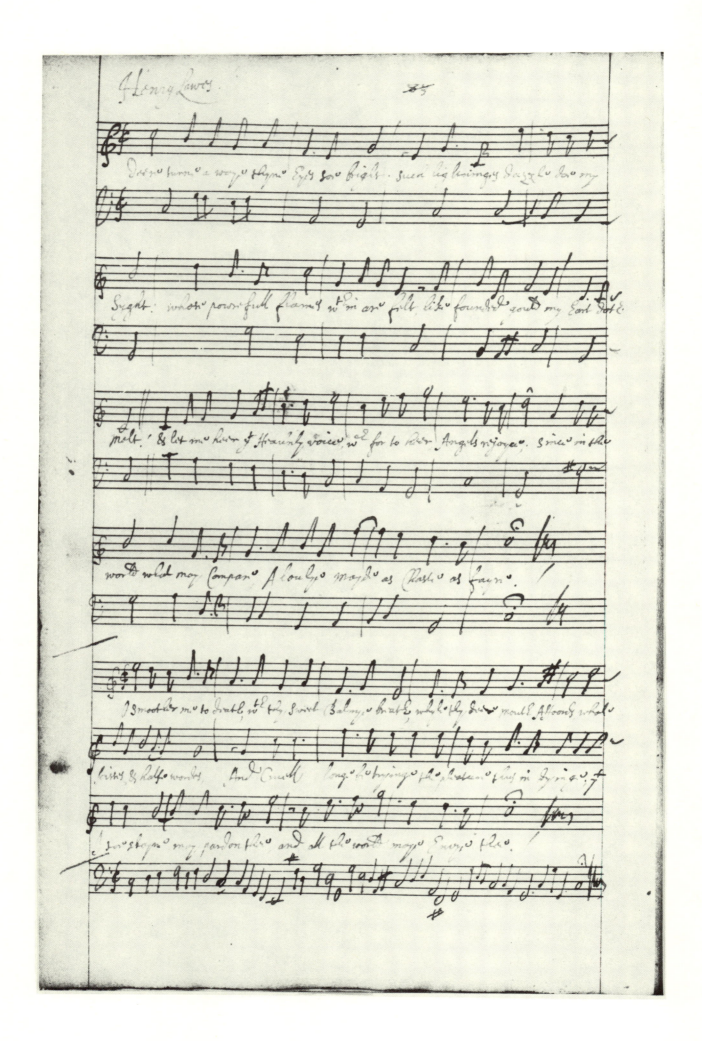

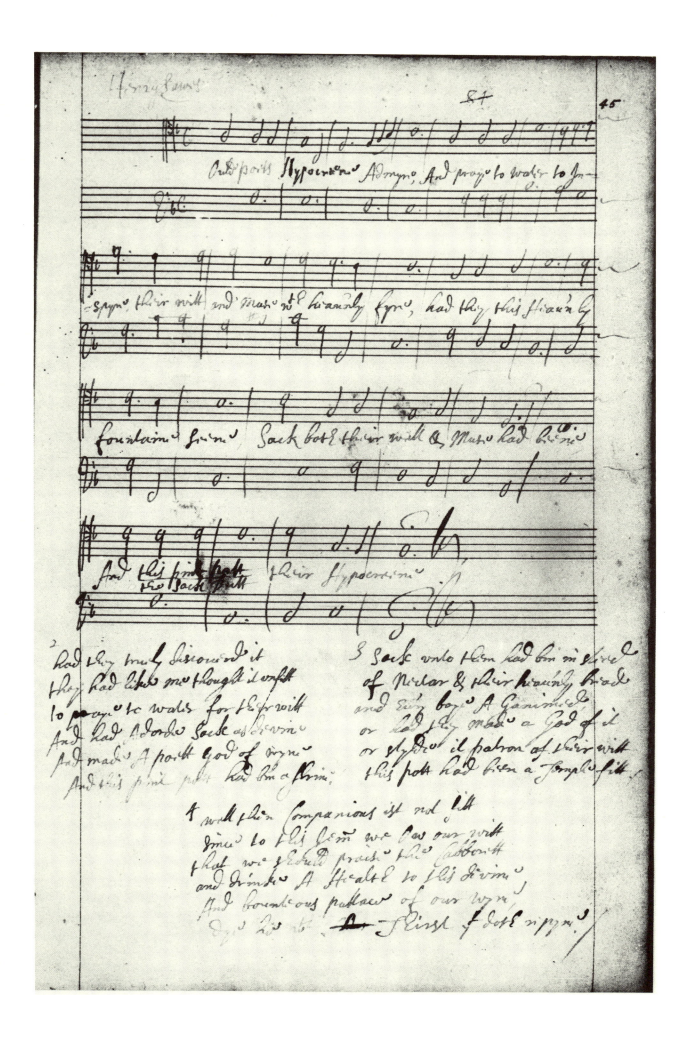

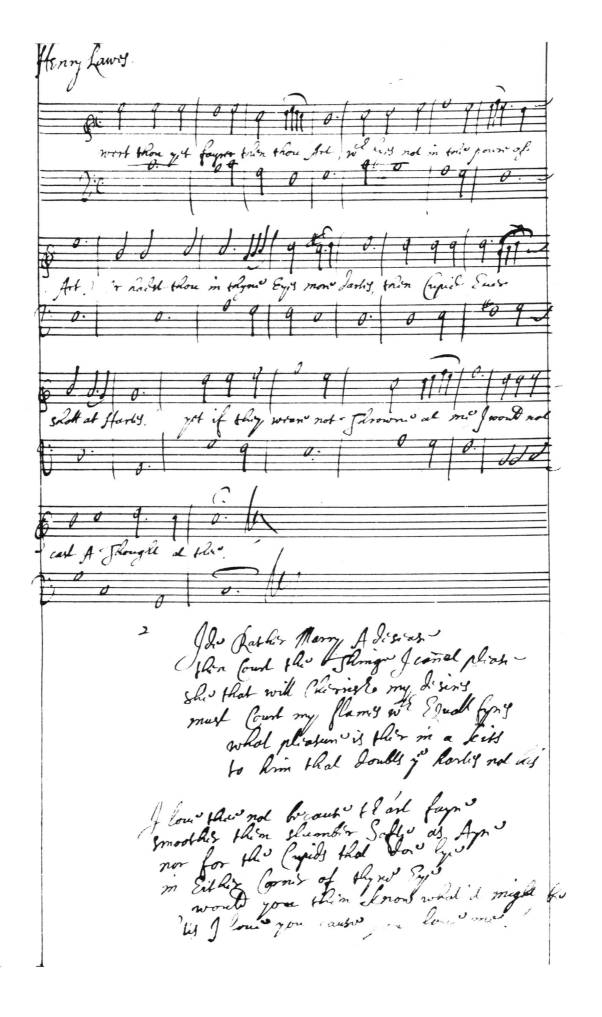

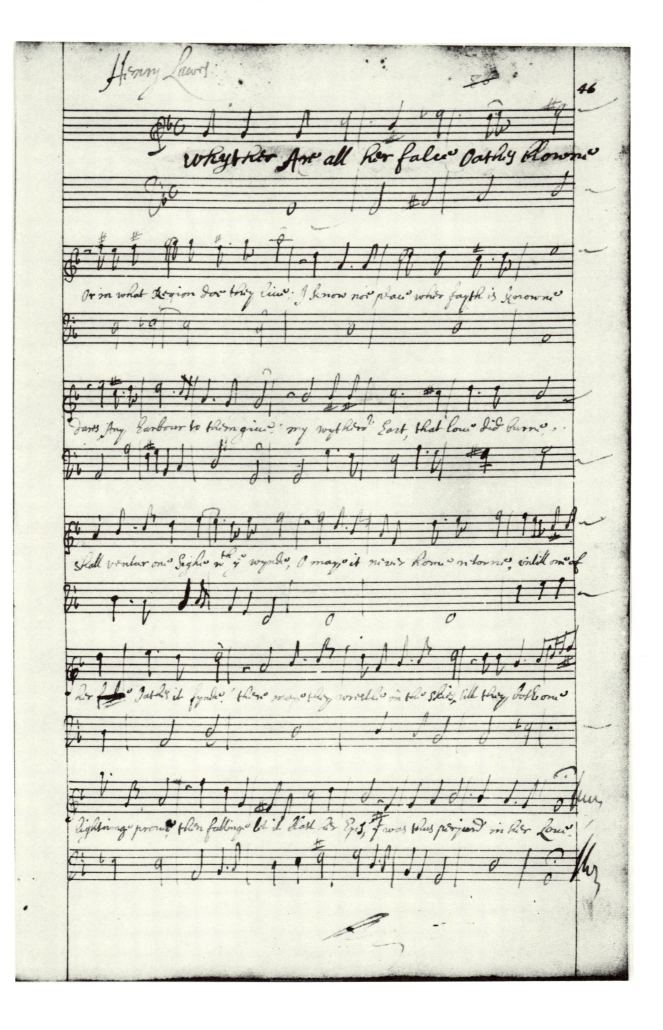

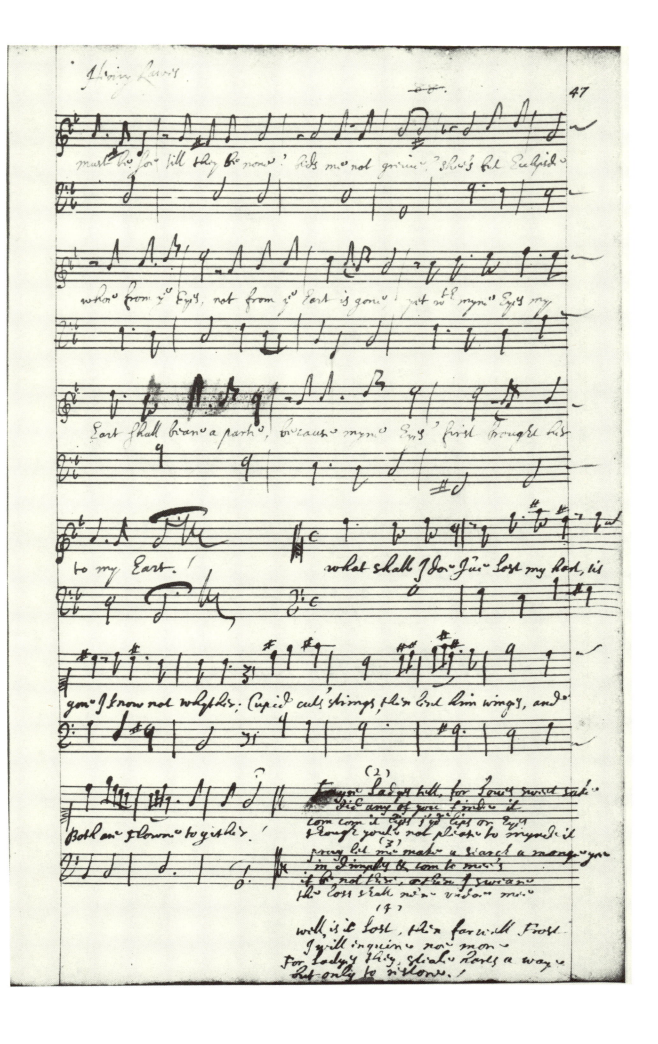

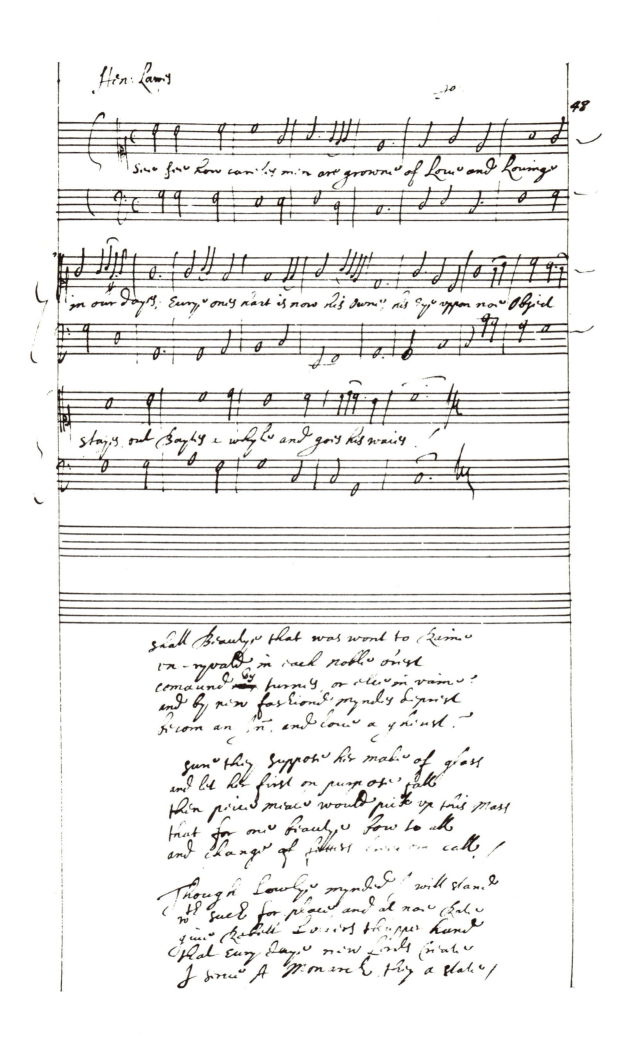

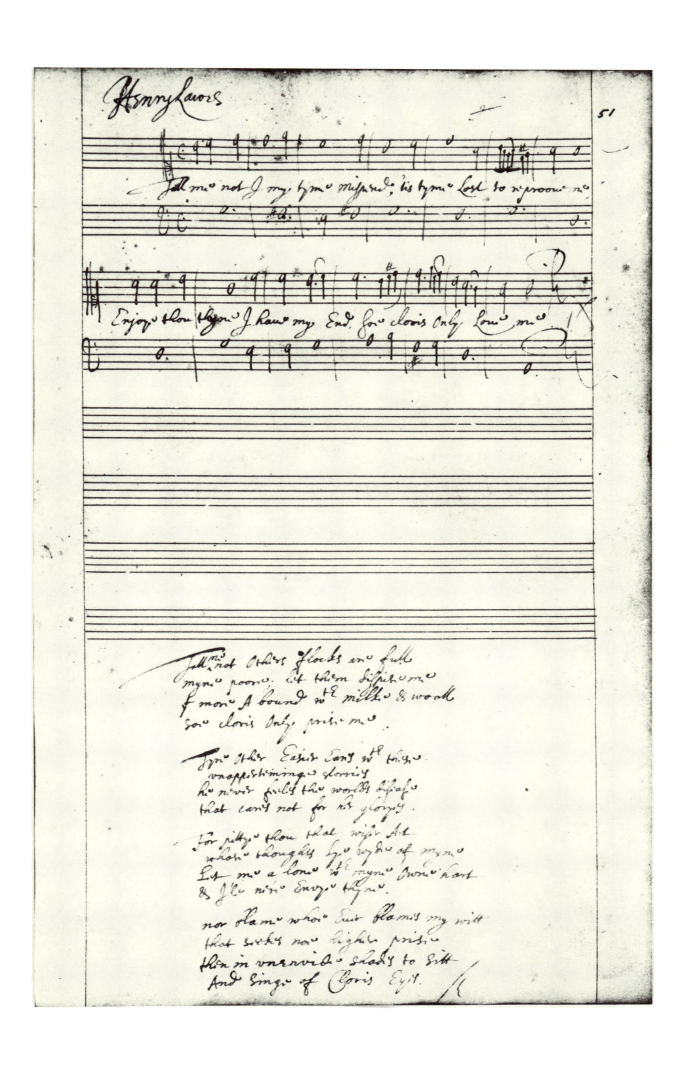

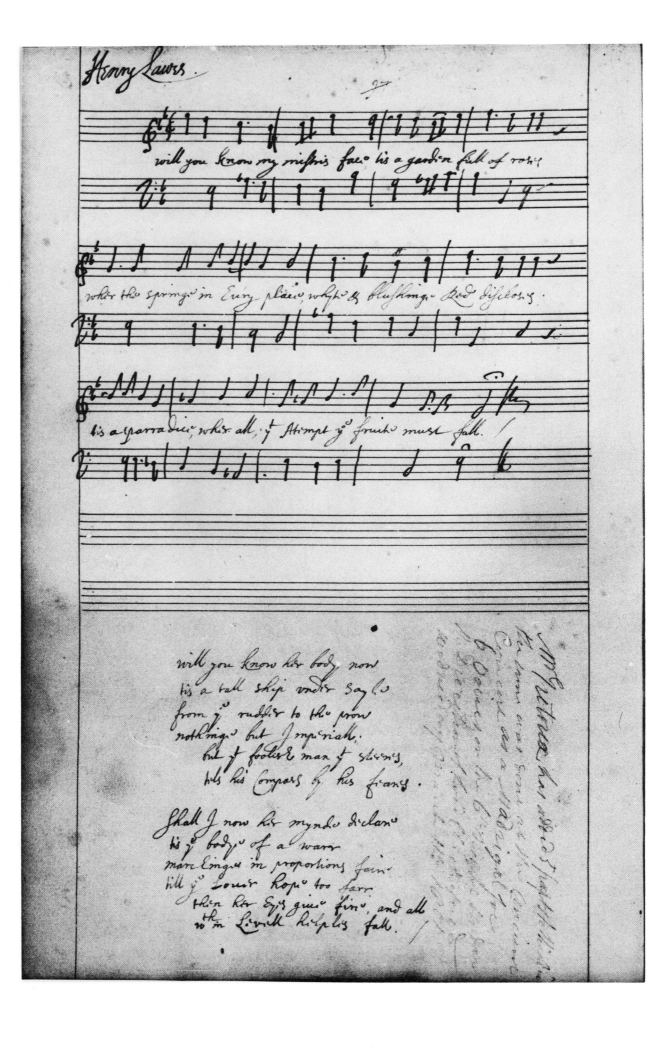

Hen: Lawes.

Com O Com I brooke noe stayes, Shee doth not Love yt can delaye.
Now this stealinge night hath blowed out yr light, and
Tapers doe supply the Daye.

2. To bee Chaste is to bee Ould
   & ye ffoolish Girle ys Cold
   is fourscore at fifteene
   Desiringe doe wrapt us greene
   and Lookes flames or youth unfold.

3. See ye first Taper is almost gone
   thy flame like it will quickly be none
   and I as it Expires
   not able to hold fire
   Shee Looketh hymn yt Lyes alone.

4. let us cherrish these these powres
   whylst wee yet may call them ours,
   their wee best spend our tyme
   when noe Dull zealous Chyme
   but sprightfull kisses strike ye Howres.

Henry Lawes

O Now the Certaine cause I know, whence the
Rose and Lillys grow, in yr faire cheekes, the Ofspring, shewrs
wch your eyes have cause those flowrs.

If yt the Floods could Venus bringe
And warlike Mars from flowers springe
Why may not hence two Gods Arise
this from yr cheekes, that from yr Eyes

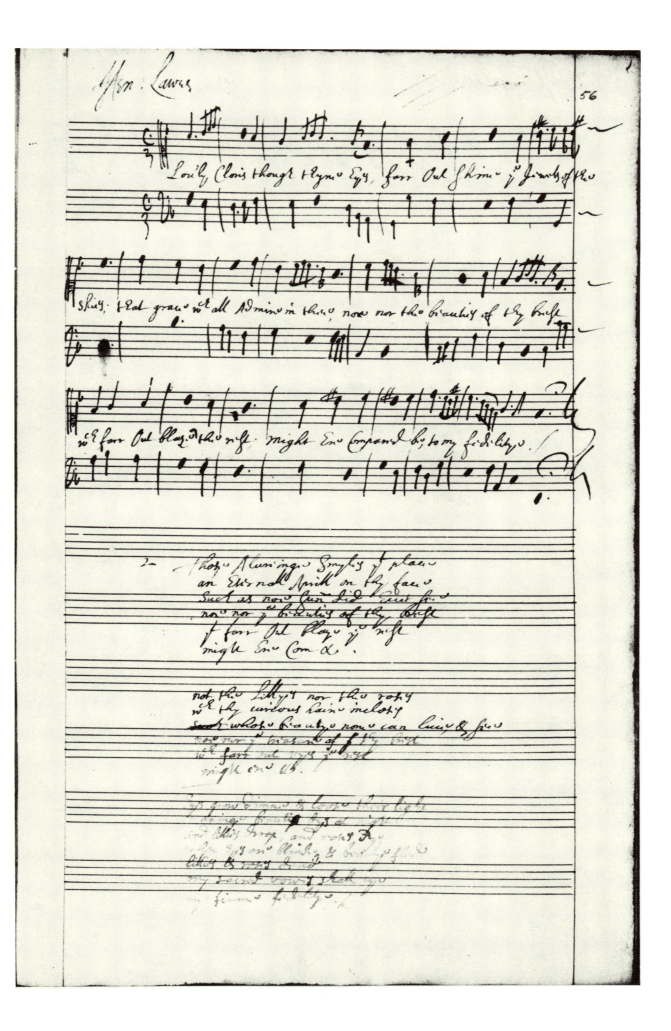

Hen: Law:

Sure thou framed wert by Art
purposely to take my hart   for such lookes were
Ever made. Only for that Cheatinge trade

all thy oathes & fondled Armes
Sighinge flatts bewitchinge charmes
Every thought thou tendst that wayes
was only bent mee to betray.

False (alas) they are that sweare
all loues bargaines are not deer
know then flatterer that J must
heer noe more then J dare trust.

you may promise, sweare, & say
what perhaps you meane to day
but Ere morrowes Sun be sett
you An other loue will gett.

hadst thou left mee then vntride
thou hadst never bin denied
And J will for my loues sake
noe Ere better bargaine make.

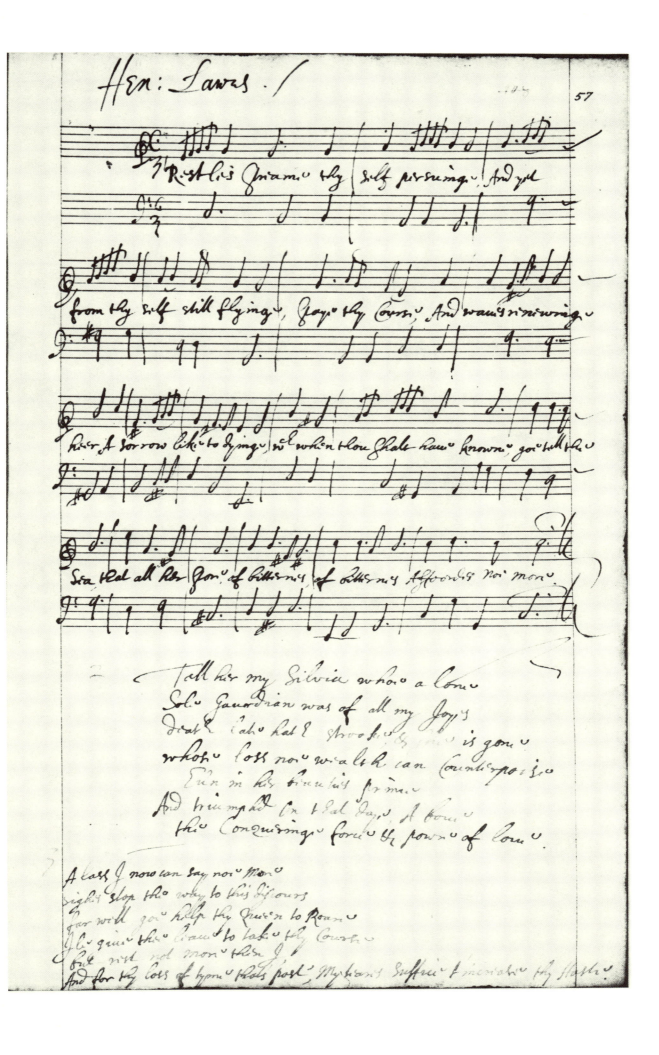

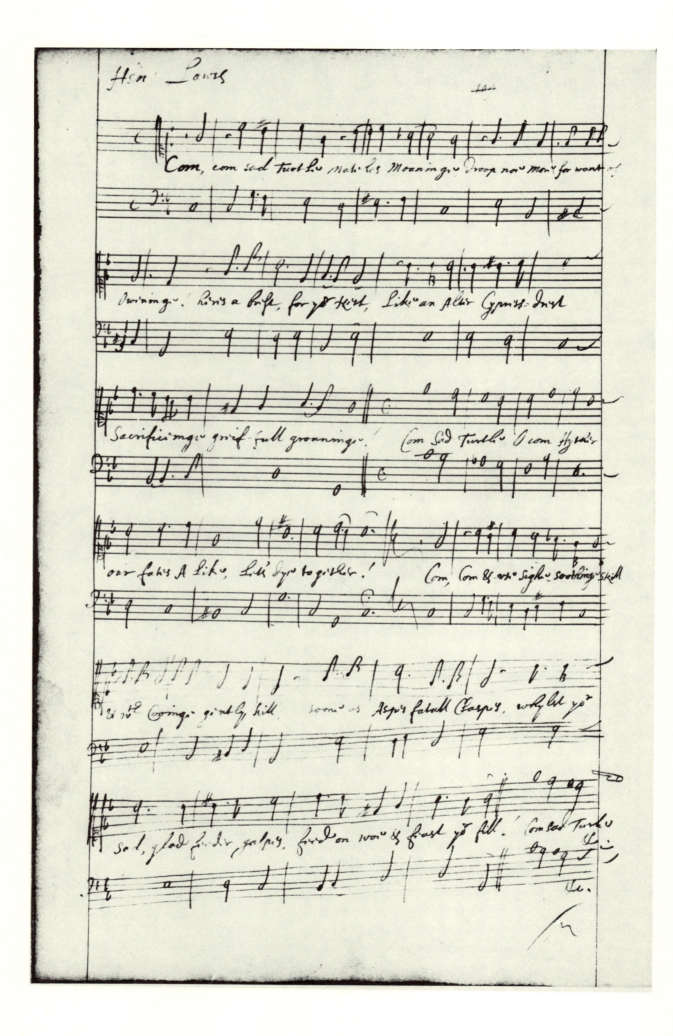

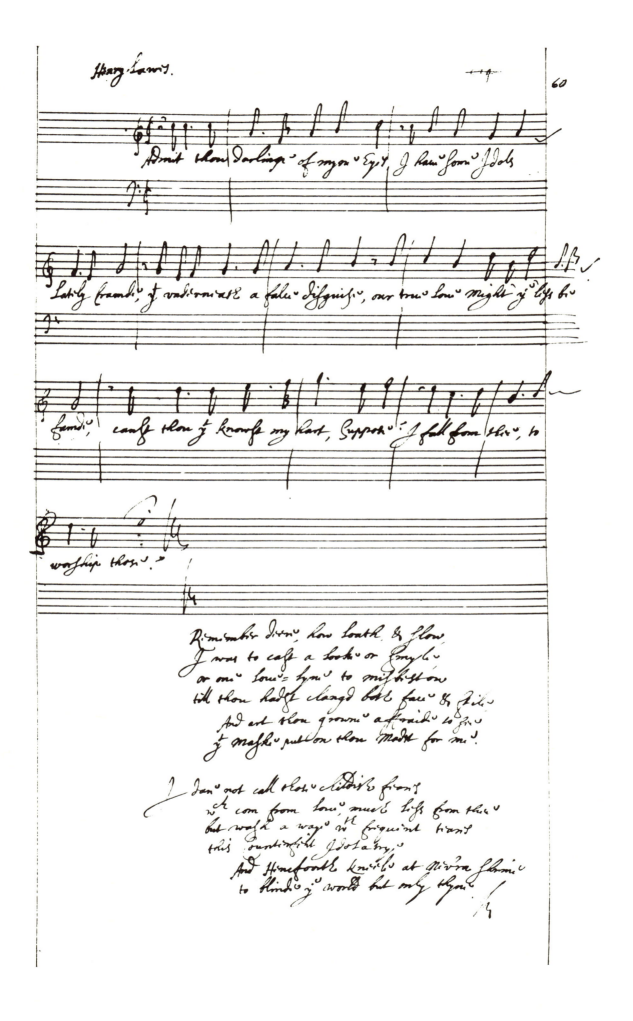

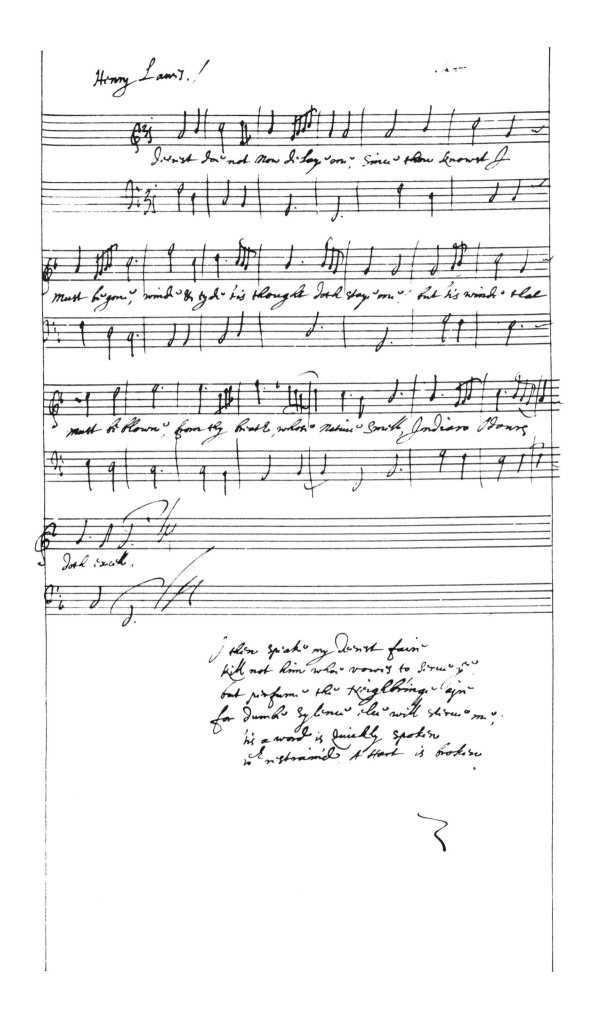

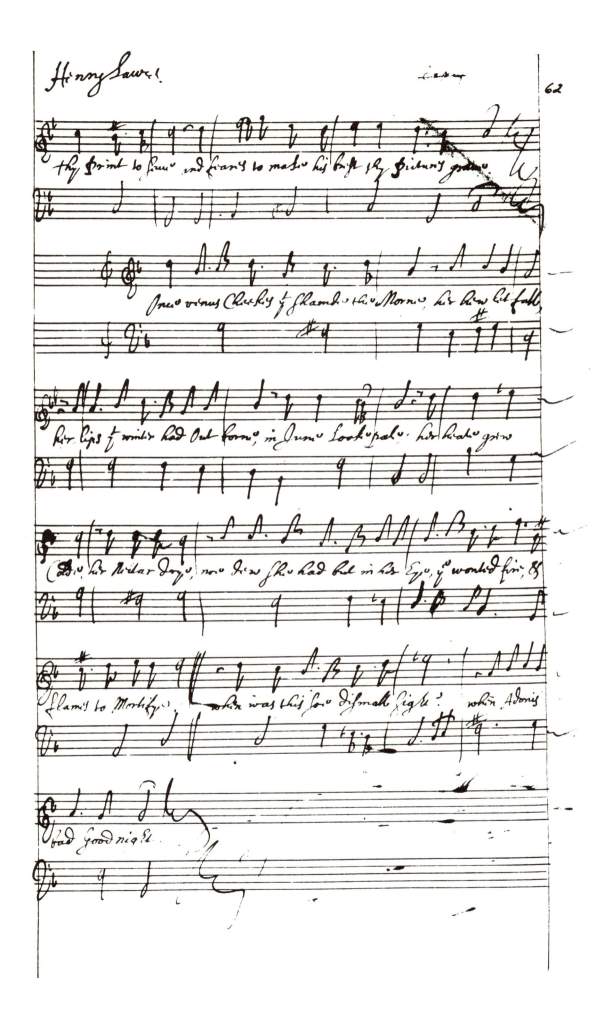

Hen: Lawes

Ladyes, you yt seeme so nice, & as Cold in show as Ice, & perhaps haue

hild out thrice; Dare not thinke but in a trice, one or other may intice

And at last by some deuice, sett yor Honors at a price.

you whose smooth & dainty skin
rosye lips, or cheekes, or chin
oft gaz'd upon you win
yet insult not speedy'ly wthin
slowly'e burne, no flame's begin
And presumption still hath bin
hild a most notorious sin.

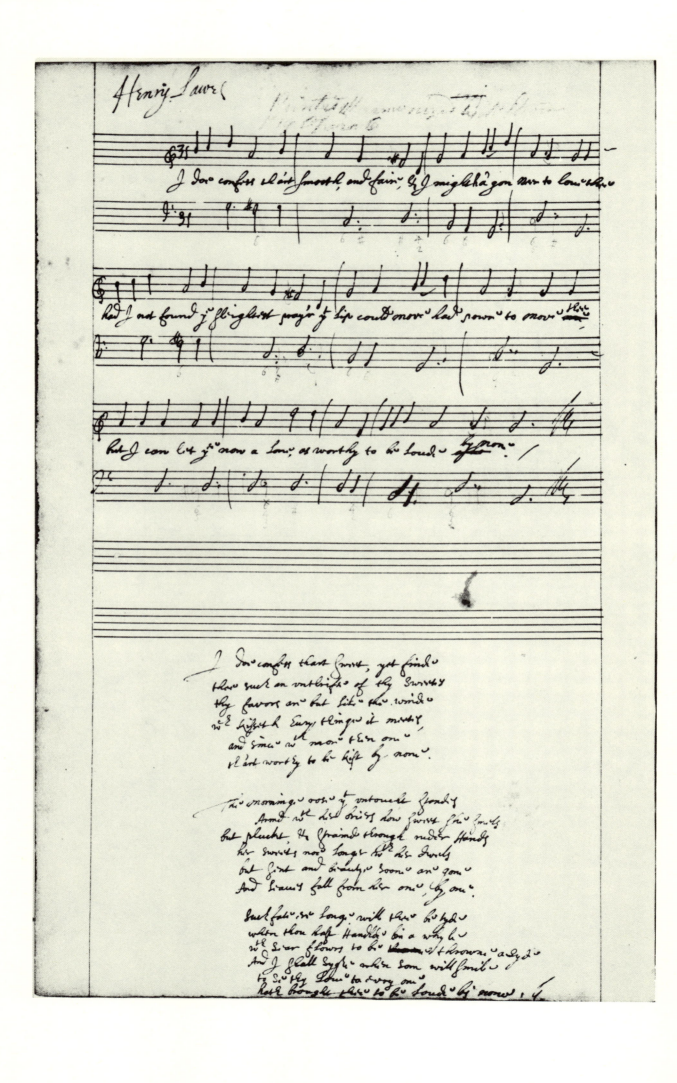

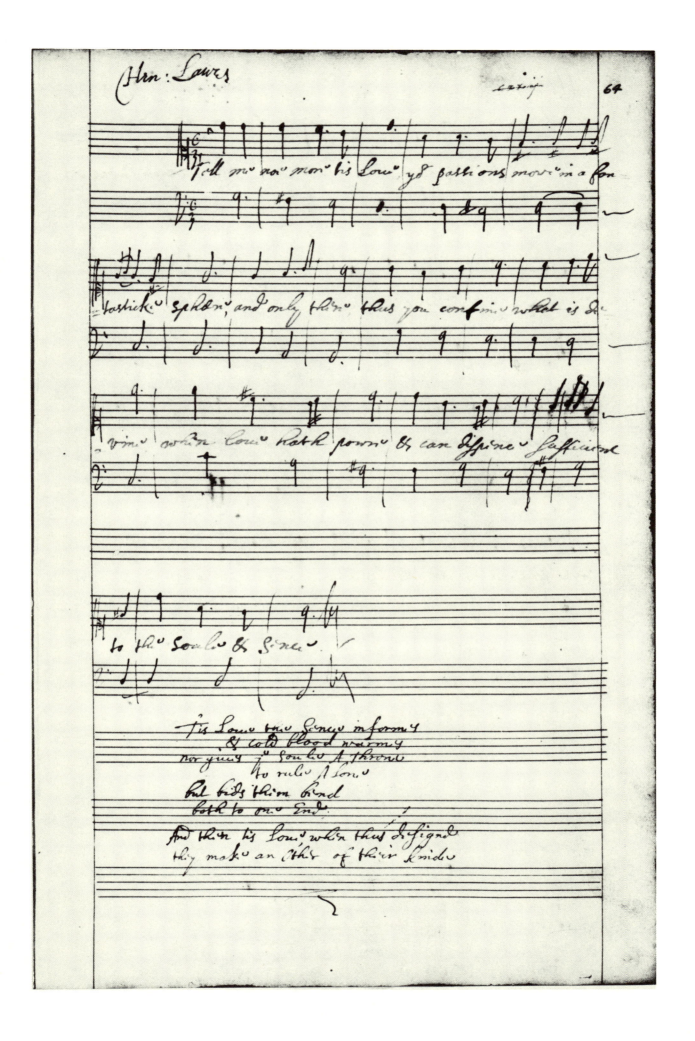

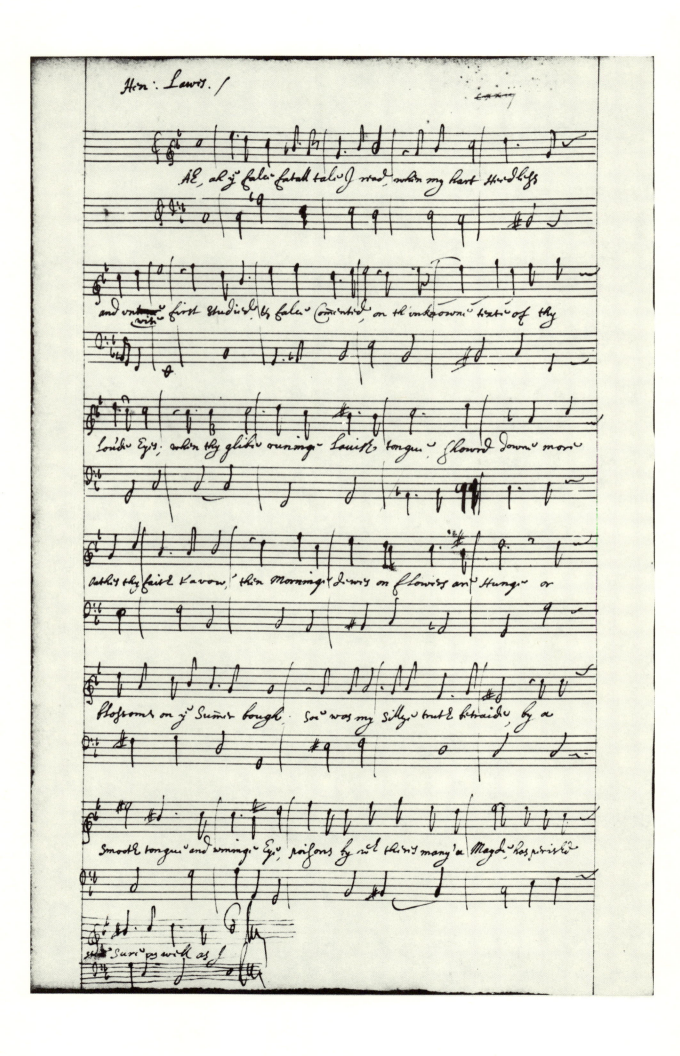

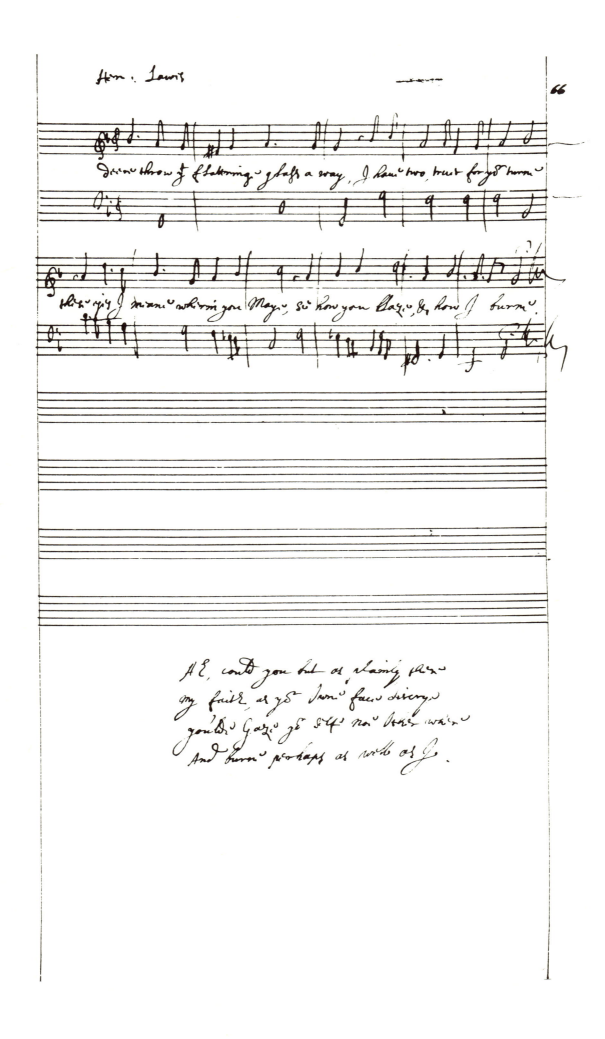

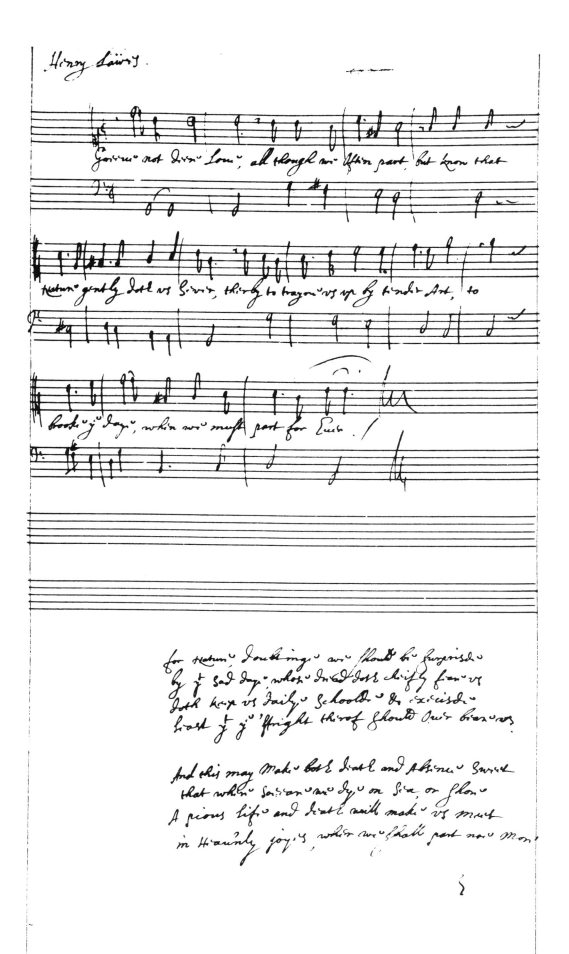

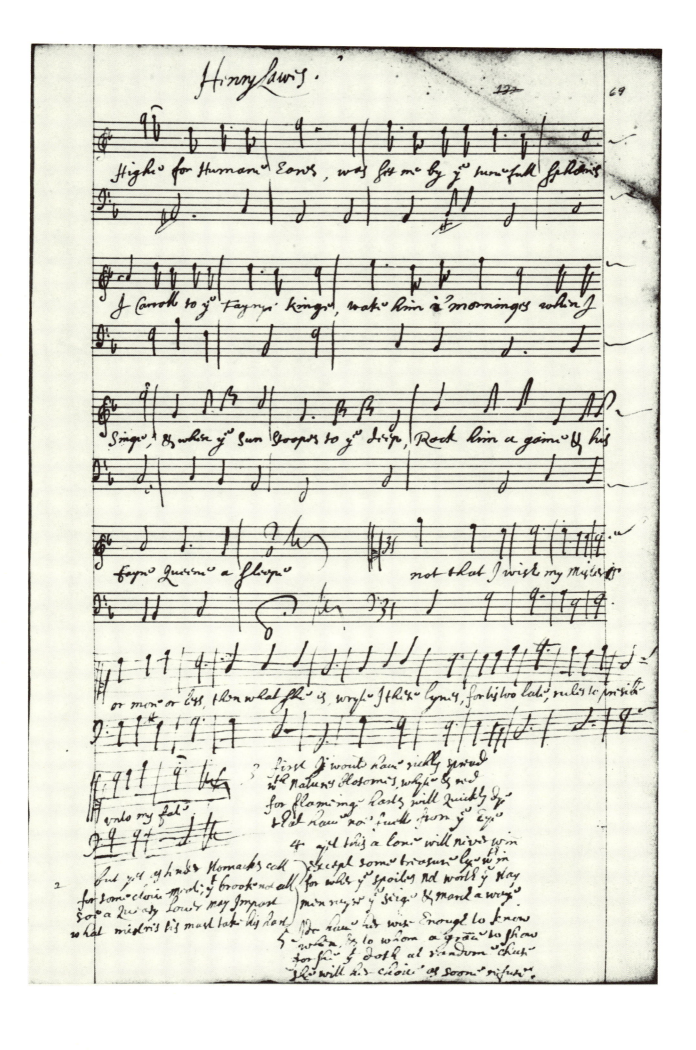

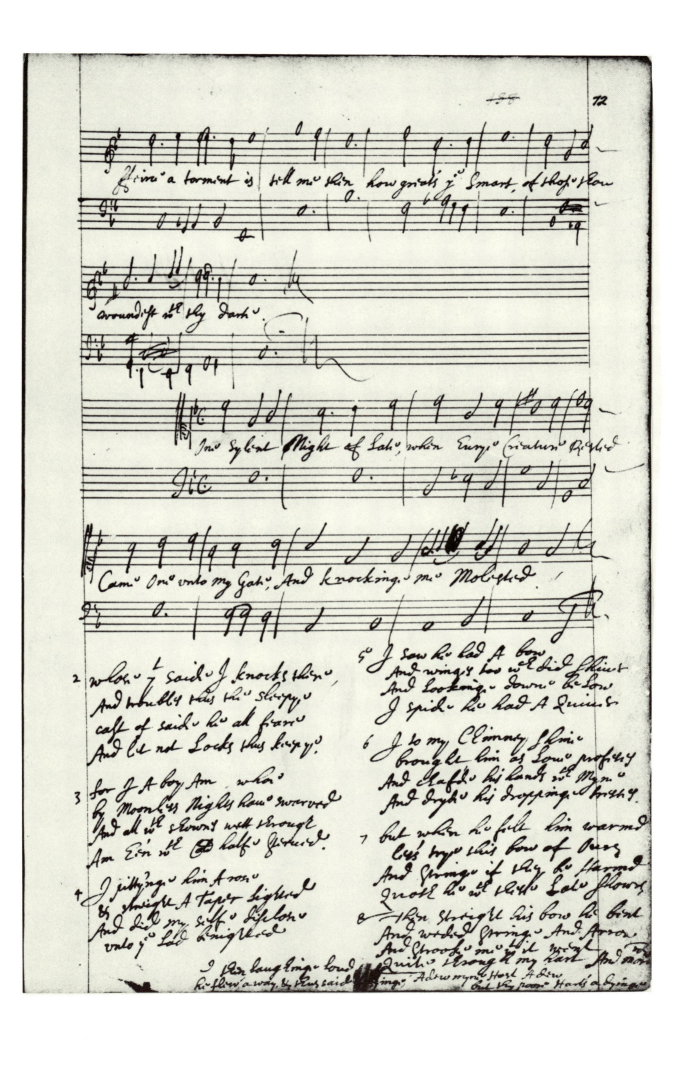

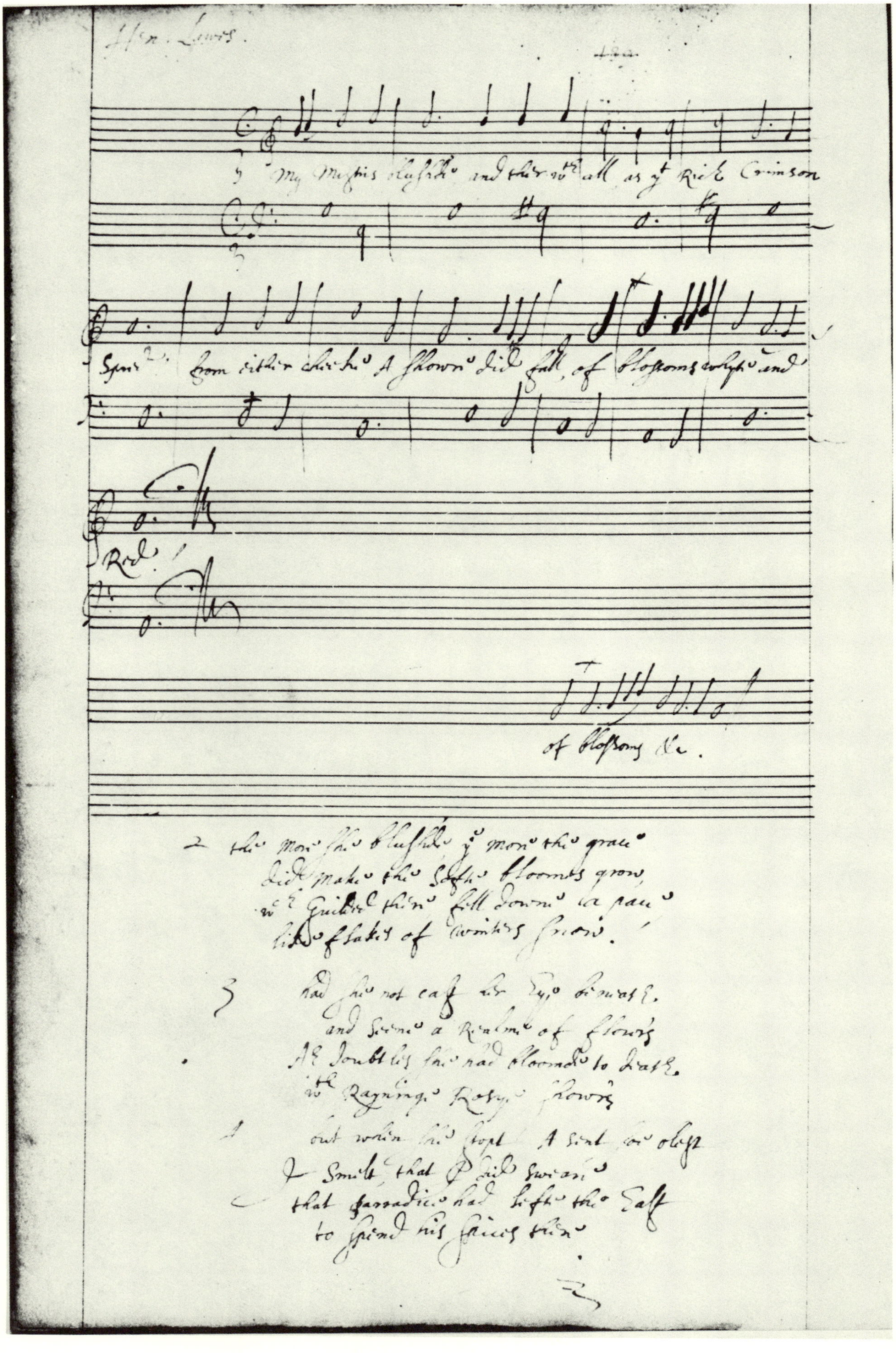

Mr̄ Lewis

My Mistris blushte and therwth all as yt Rich Crimson

Spred from either cheeke, A showr did fall, of blossoms wht and

Red

of blossoms &c.

2 the more she blushte ye more the grace
   did make the softer bloomes grow,
   wc Guilded them fell downe apace
   like flakes of winters snow.

3 had shee not cast her Eyes beneath,
   and seene a Realme of flowrs
   As doubtles shee had bloomde to death
   wth Raynings Roby showrs

4 out when shee stopt A sent or oboe
   I smilde, that I did sweare
   that paradice had left the East
   to spend his glories there.

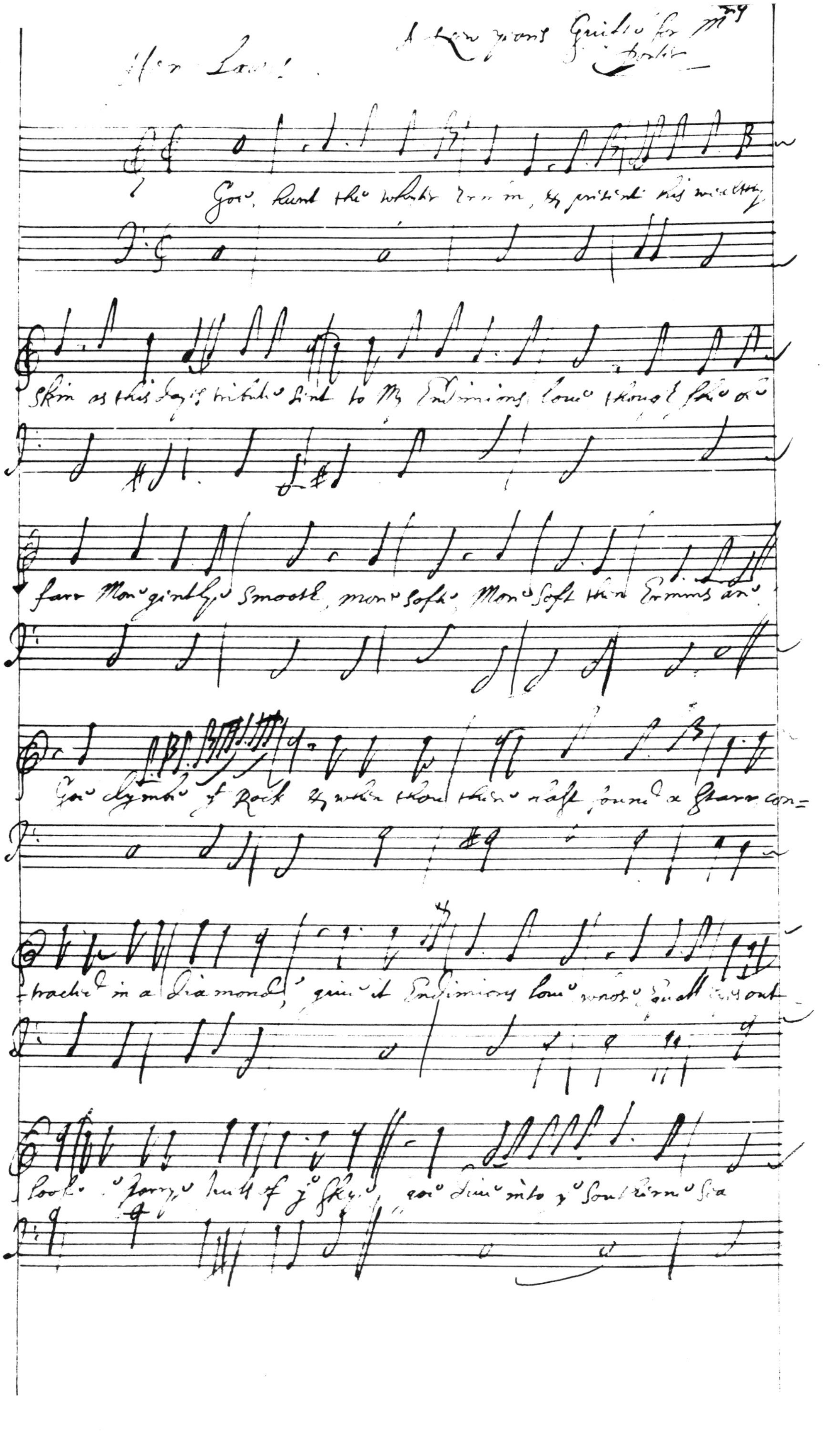

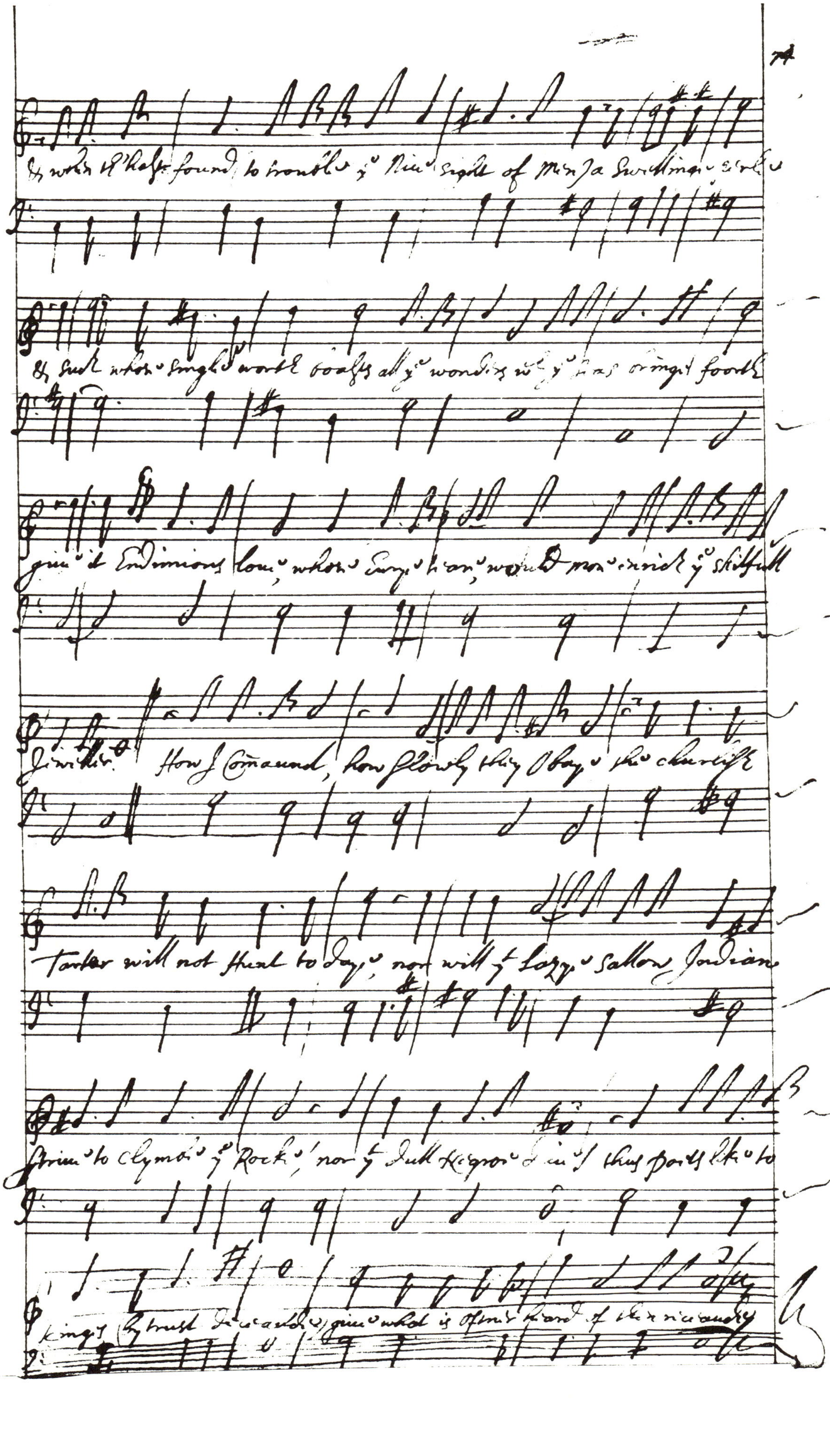

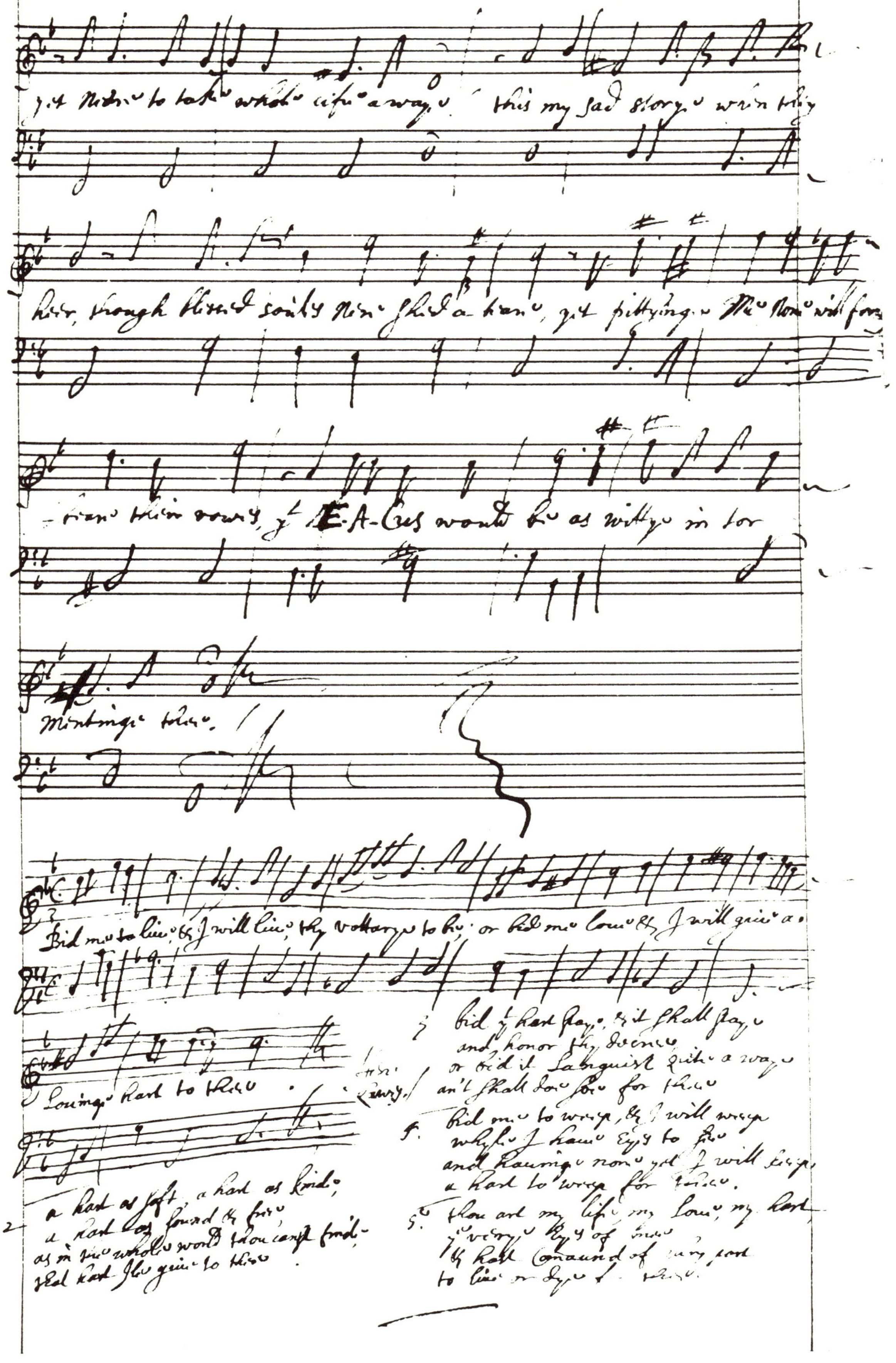

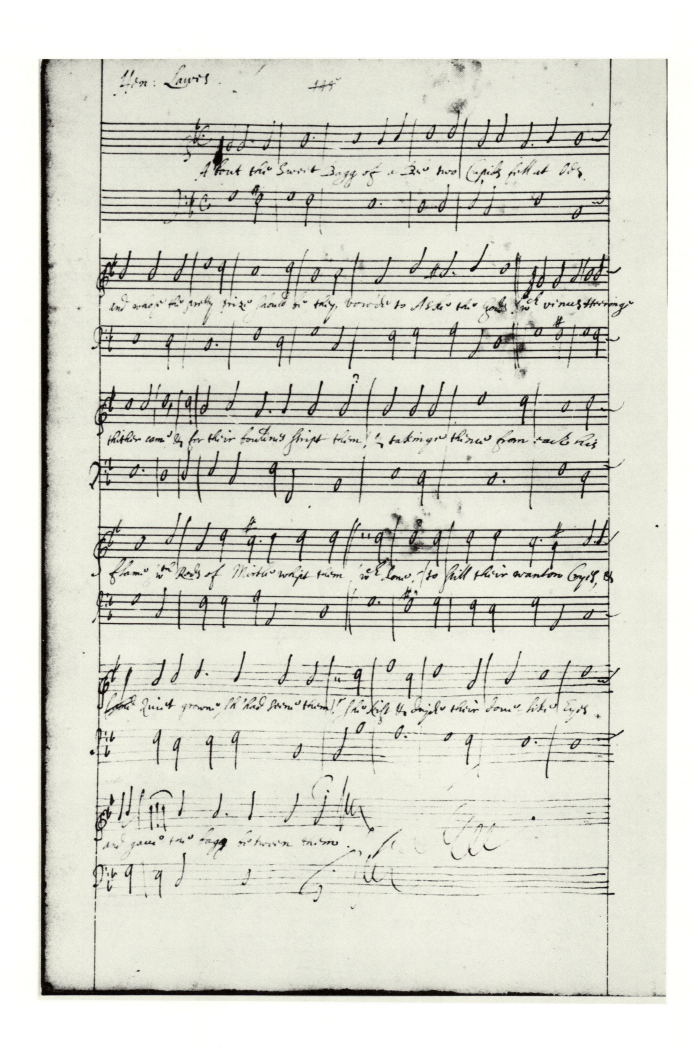

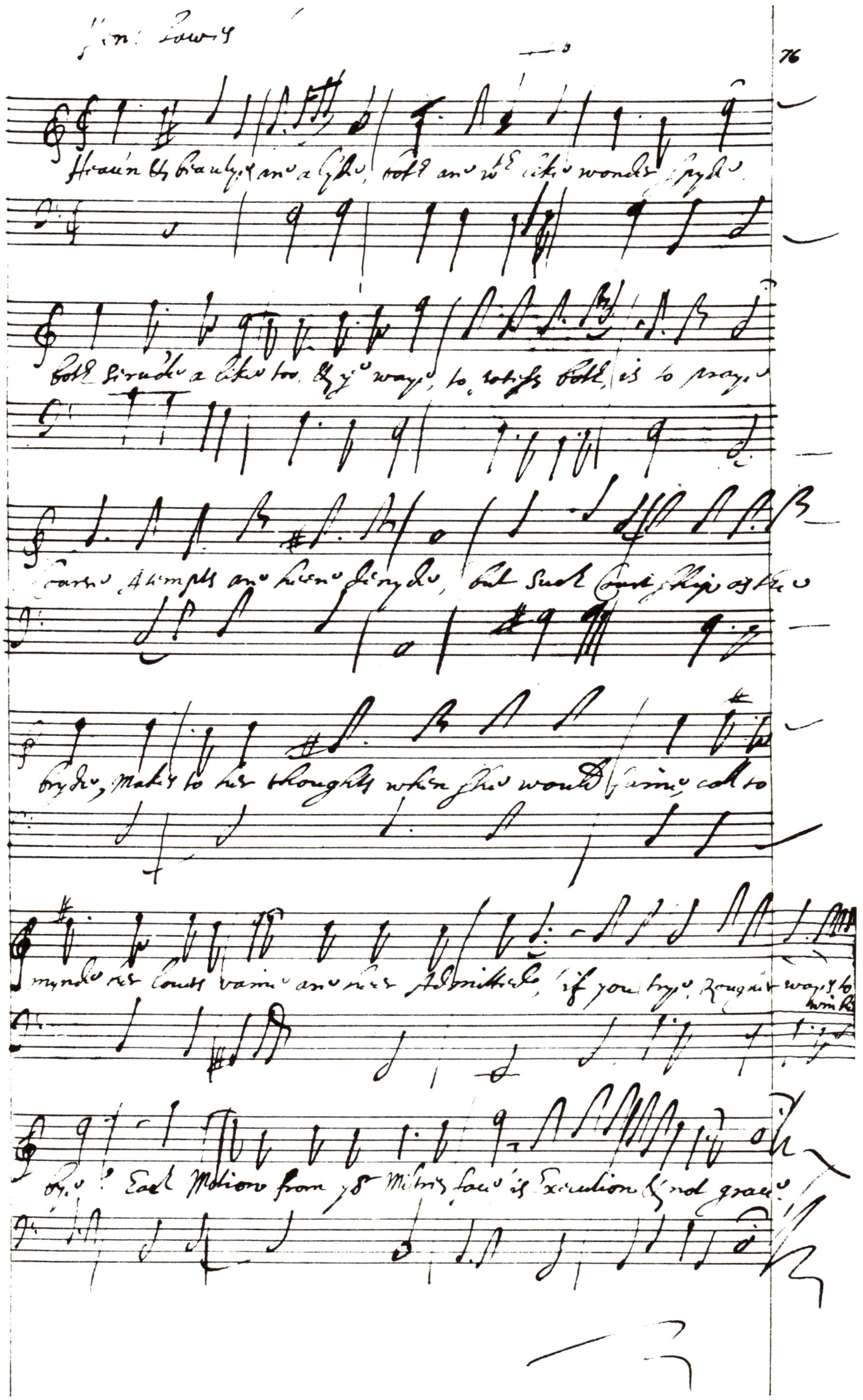

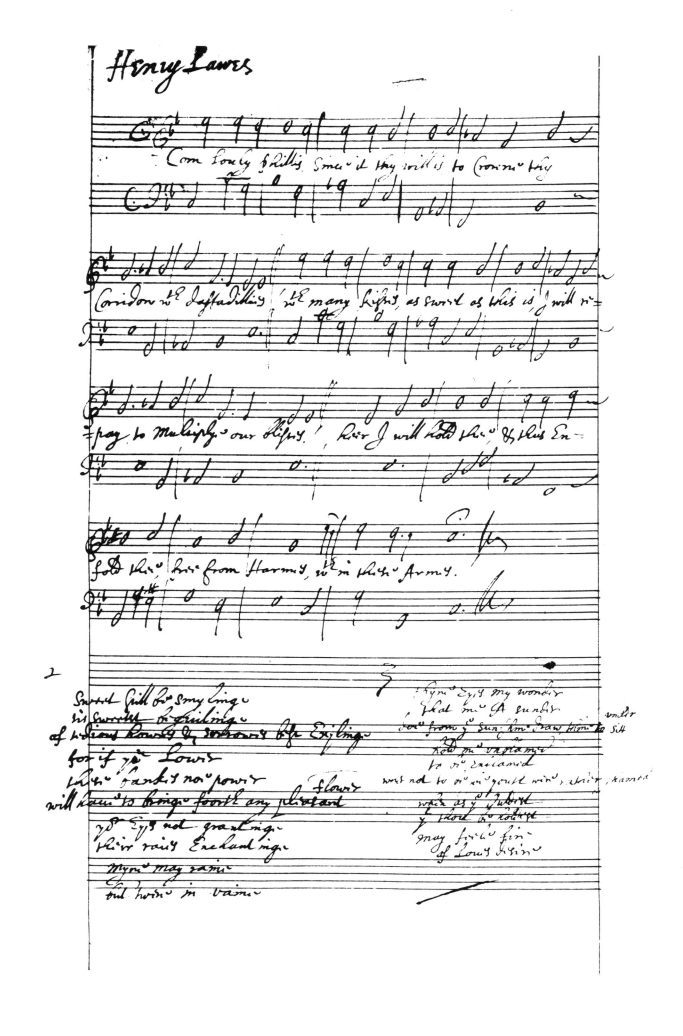

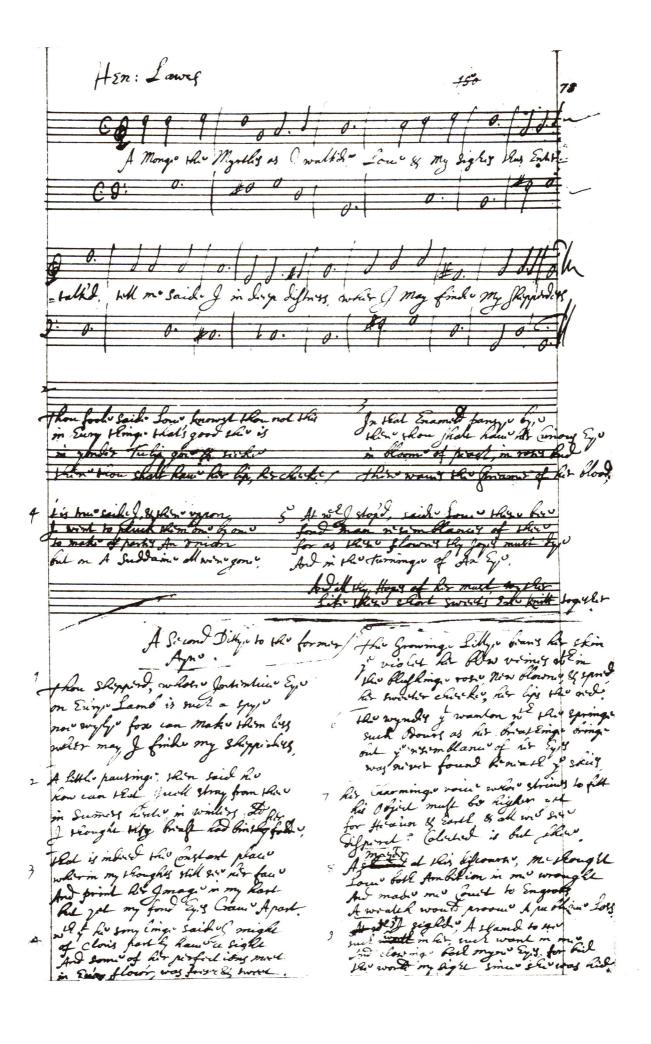

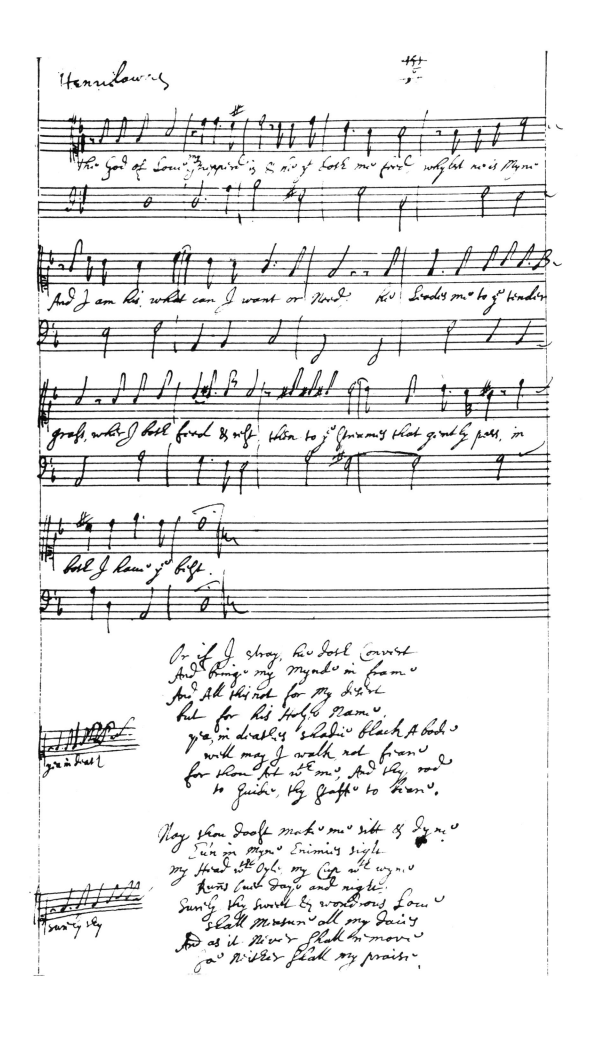

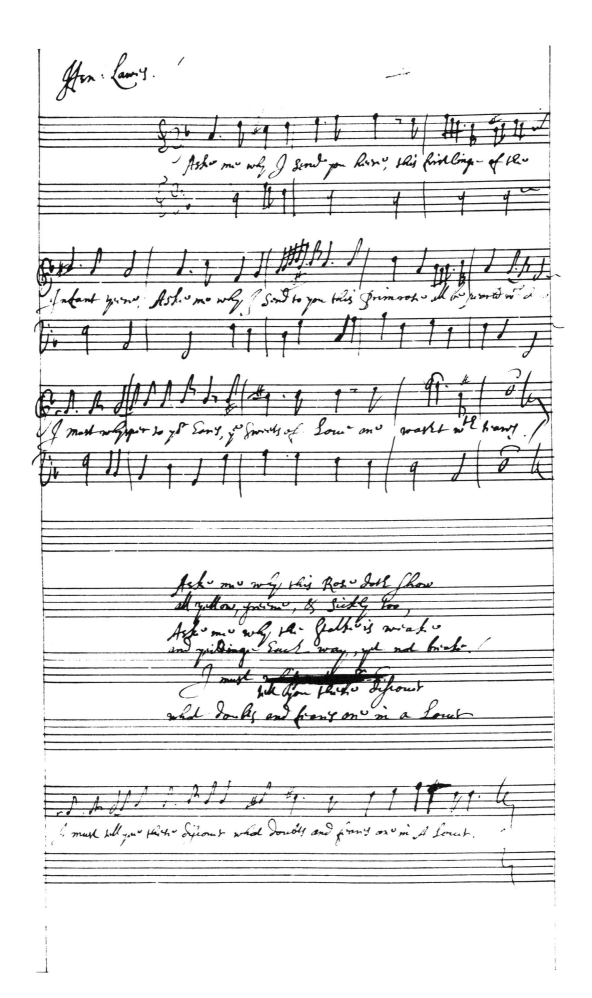

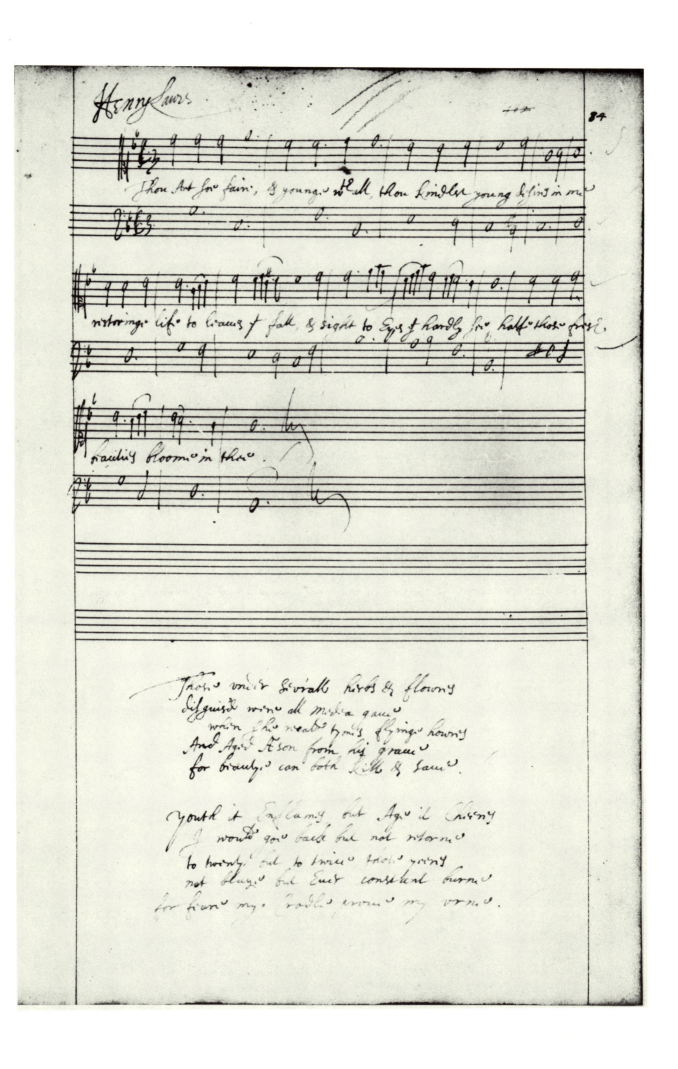

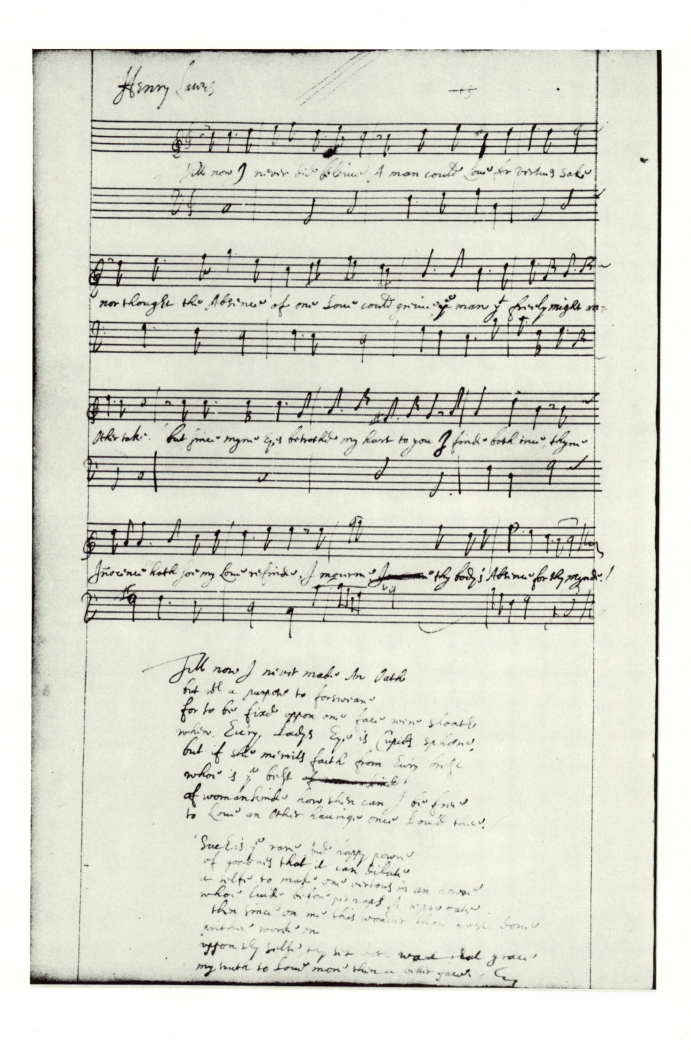

Hen: Lawes.

Though my Body be restrained from thy presence, yet my
mynde, wch no fetters can be chayned but a passage it will find to thy
Bosome, where ye Bliss of my Soule enclosed is.

what are these disasters then
lives I bound nor lives I free
cares like shaddowes vanish when
I doe feed my thoughts on thee
on thy will my life depends
that my joyes or sorrow Ends.

Then divinest beauty wonder
lett ye ——— or ———
let our soules Embrace each other
though ô bodys lies asunder
and let not Affliction smother
that sweet flame whose sacred fyre
Cupids sweares shall not Expire

Henry Lawes
86
that powerfull stroke, cals my fleeting soul away
suppress that magick sound wch destroys wthout a wound
peace, peace cloris peace or singing dye that together Love &
to heaven may goe for all we know of what ye blessed doe a
is that they sing, & that they Love.

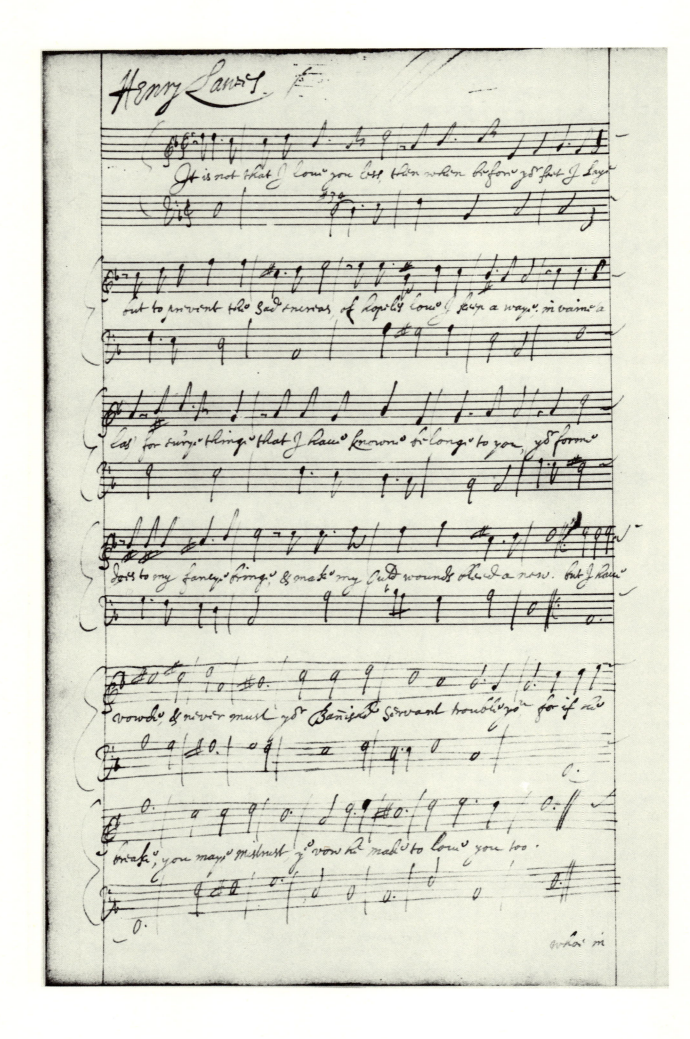

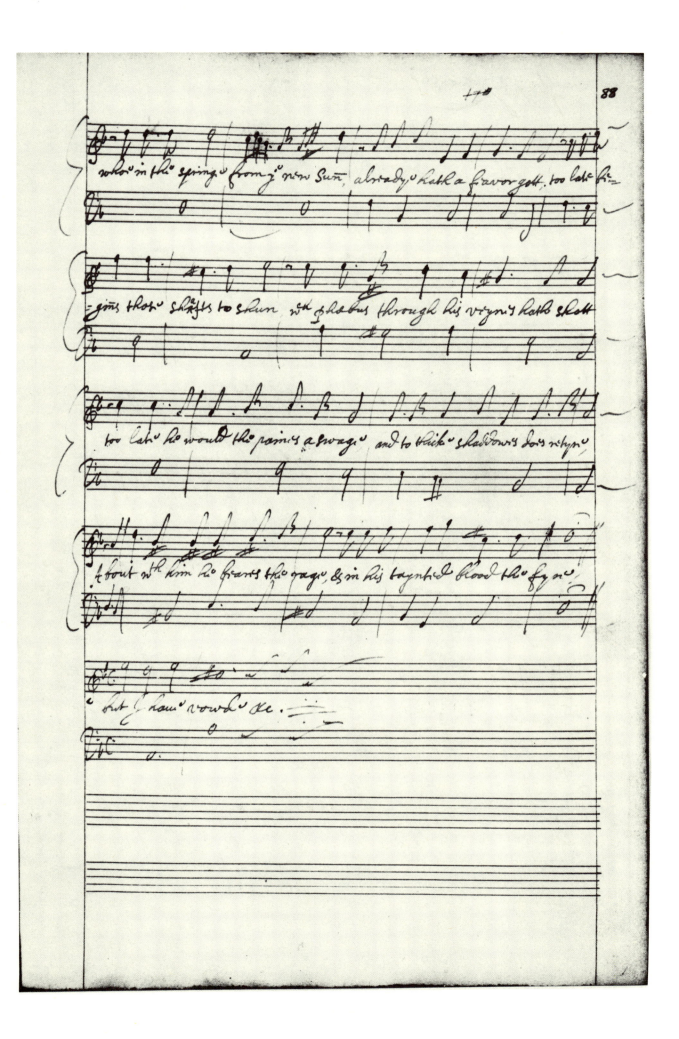

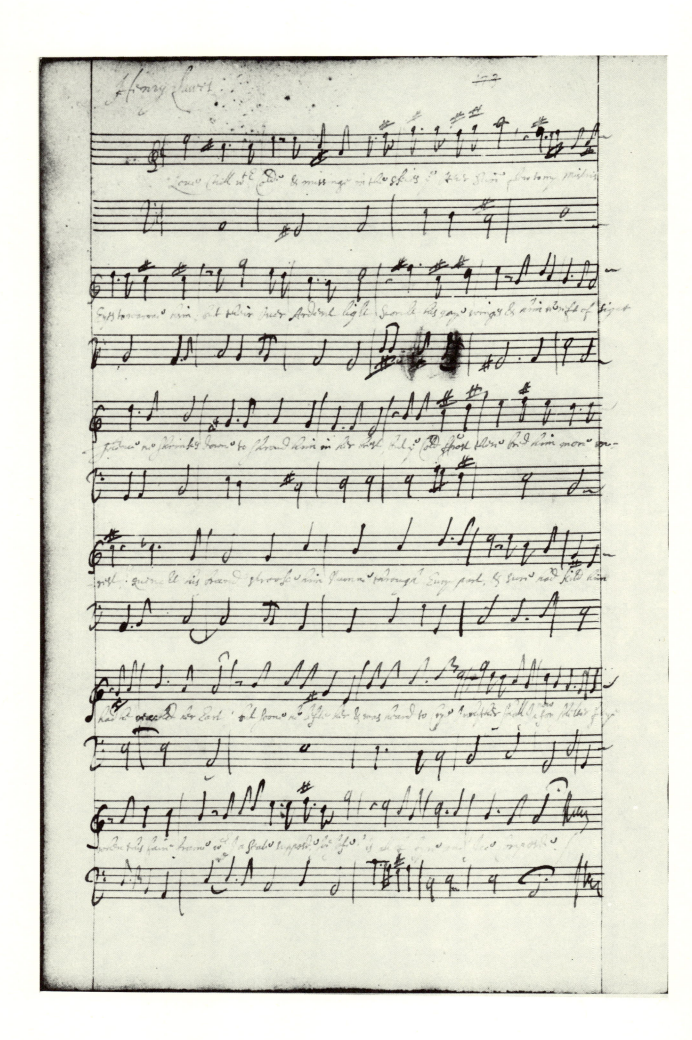

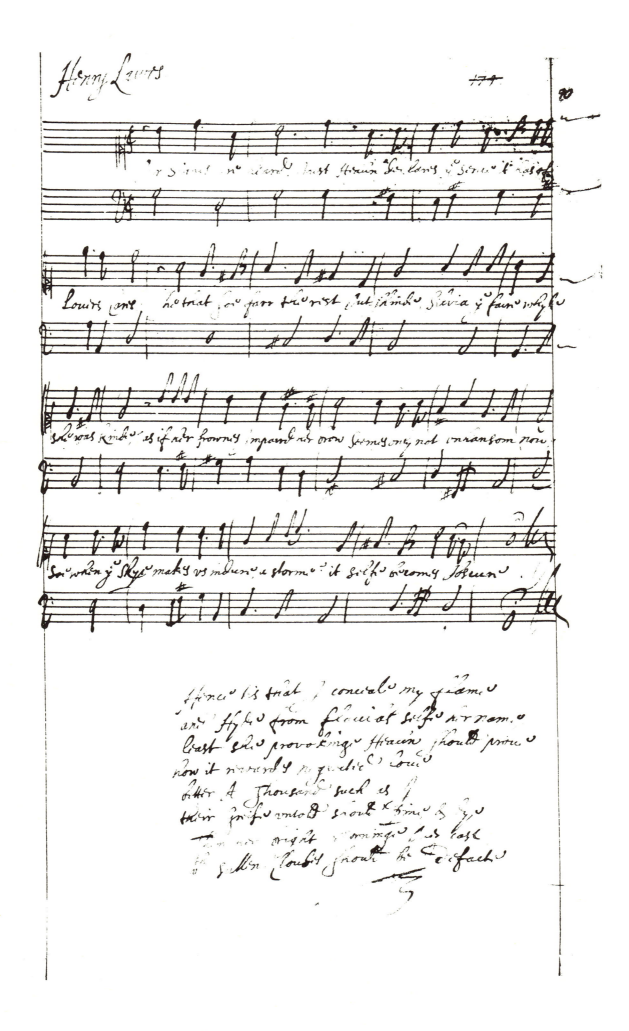

Henry Lawes
91
Leave it to ye planets too, what we shall hereafter doe
for the joys we now may prove, take advice of present love
I love thee for thy fickleness & great inconstancy, for hadst thou
bin a constant lass then thou hadst ne'er loved me

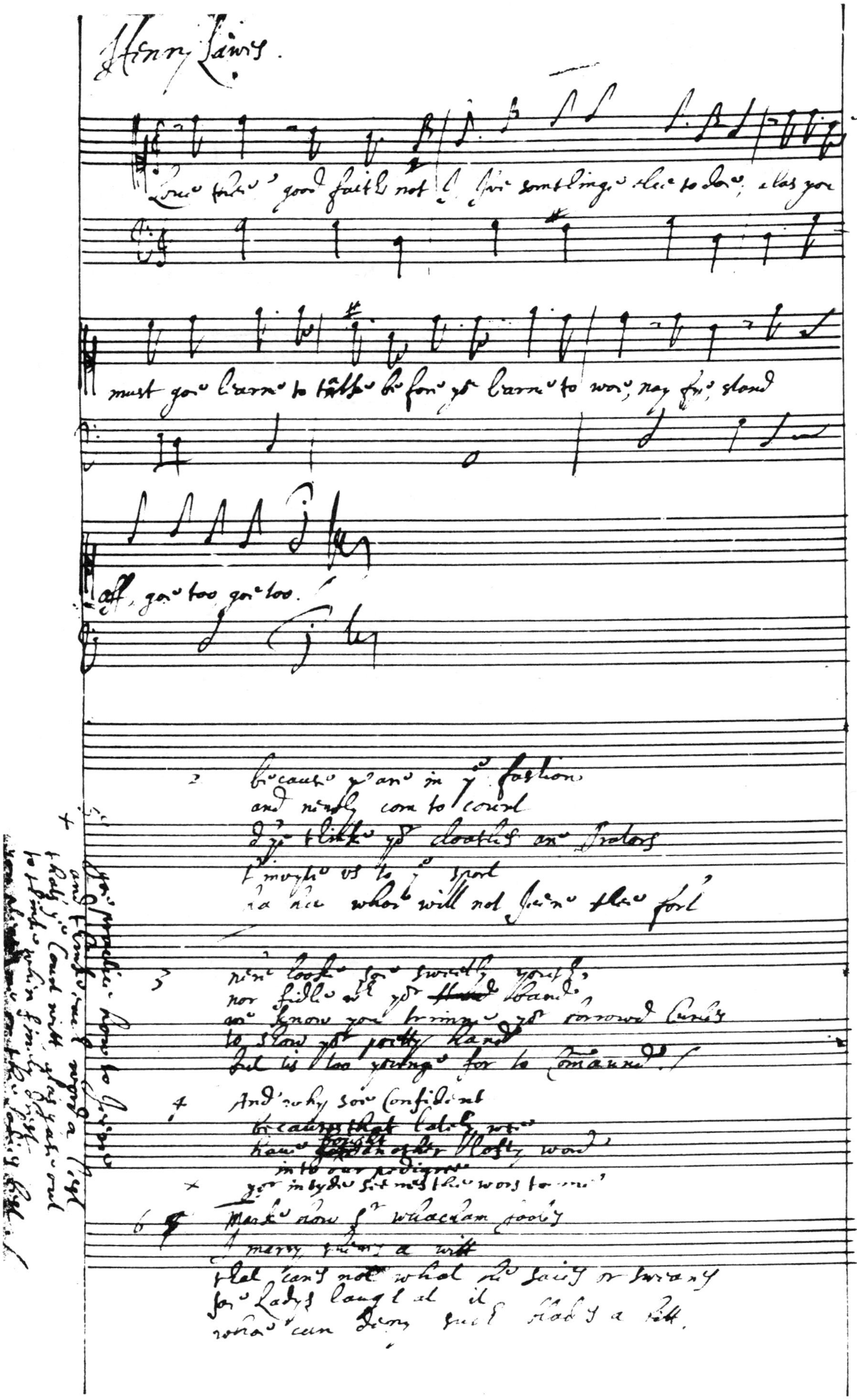
Henry Lawes.
Love thee good faith not I Ive somthinge else to doe; alas you
must you learne to talke before you learne to woe, nay fie, stand
off, goe too goe too.

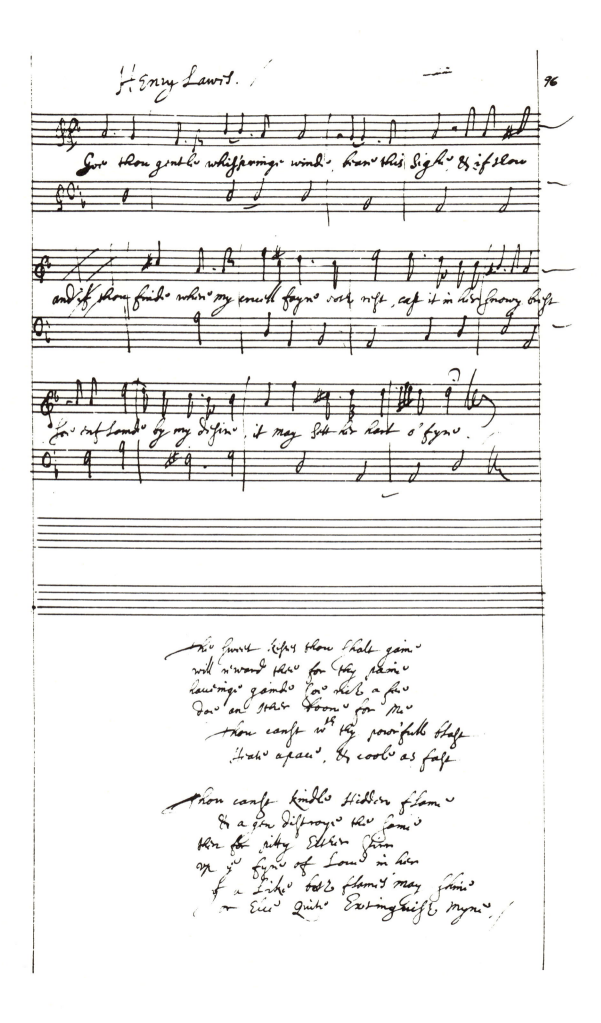

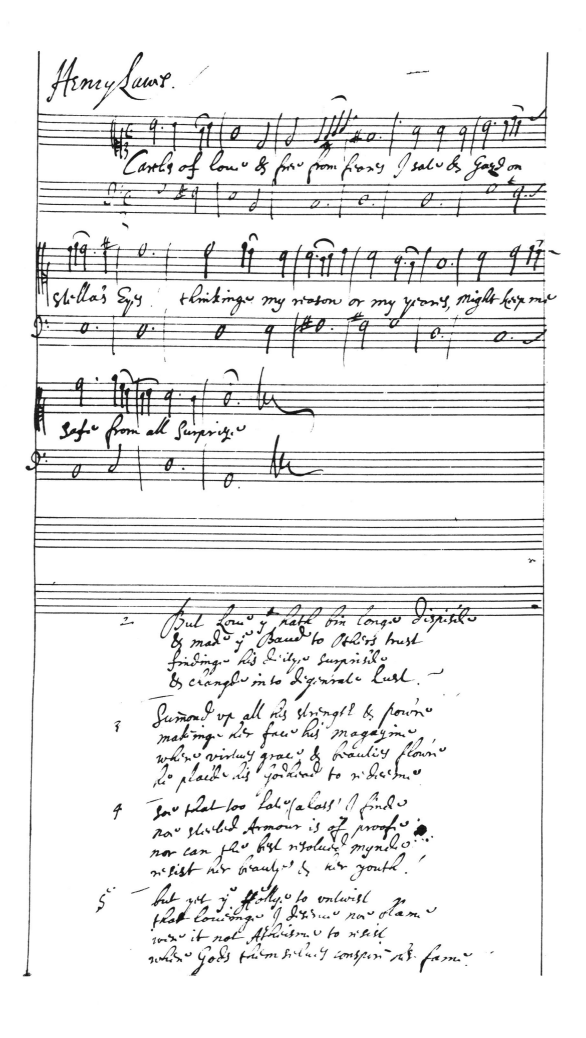

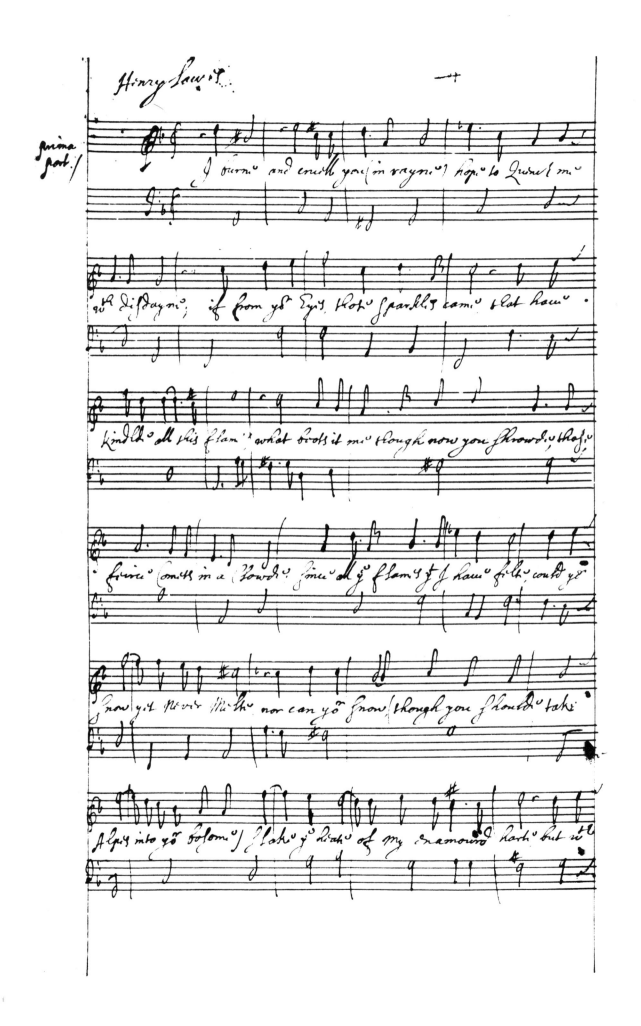

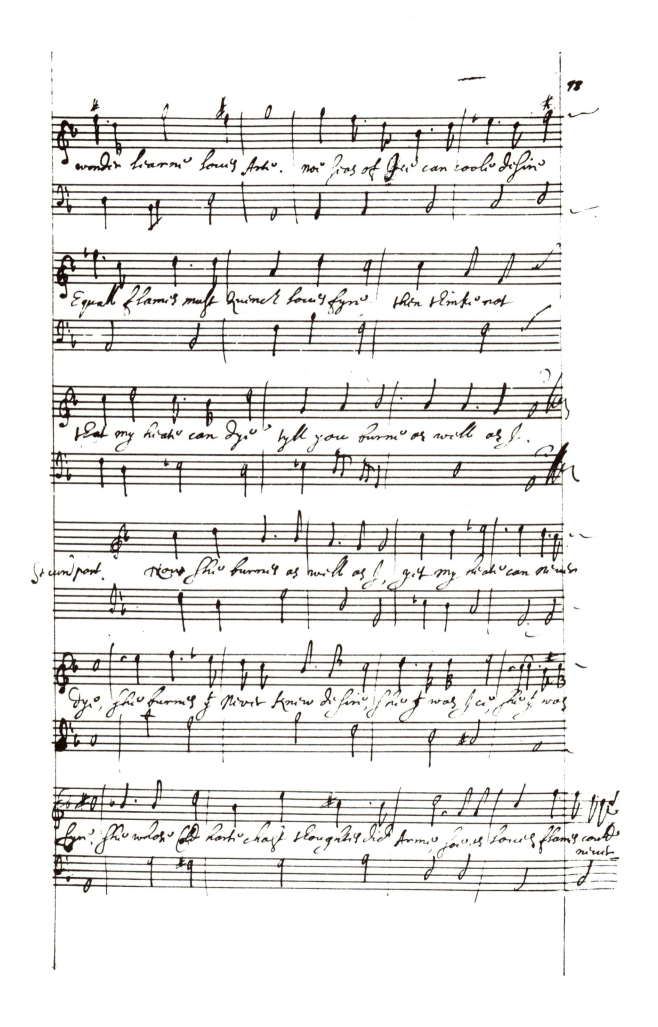

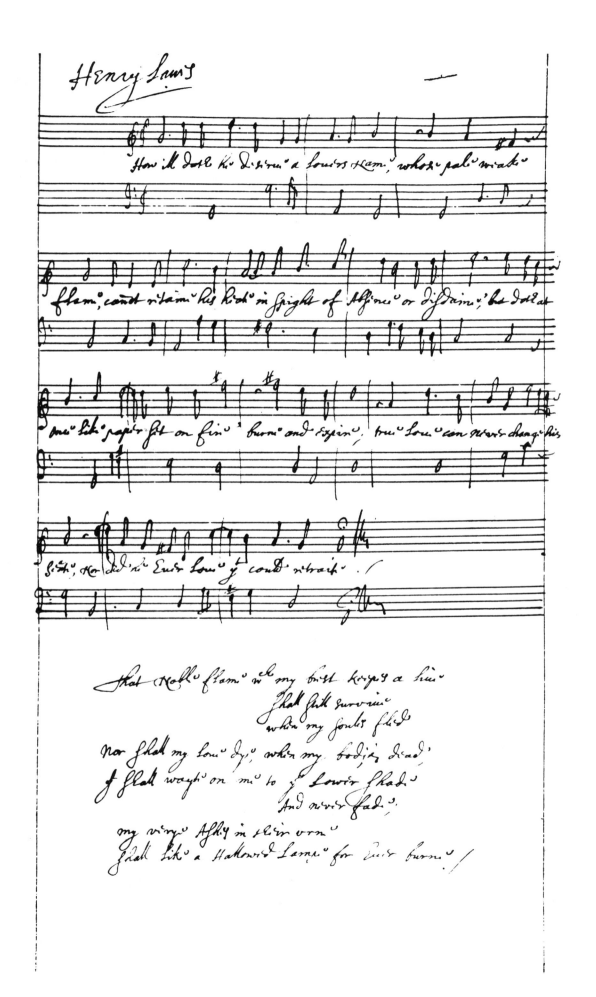

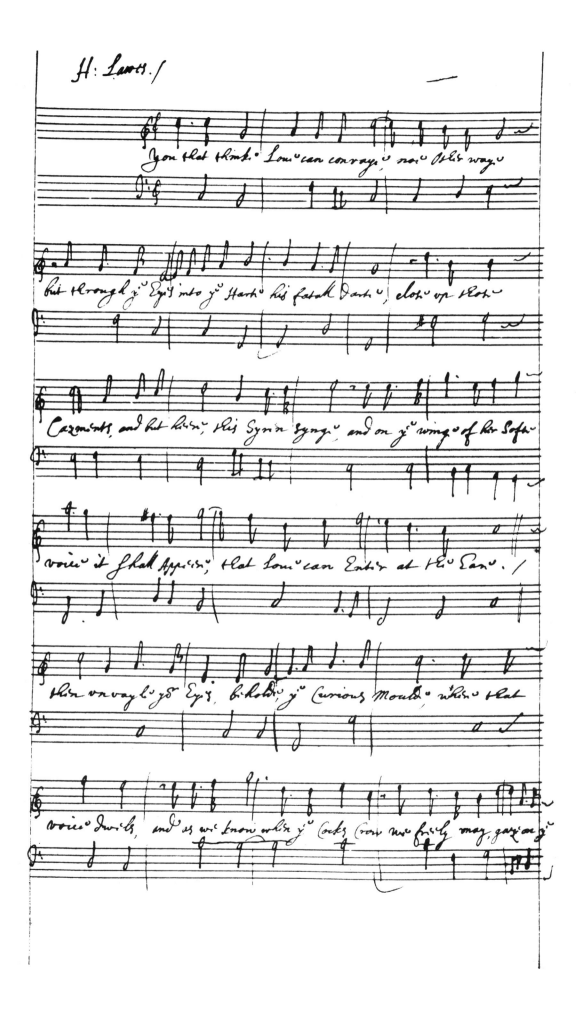

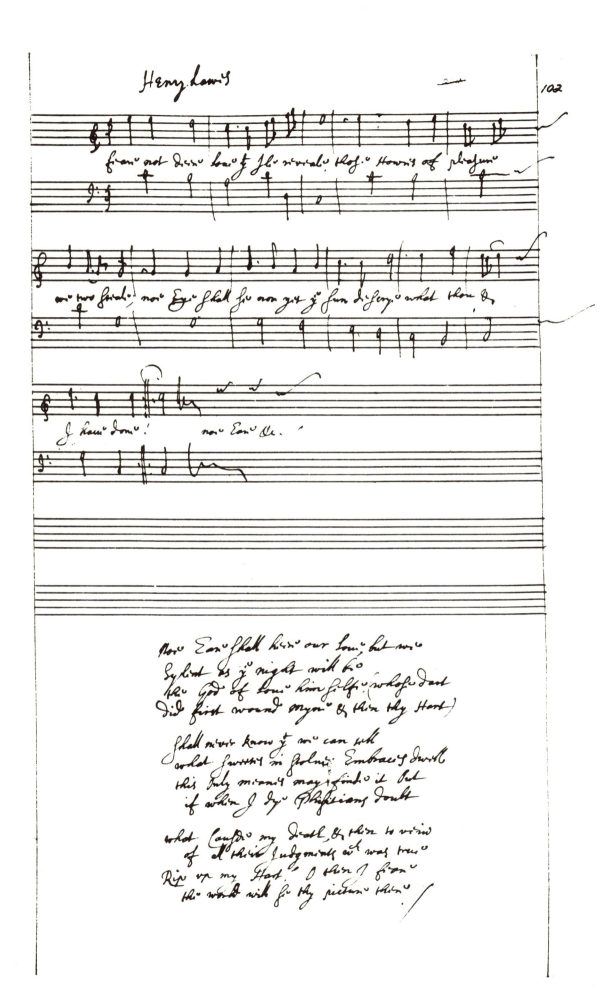

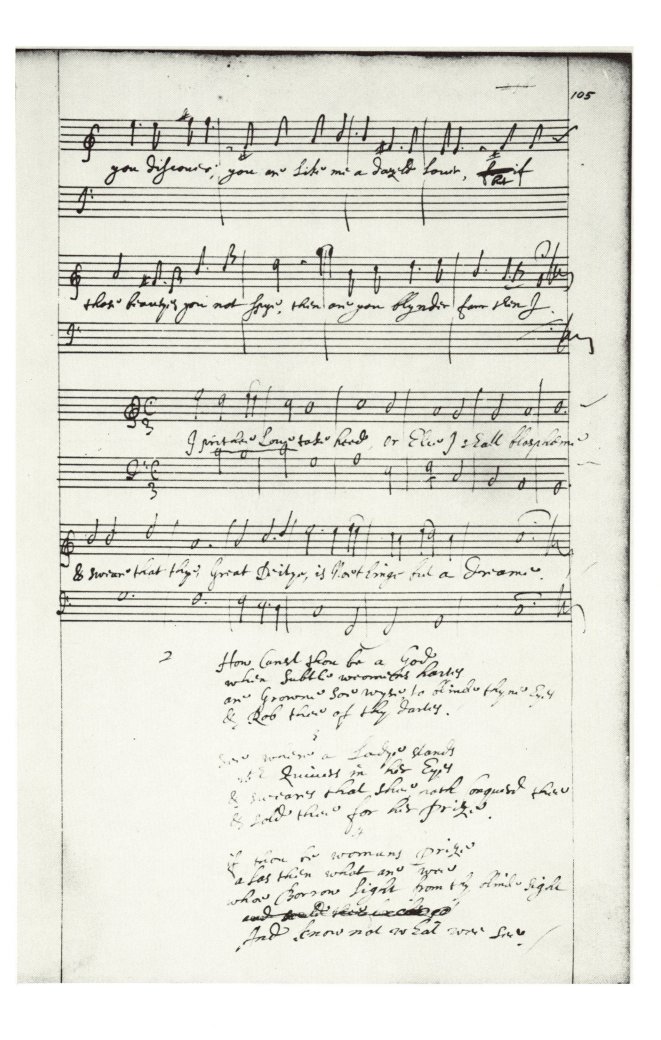

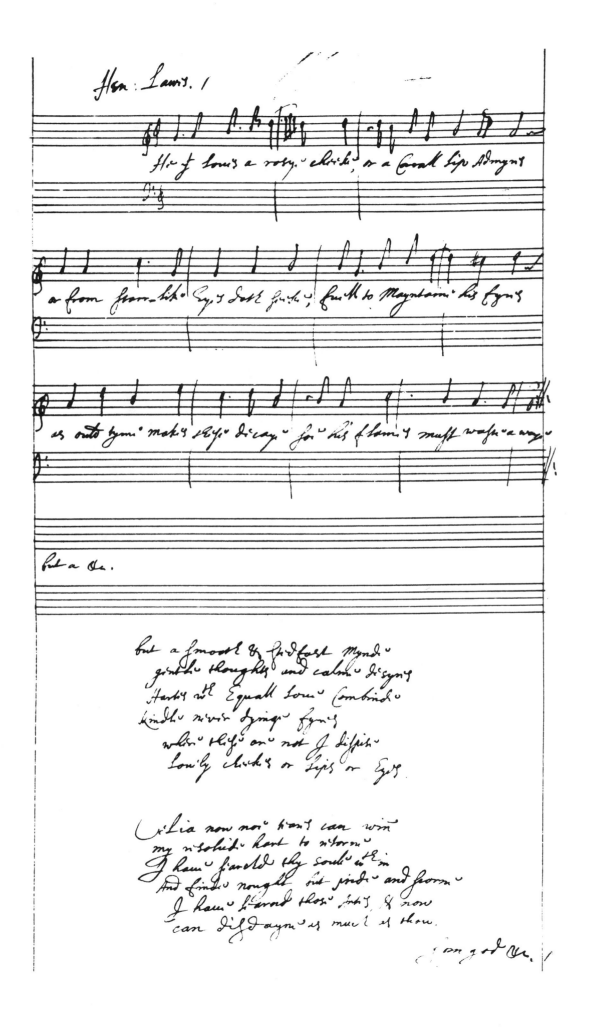

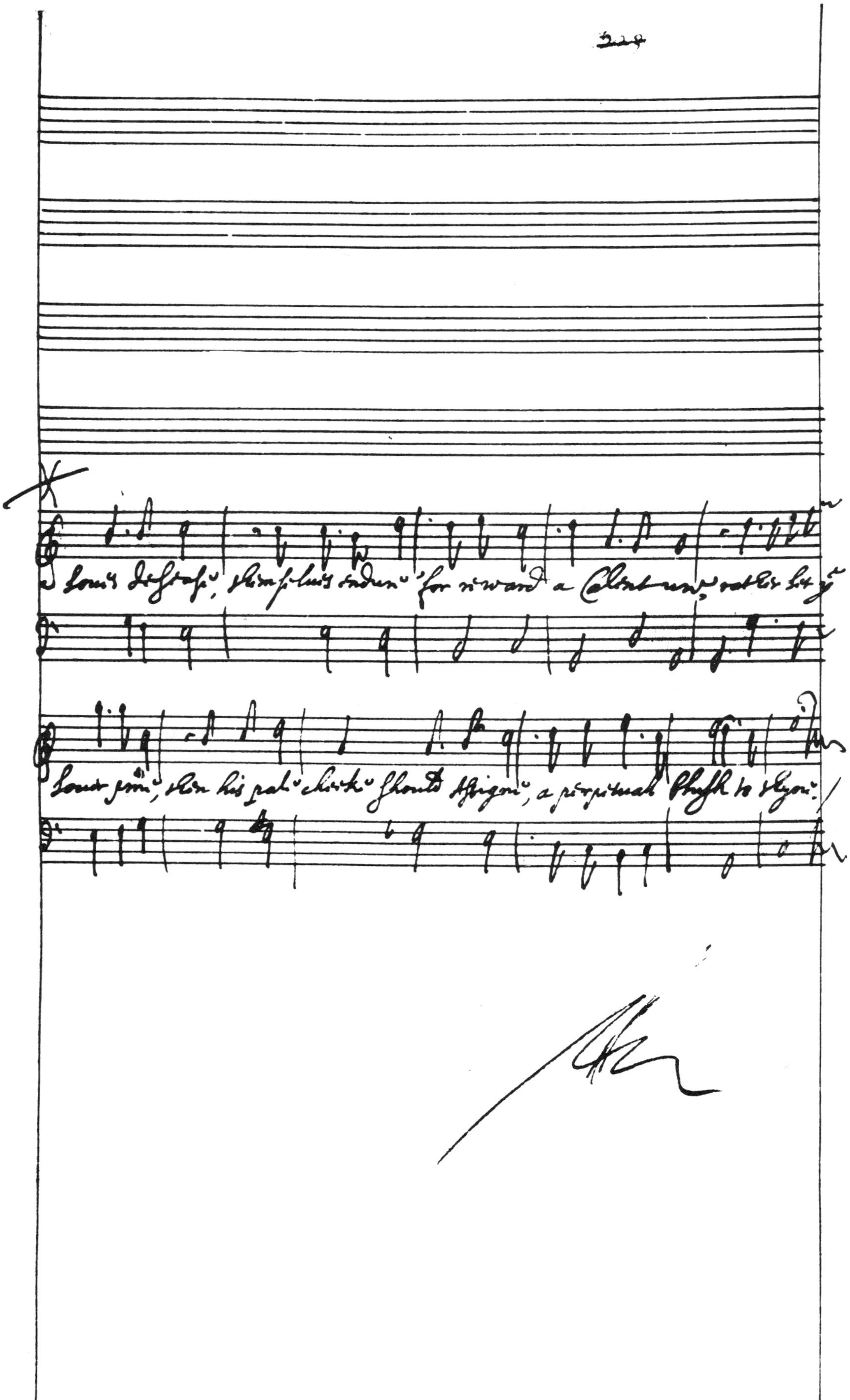

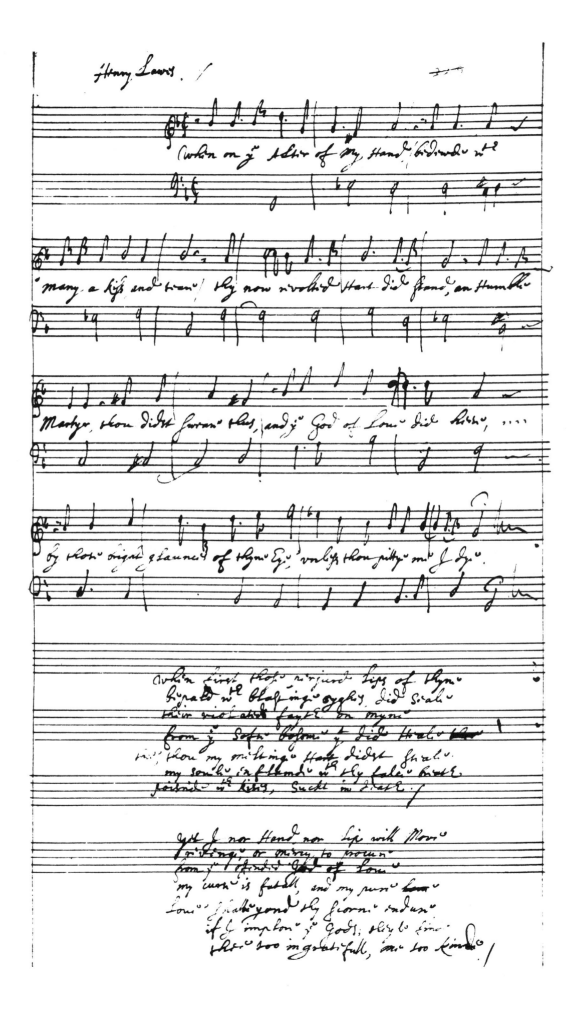

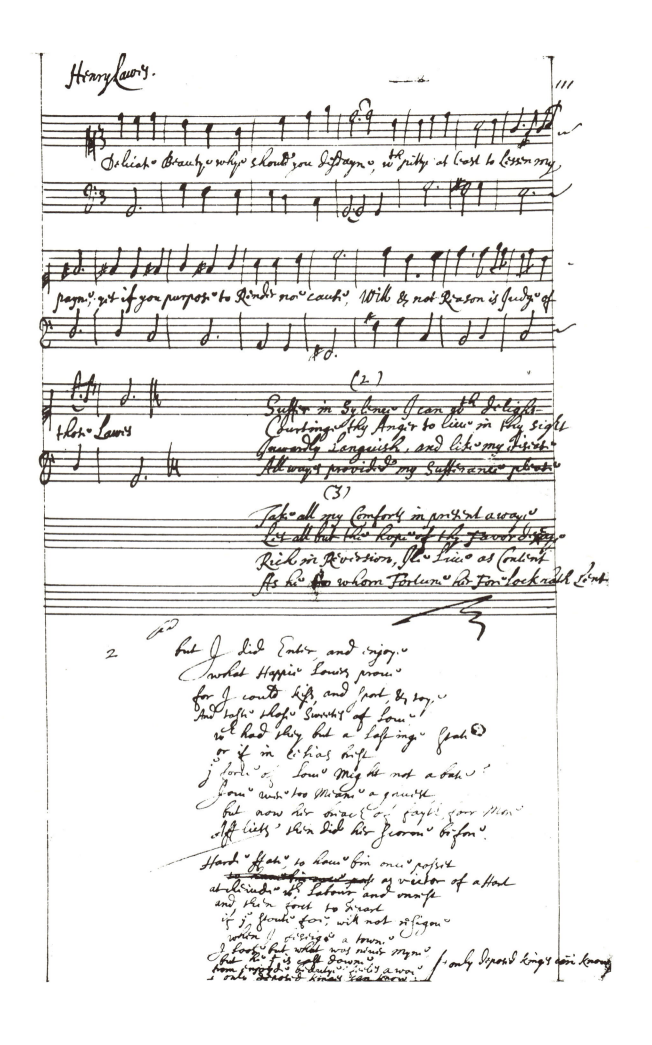

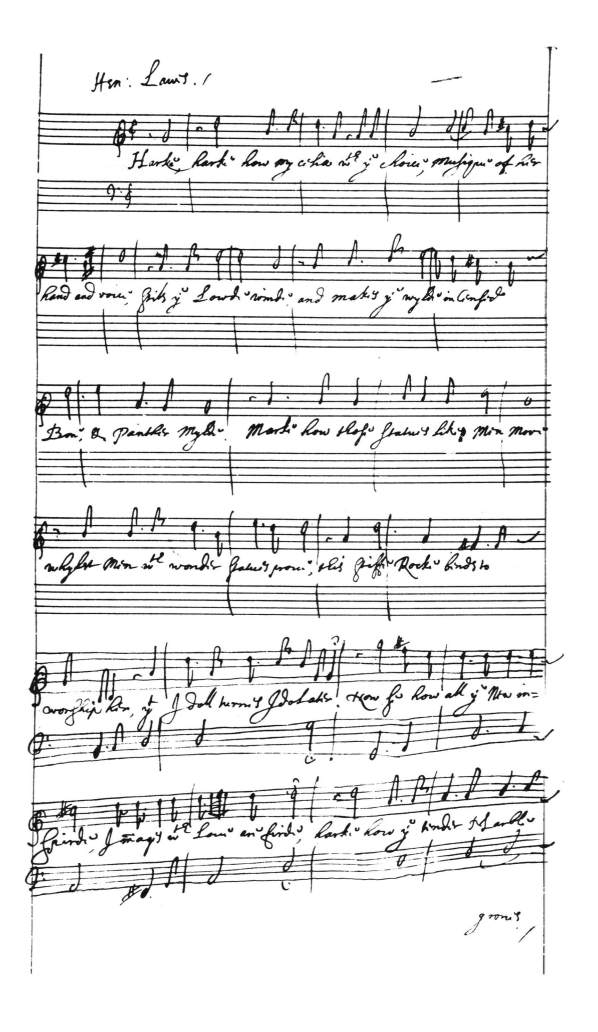

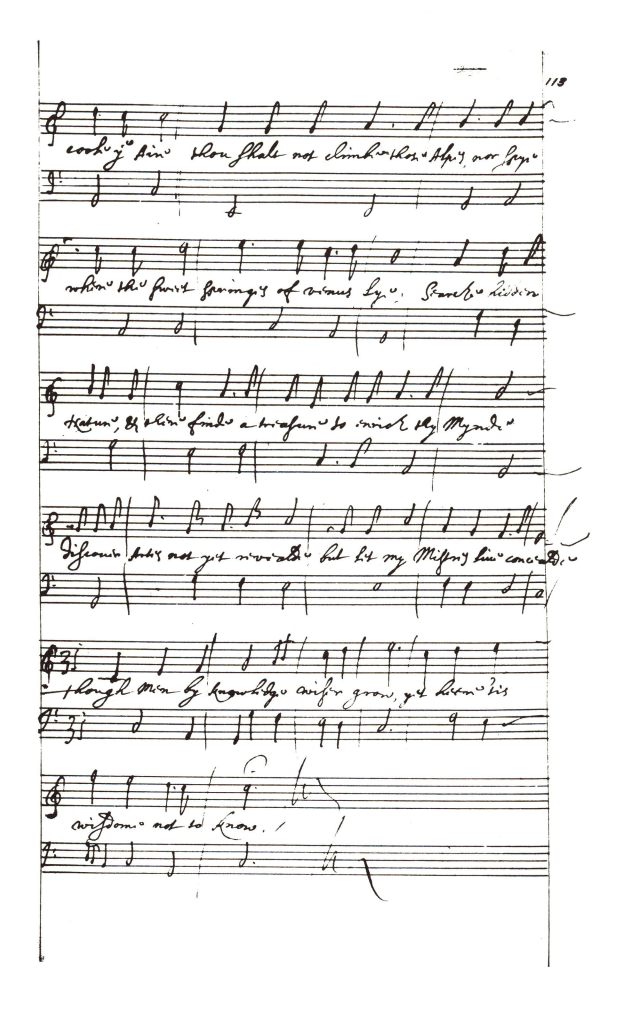

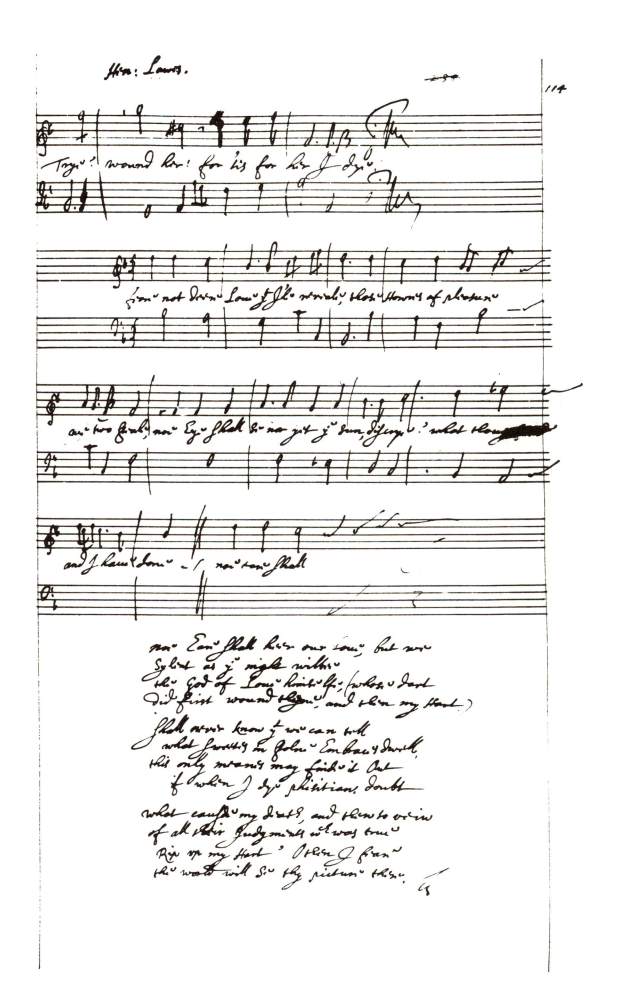

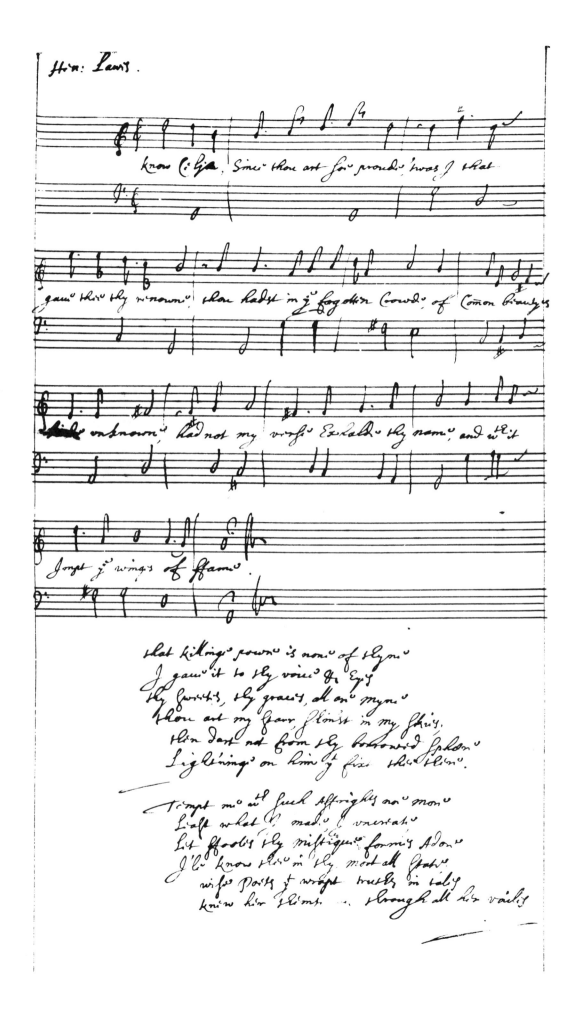

Hen: Lawes
Staye Coward blood, & doe not yield to thy
pale Sister beautys field. where then displaying round her whyte
Ensignes hath usurp'd thy right, invading thy peculiar
throne, ye lip, where thou shouldst rule alone. & on the
cheeke where Natures care, Allotted each an Equall share
her spreading Lilly only growes, whose Milky deluge drownes

thy joy. Quitt not the field: faintt blood nor rush in ye
short sally's of a blush uppon thy sister foe: but
Strive to keepe an Endless warr alive, though peace doe
Safety fast maintayne, lett warr alone Make beauty Reigne

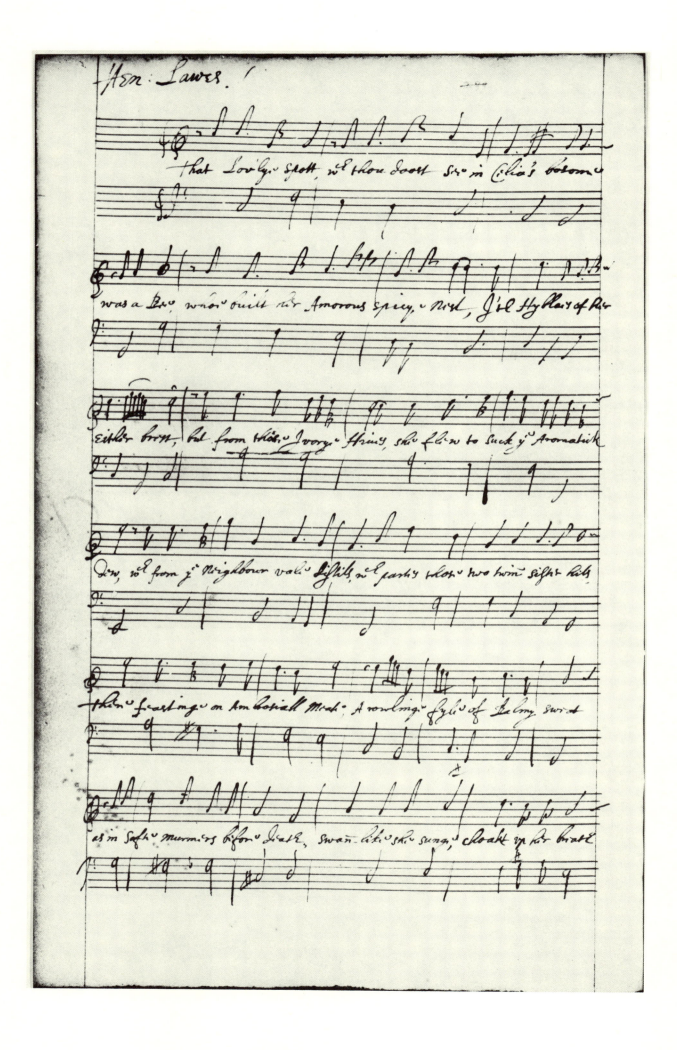

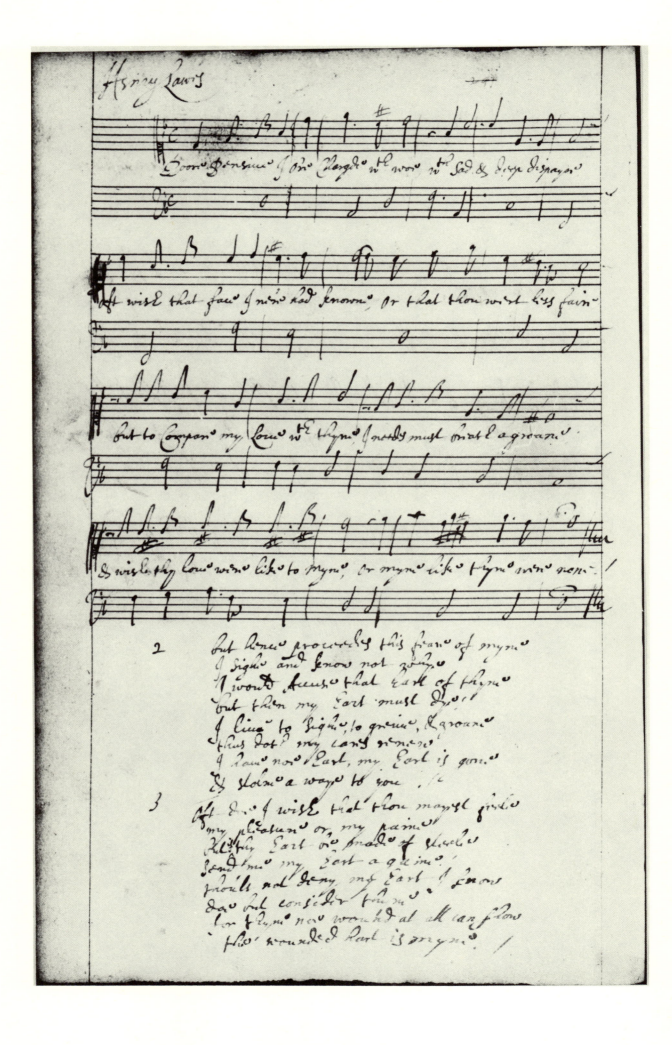

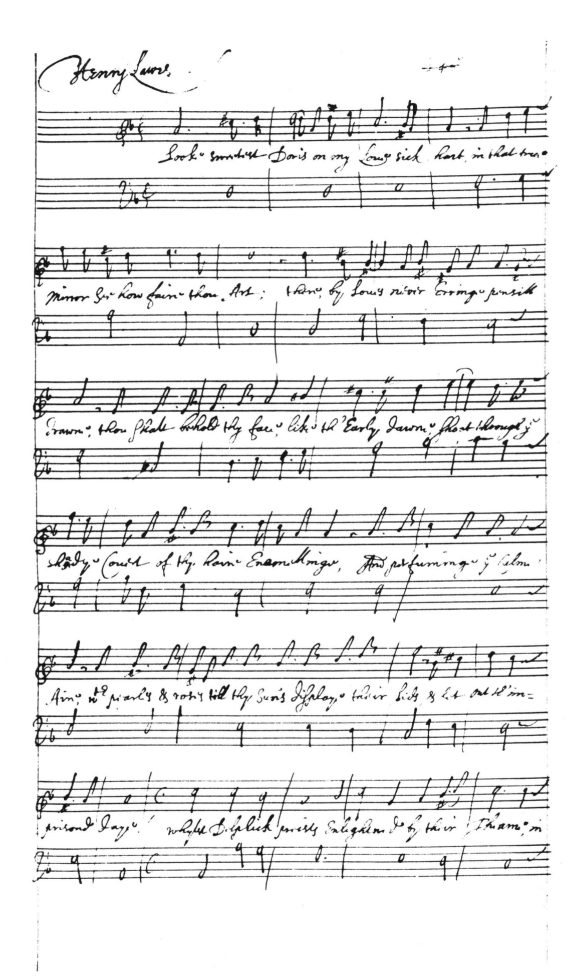

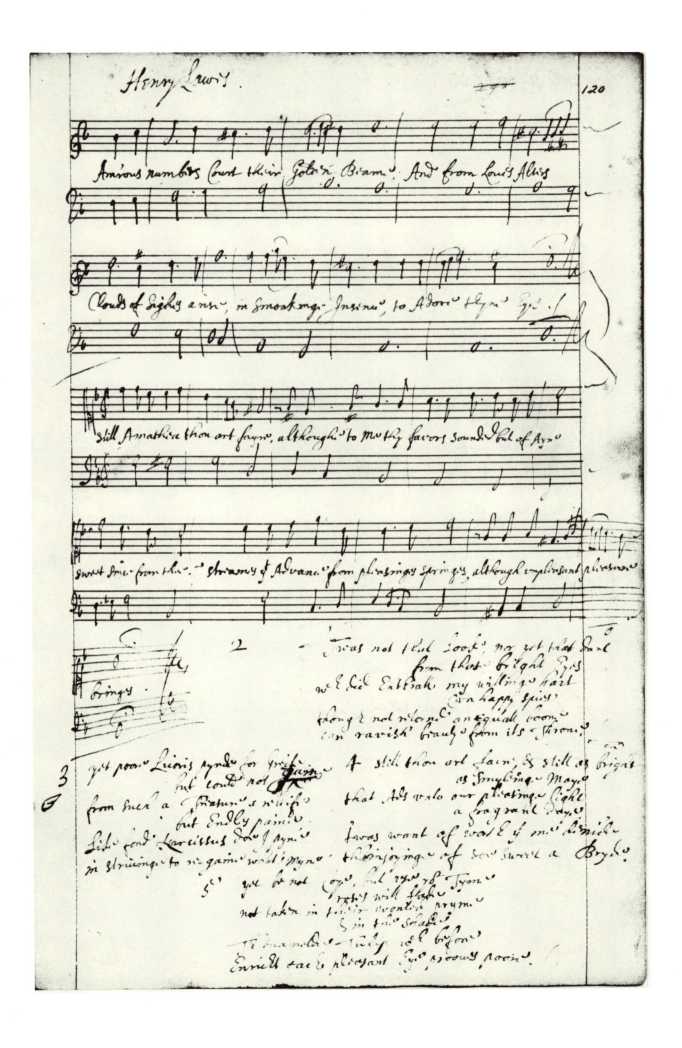

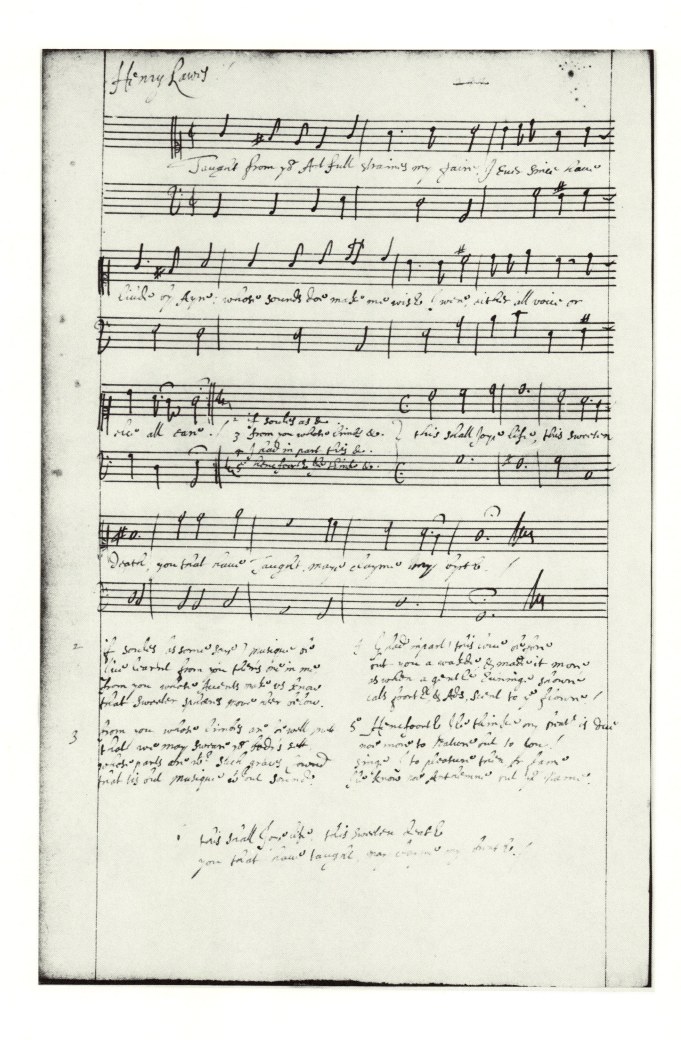

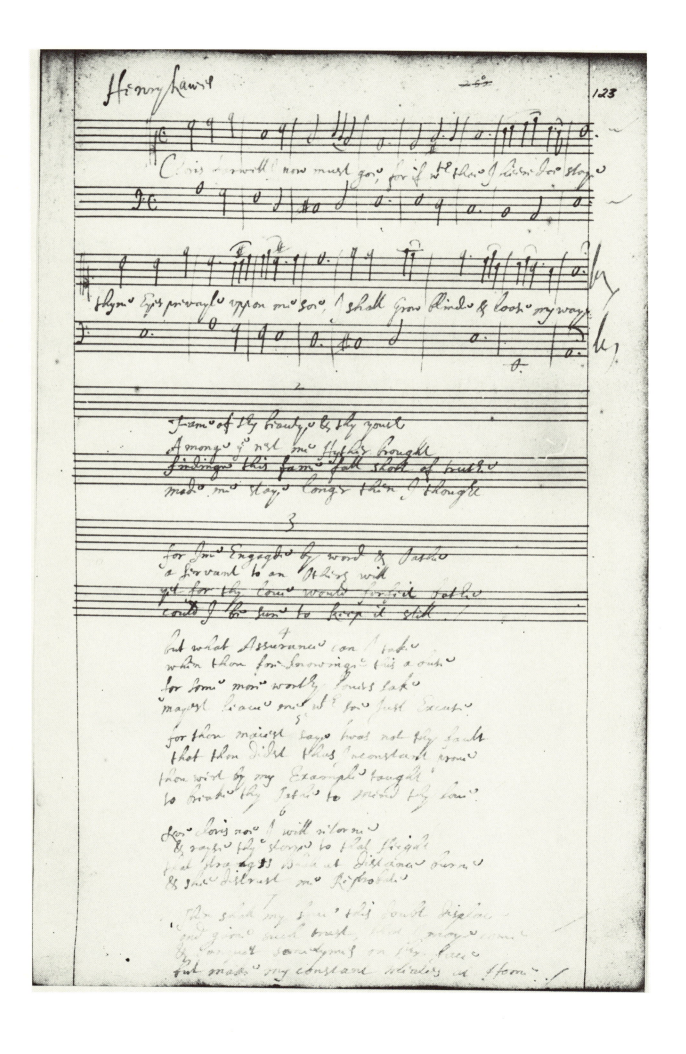

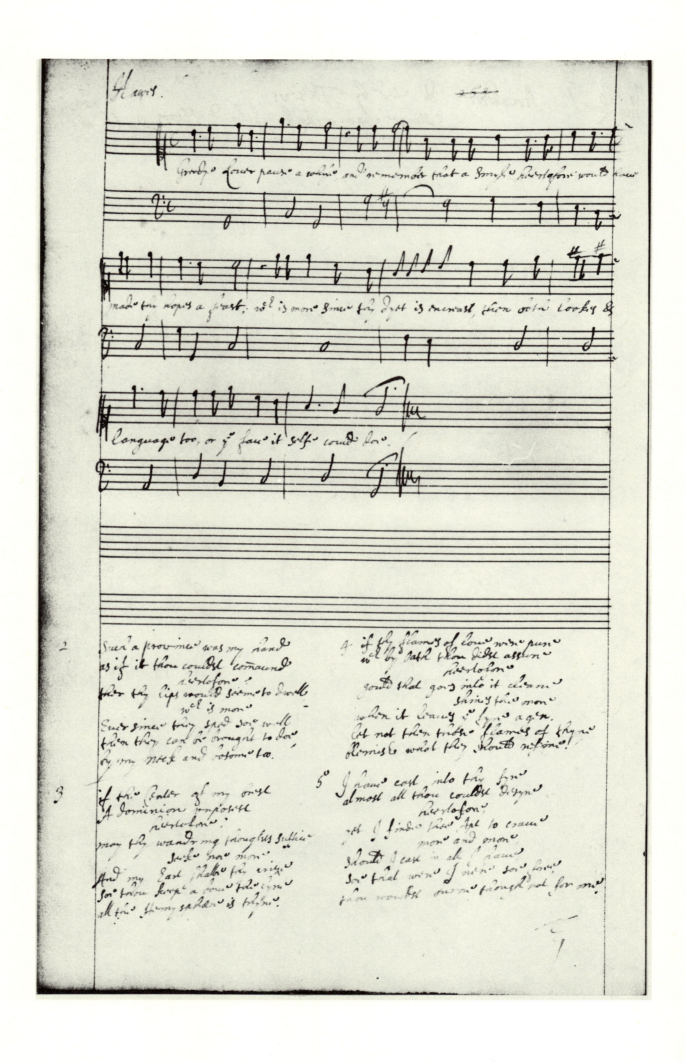

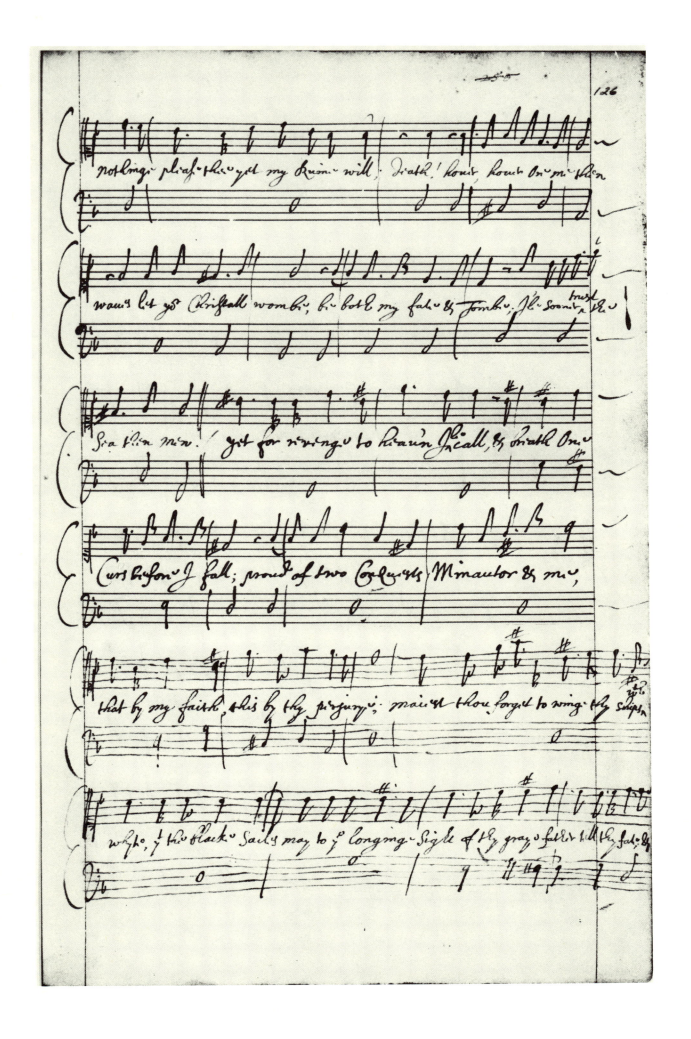

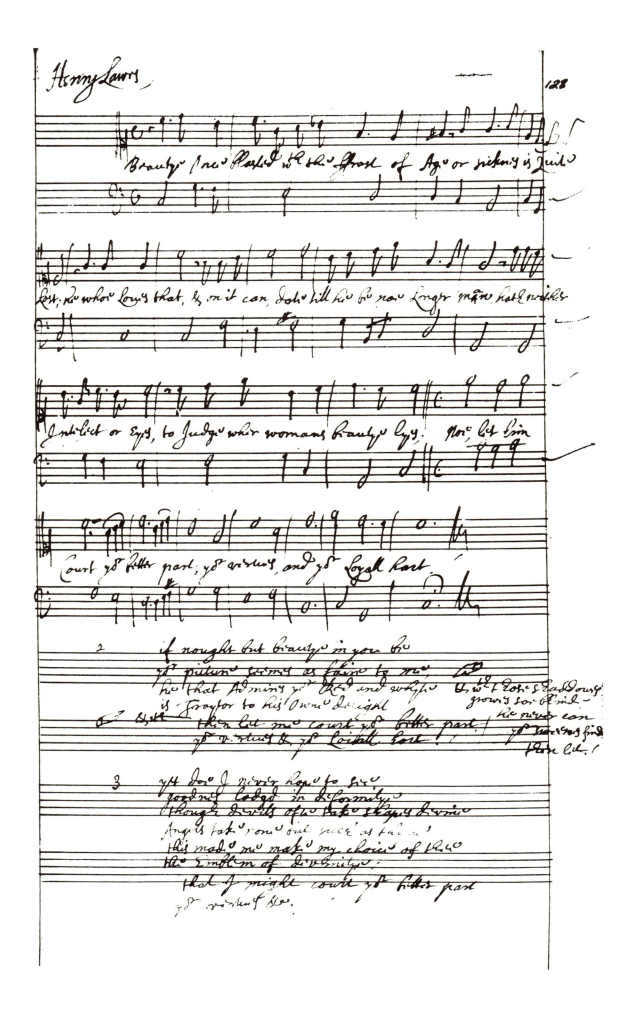

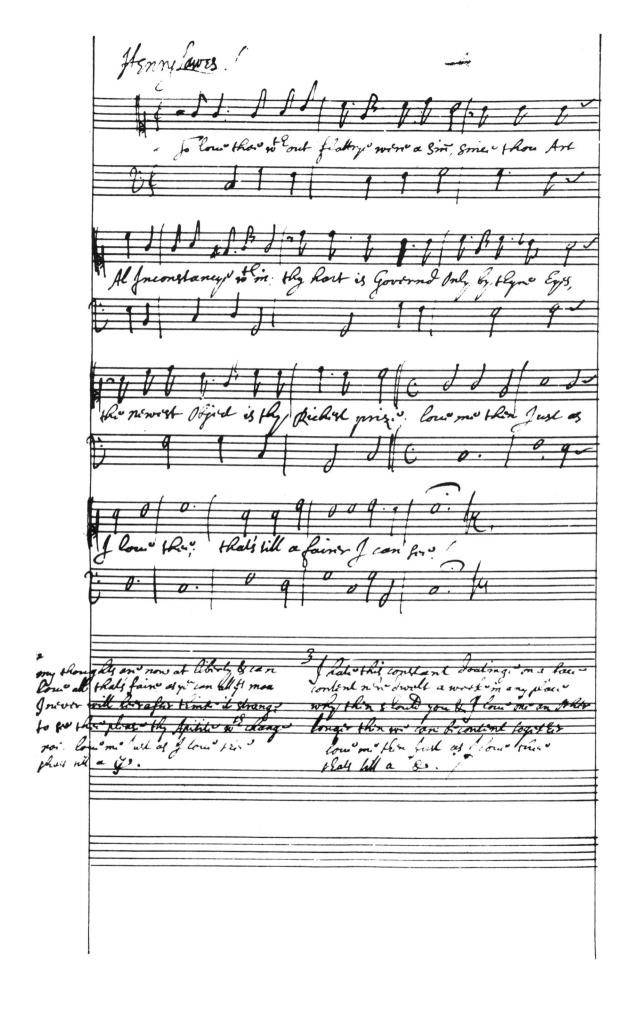

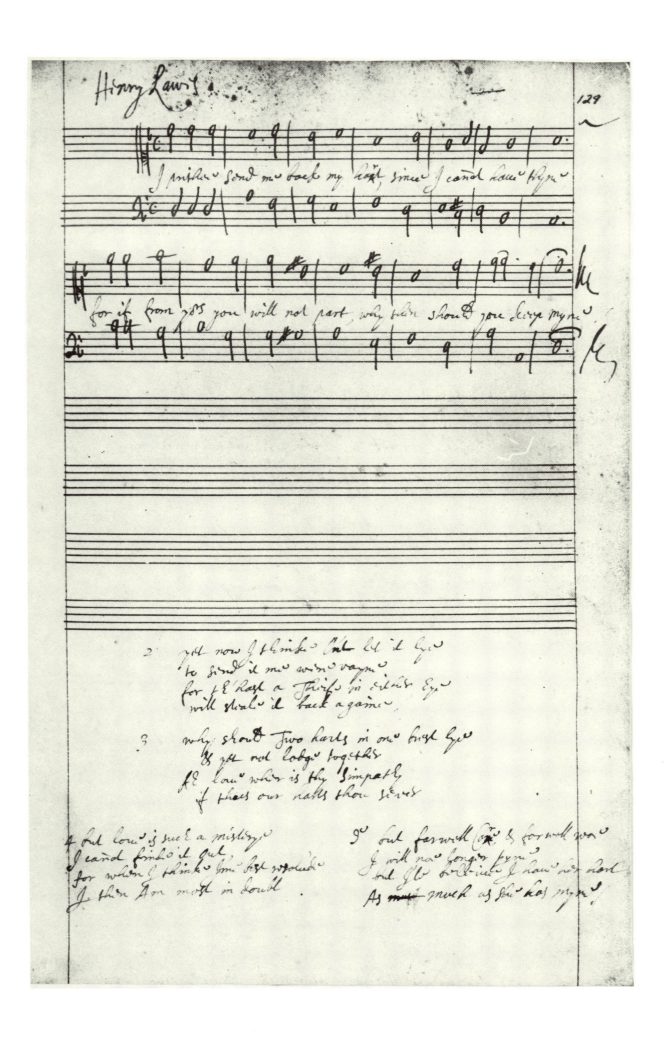

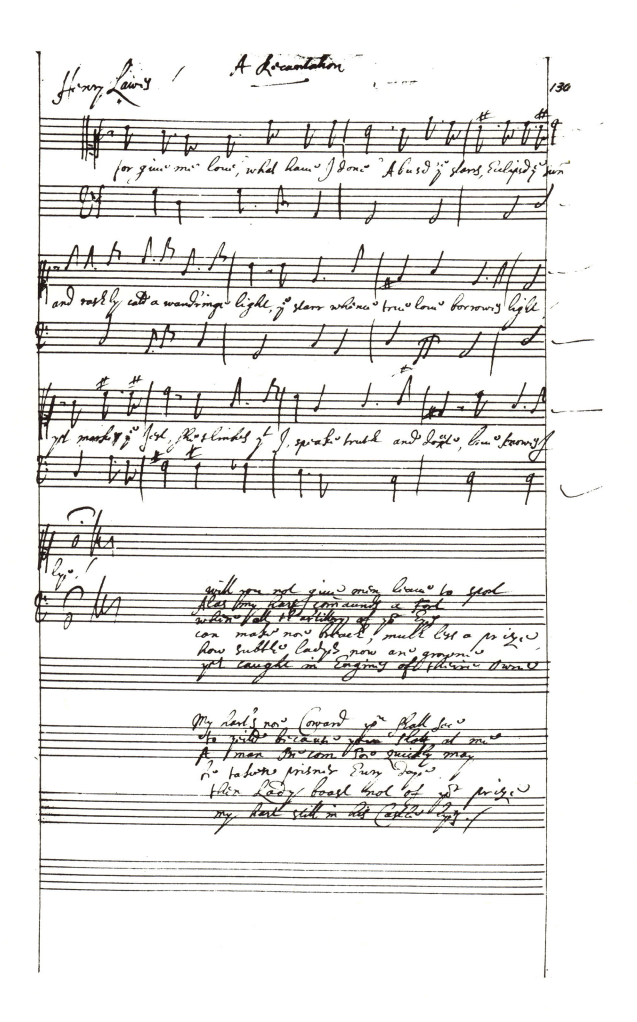

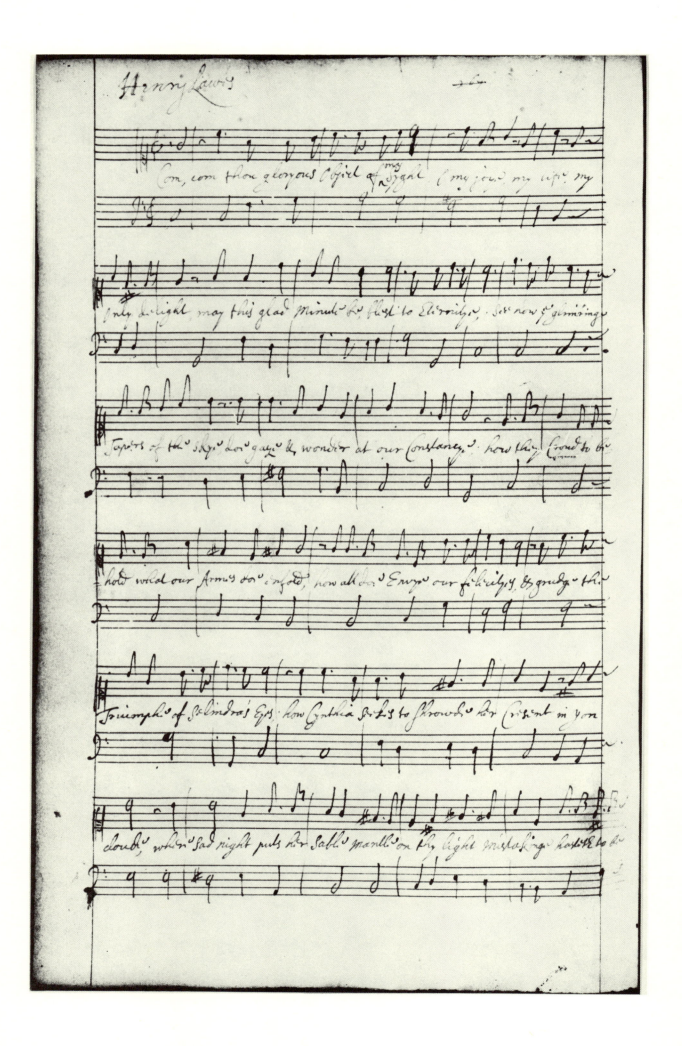

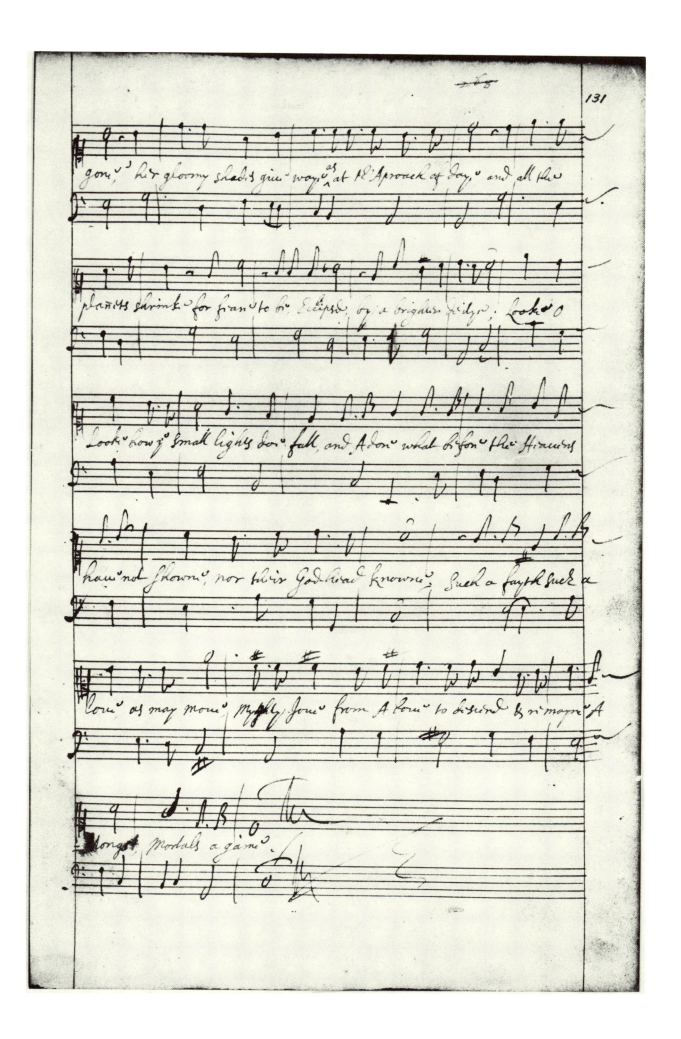

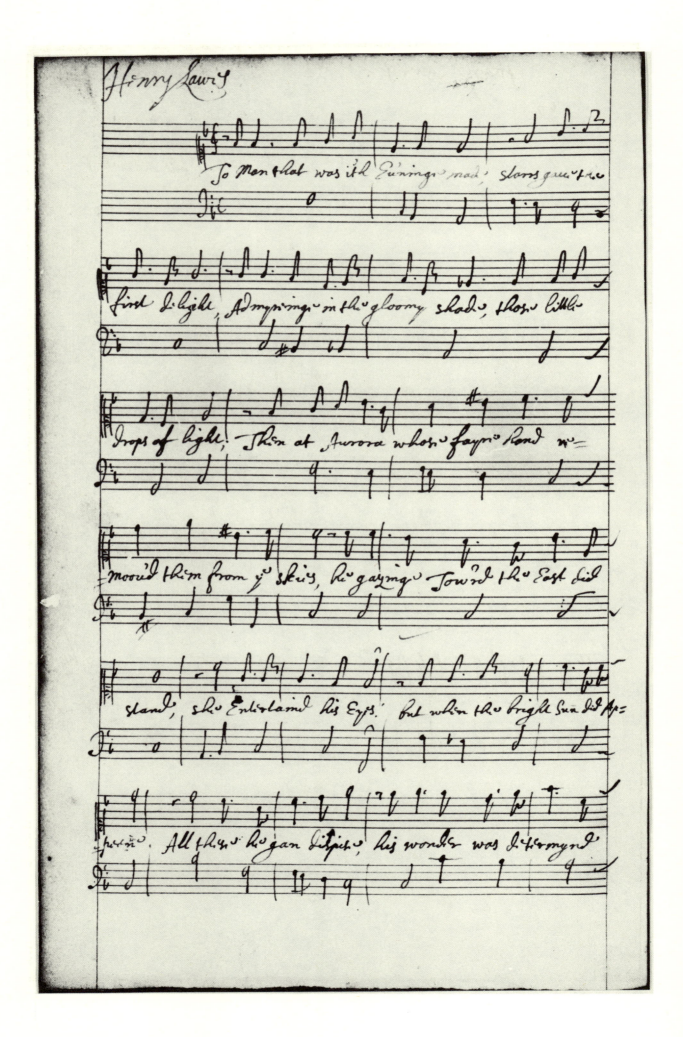

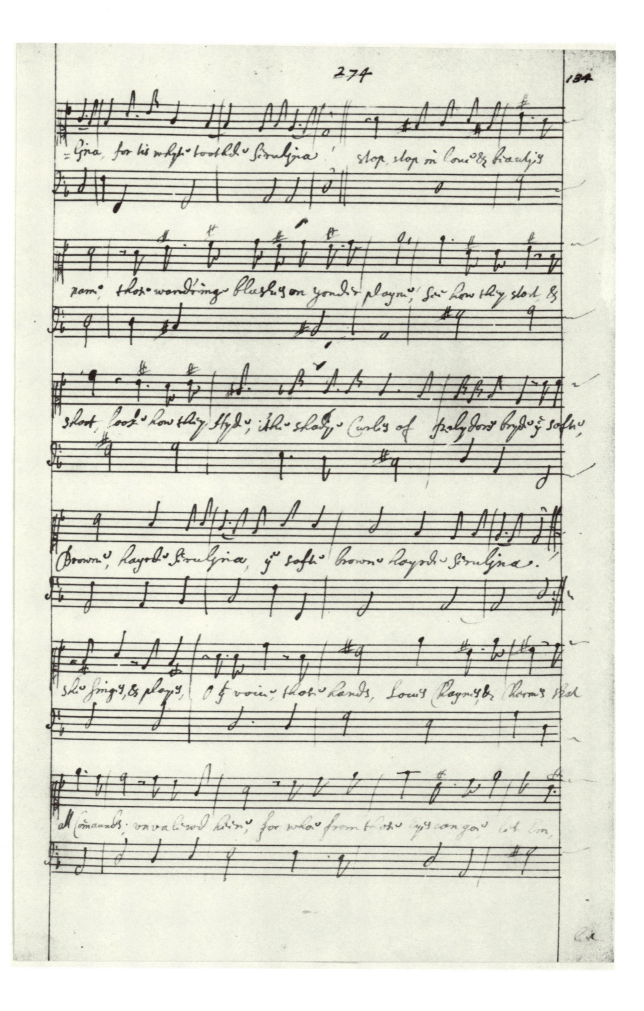

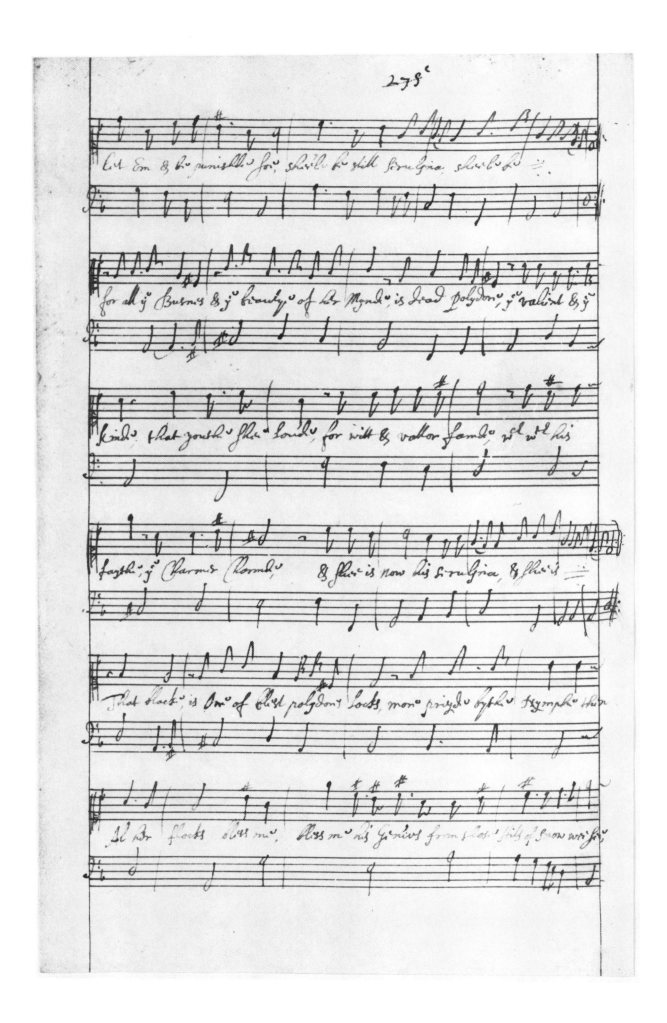

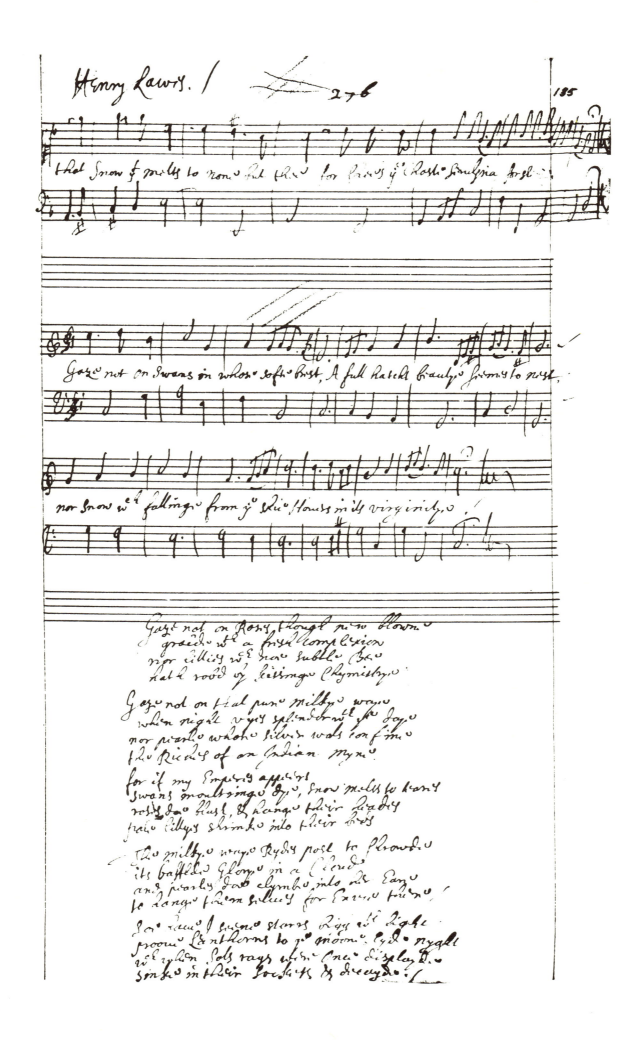

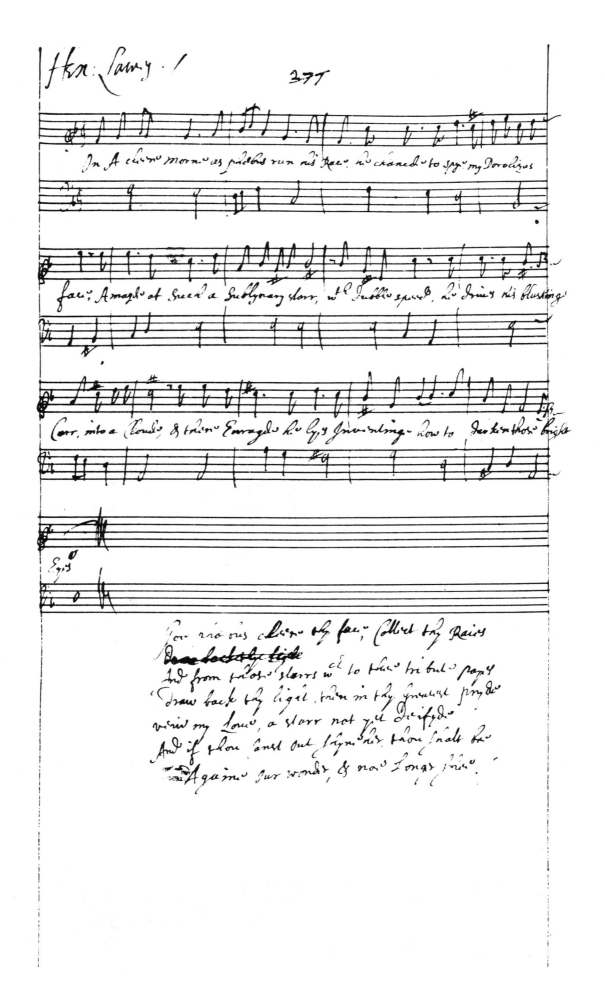

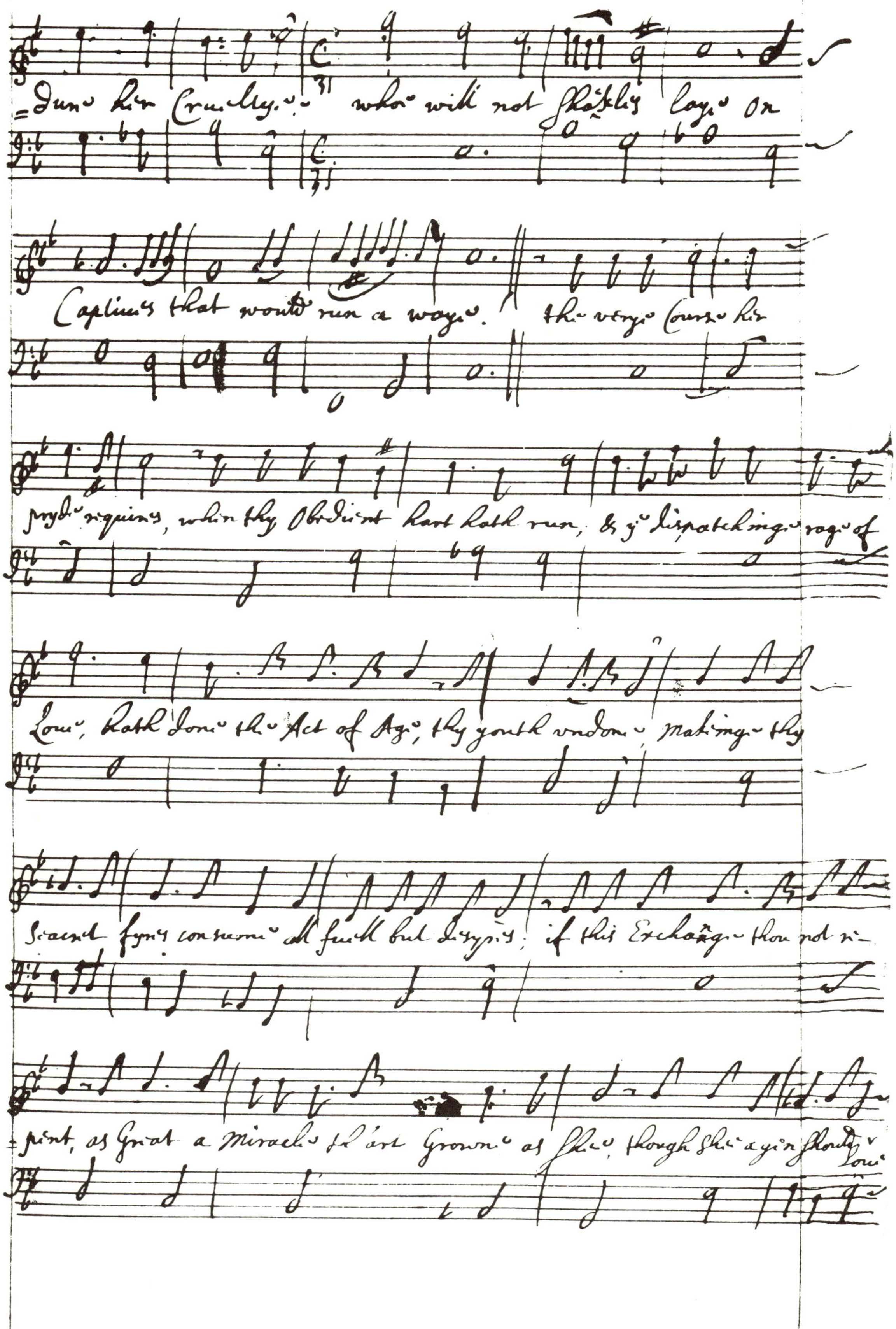

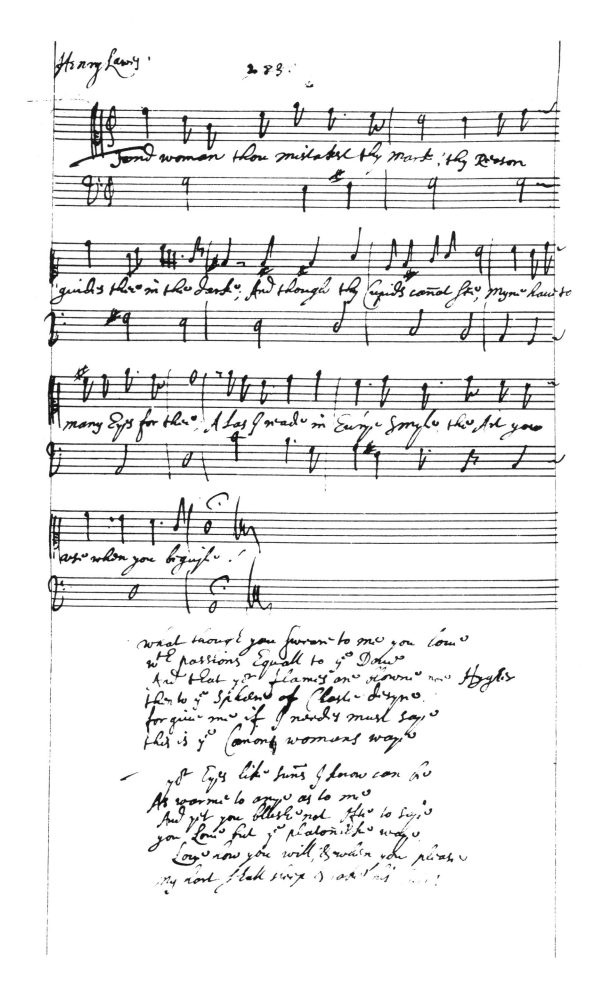

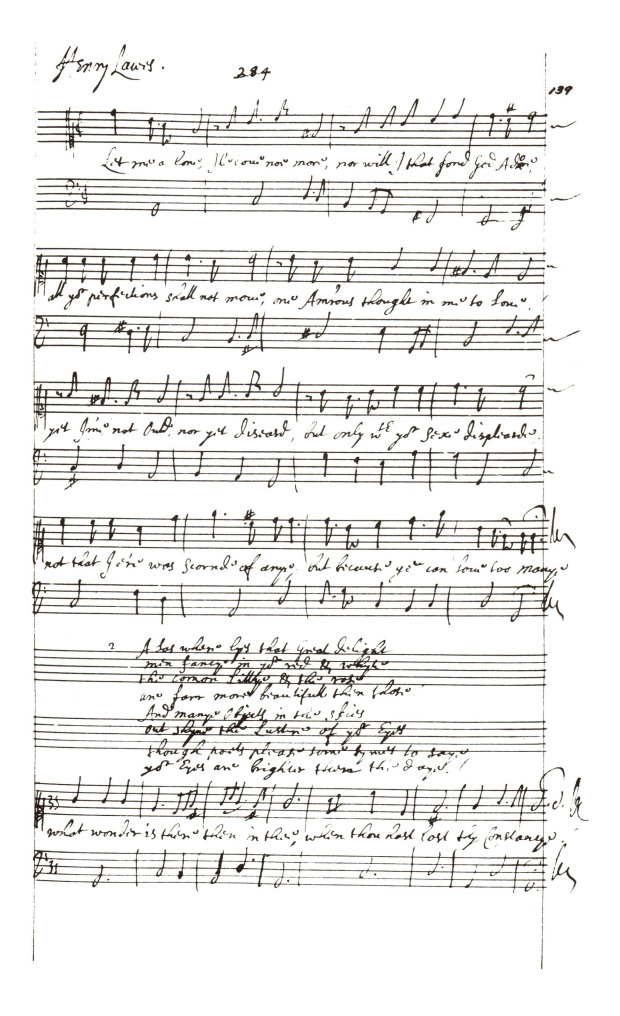

289

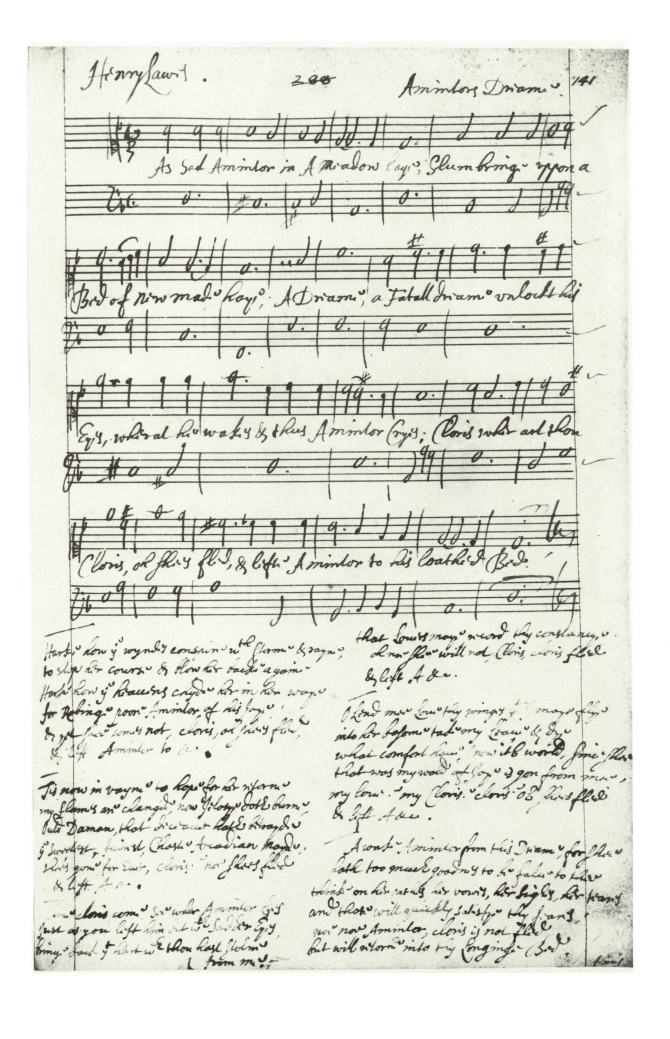

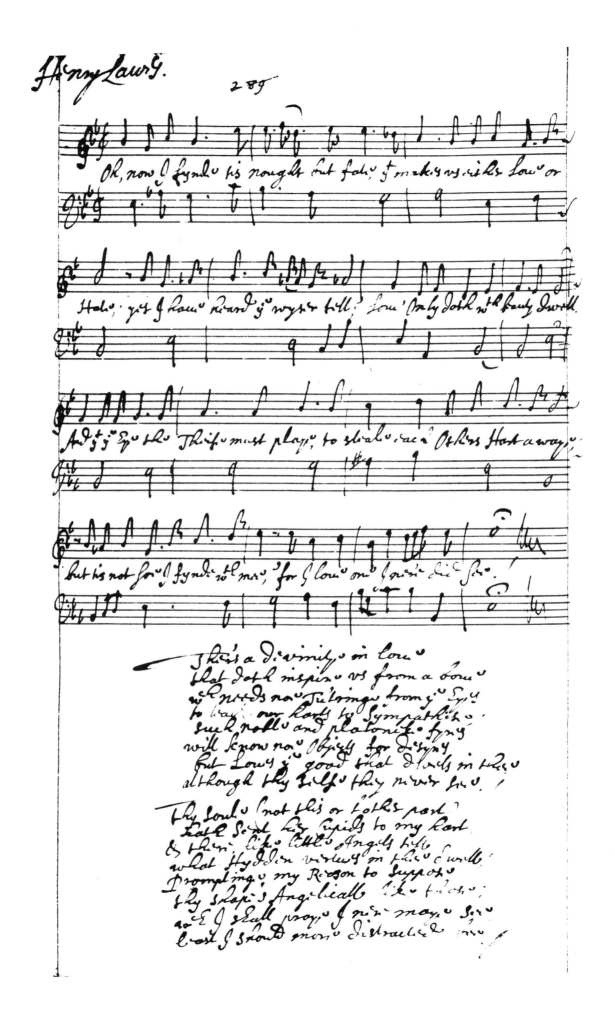

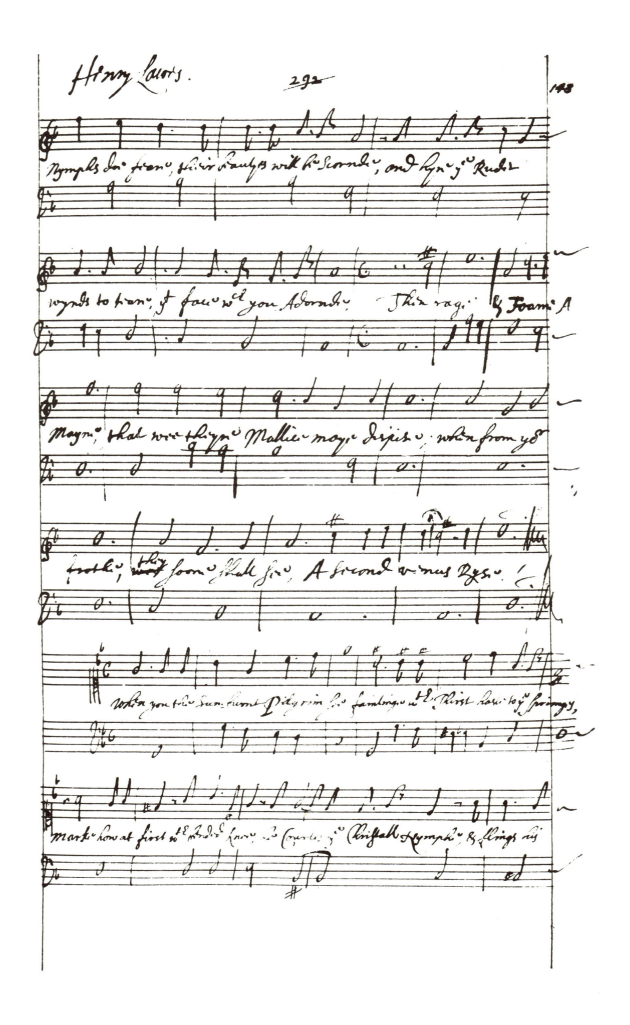

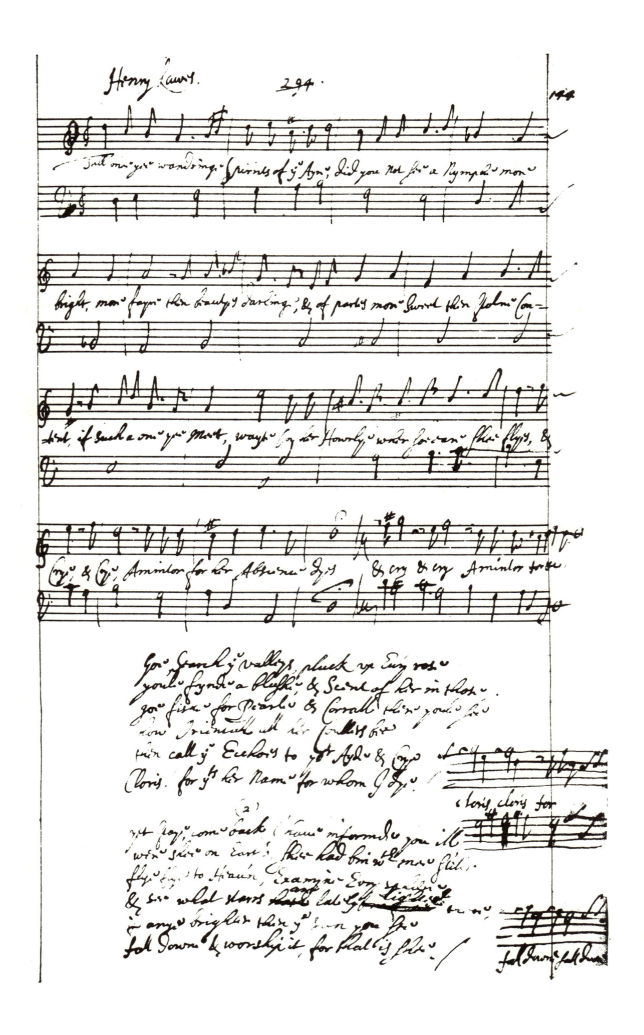

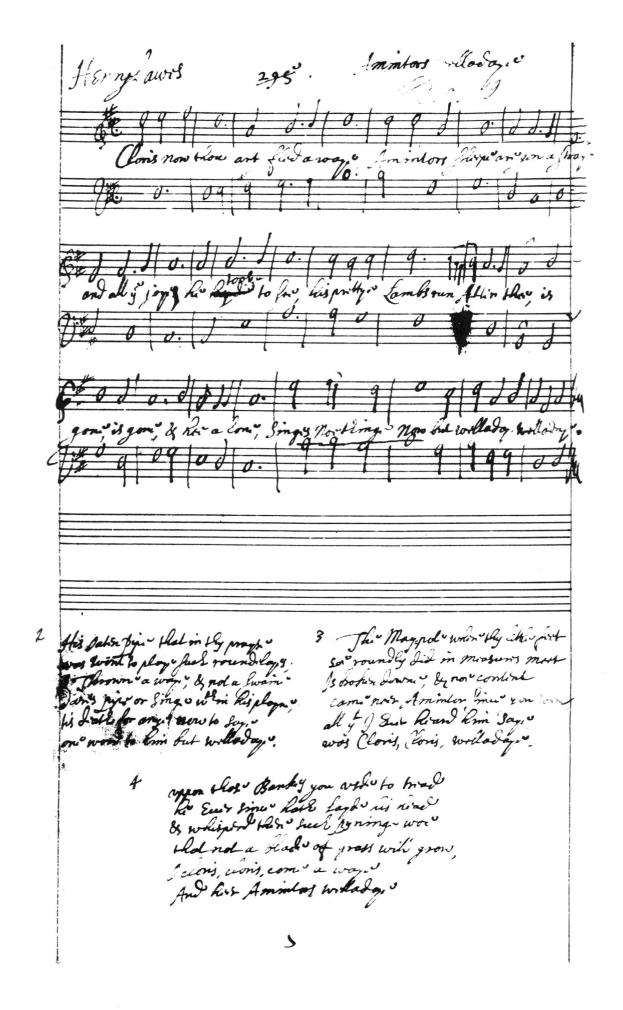

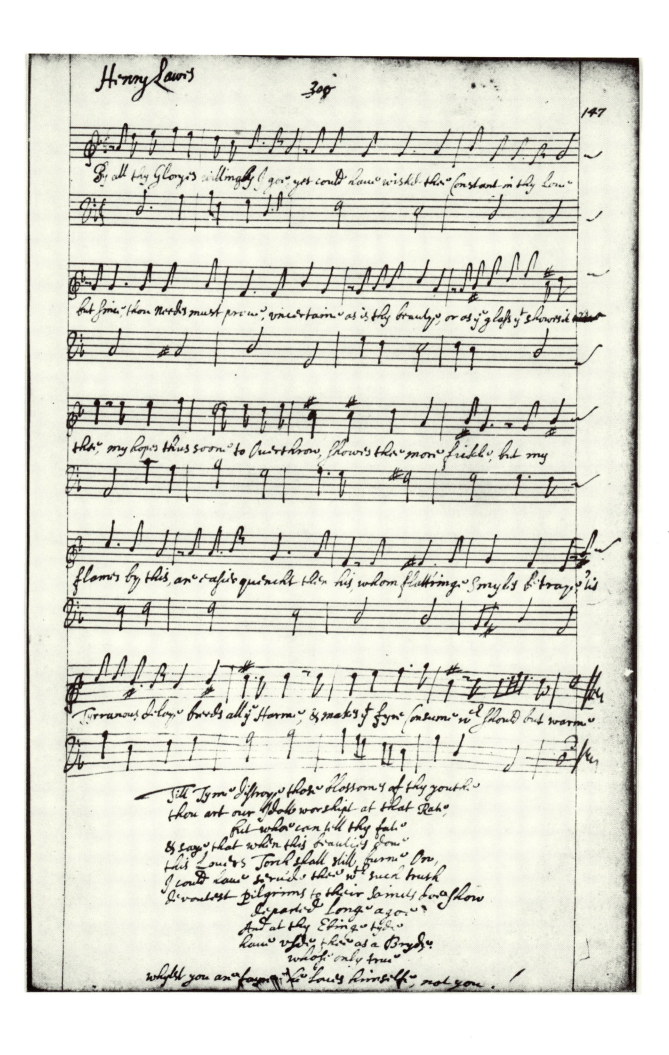

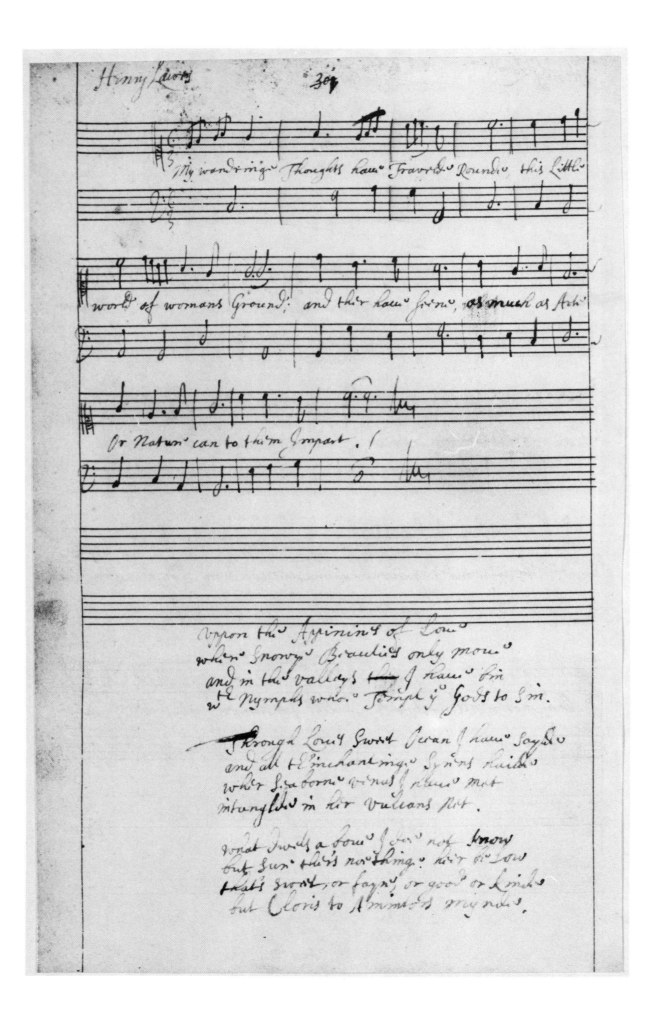

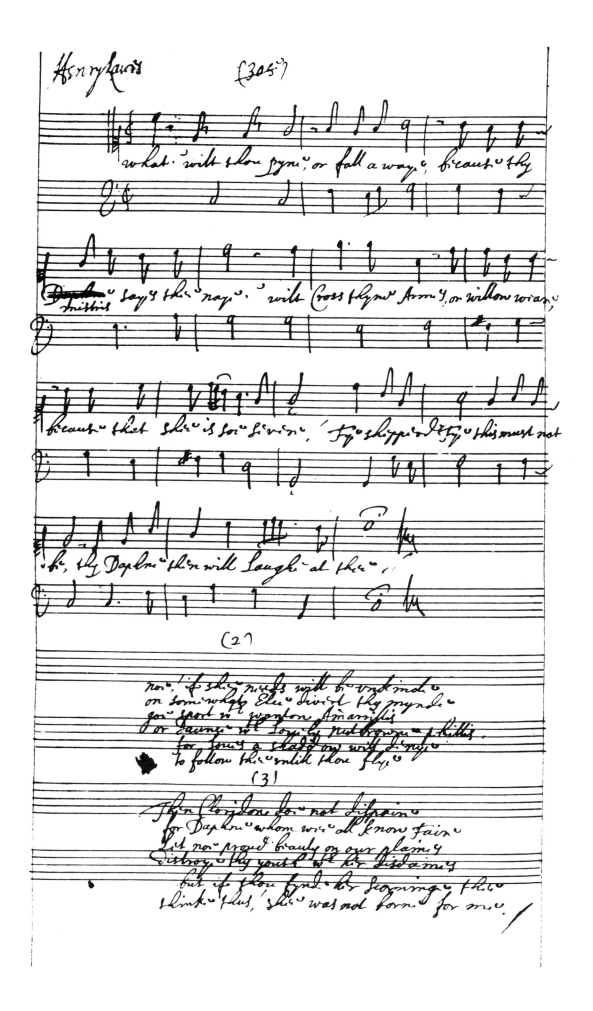

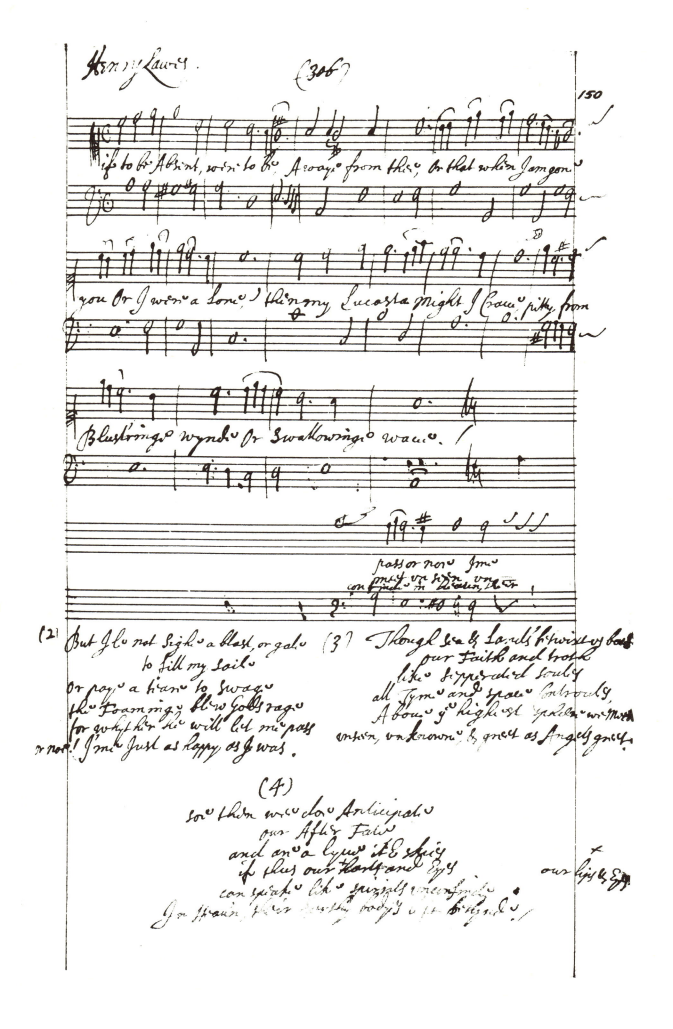

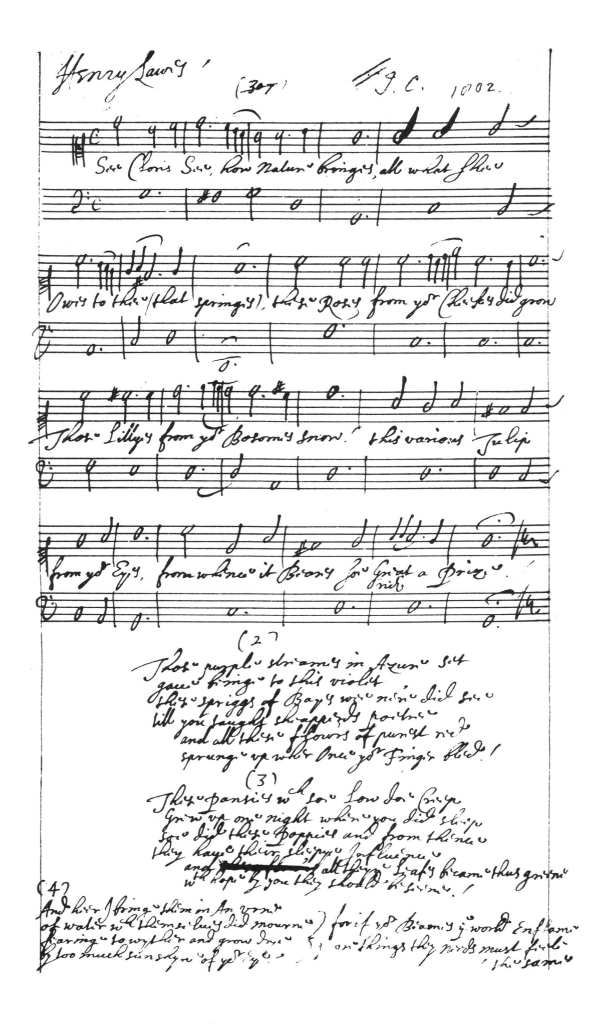

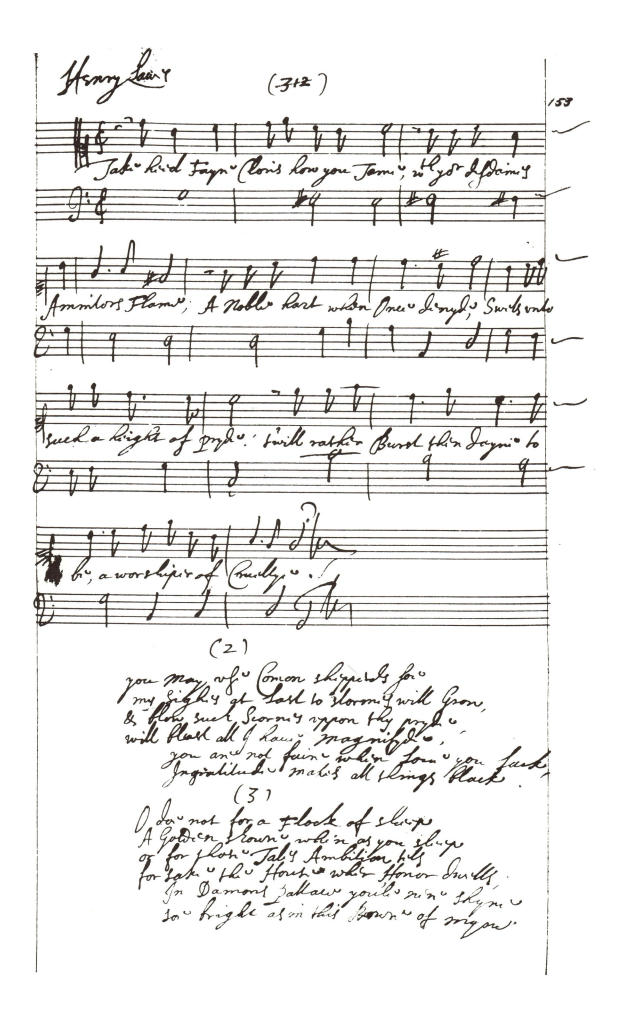

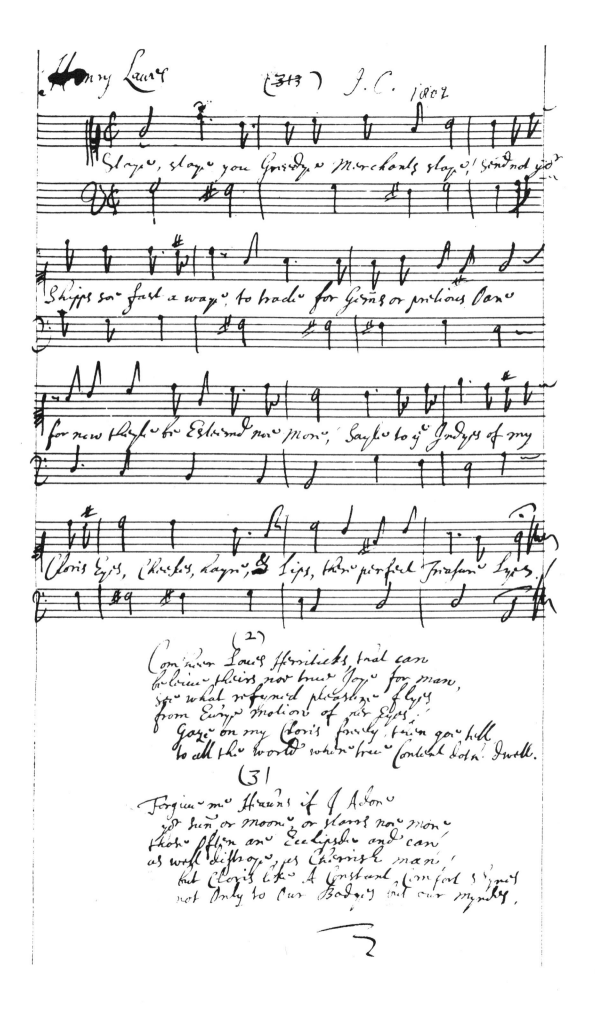

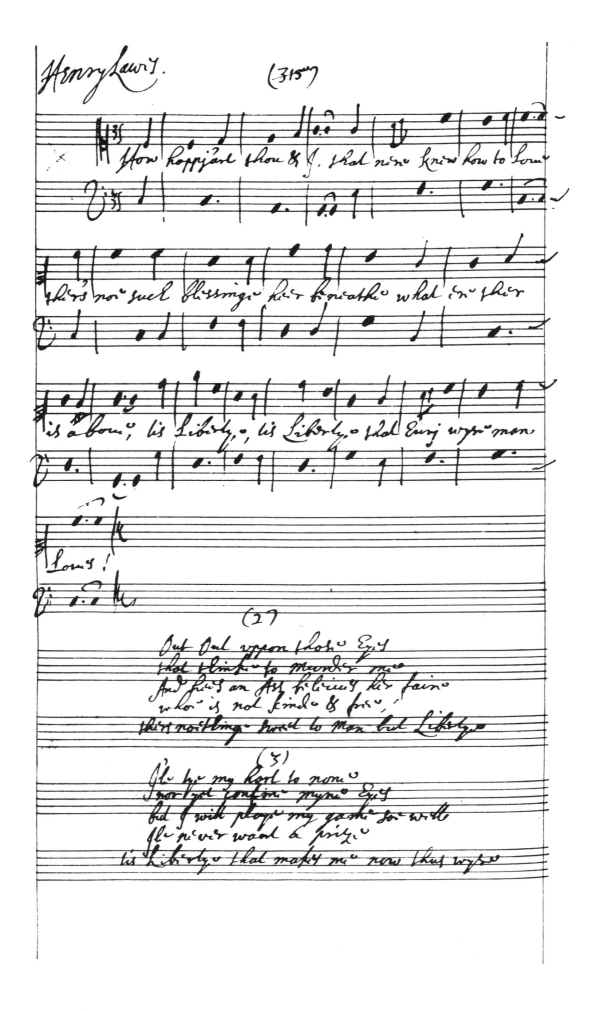

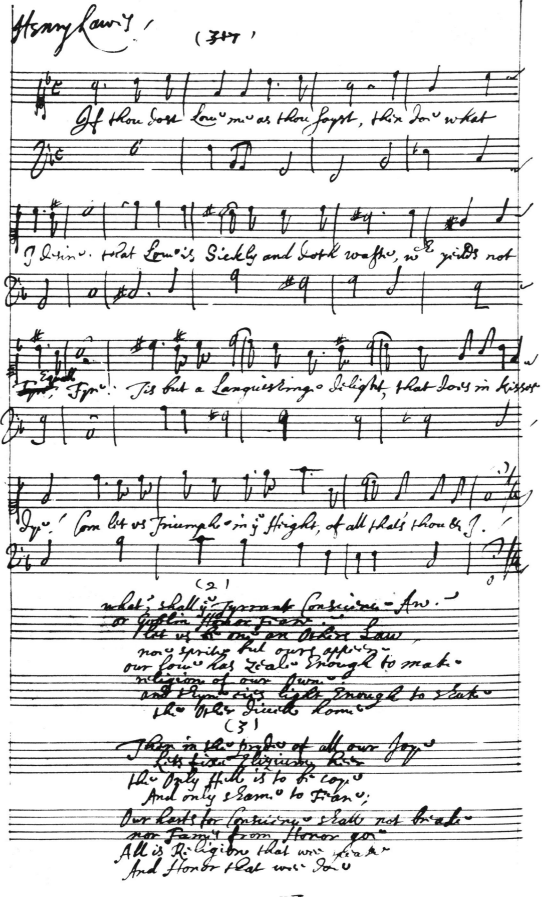

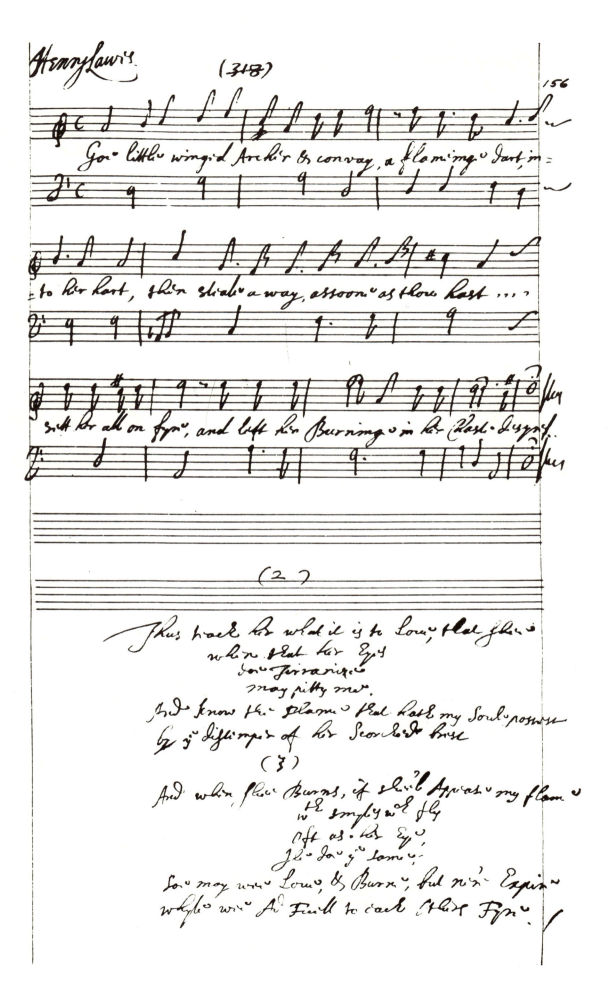

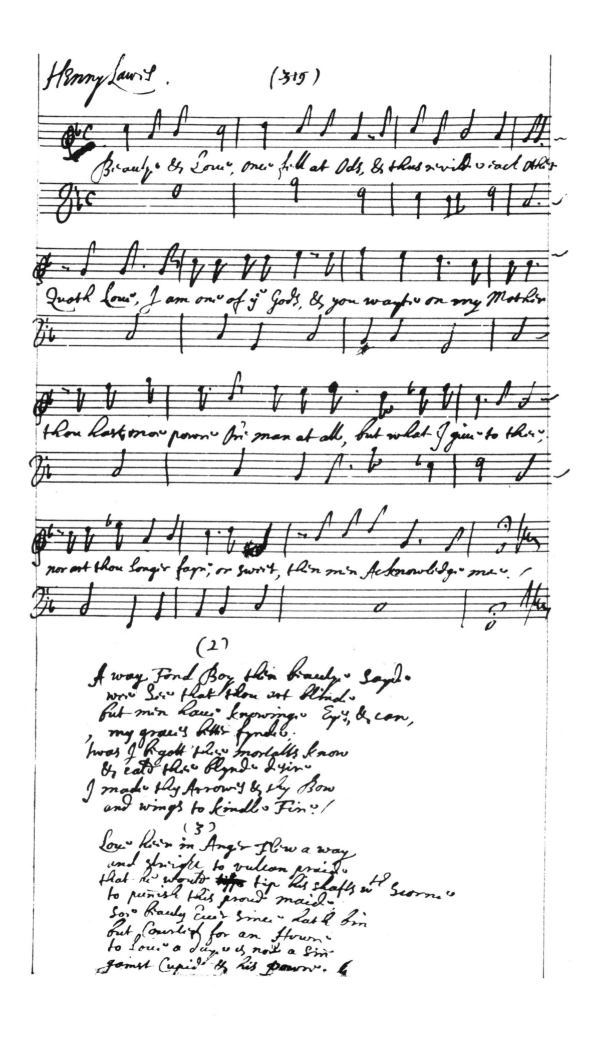

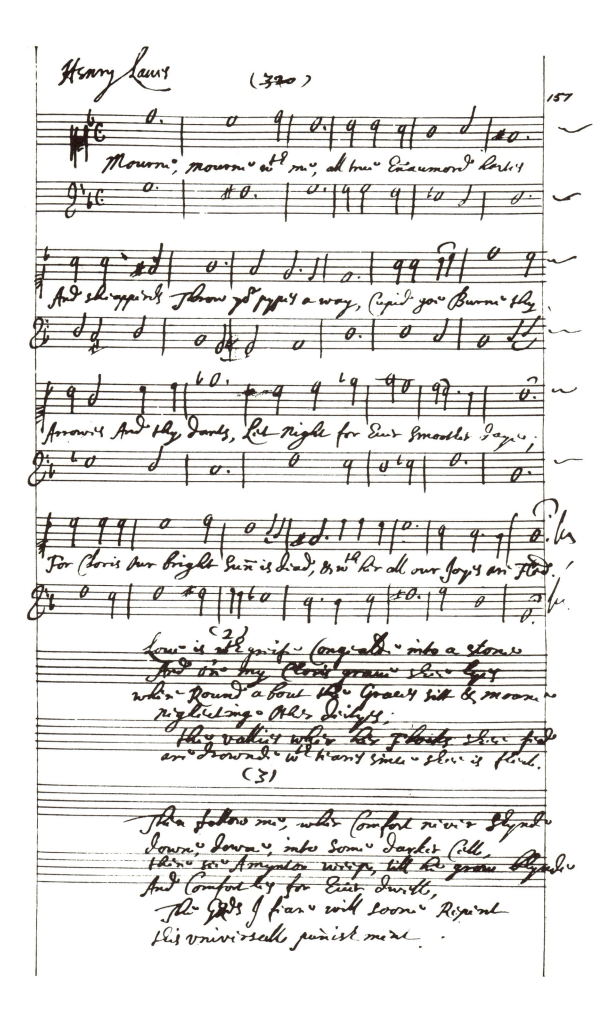

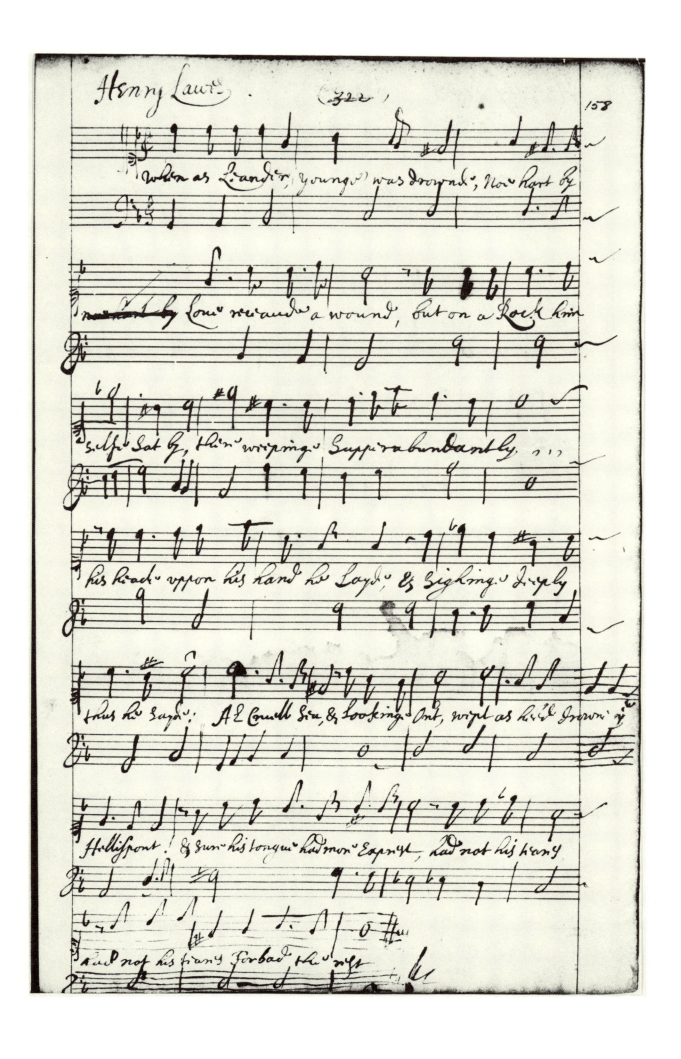

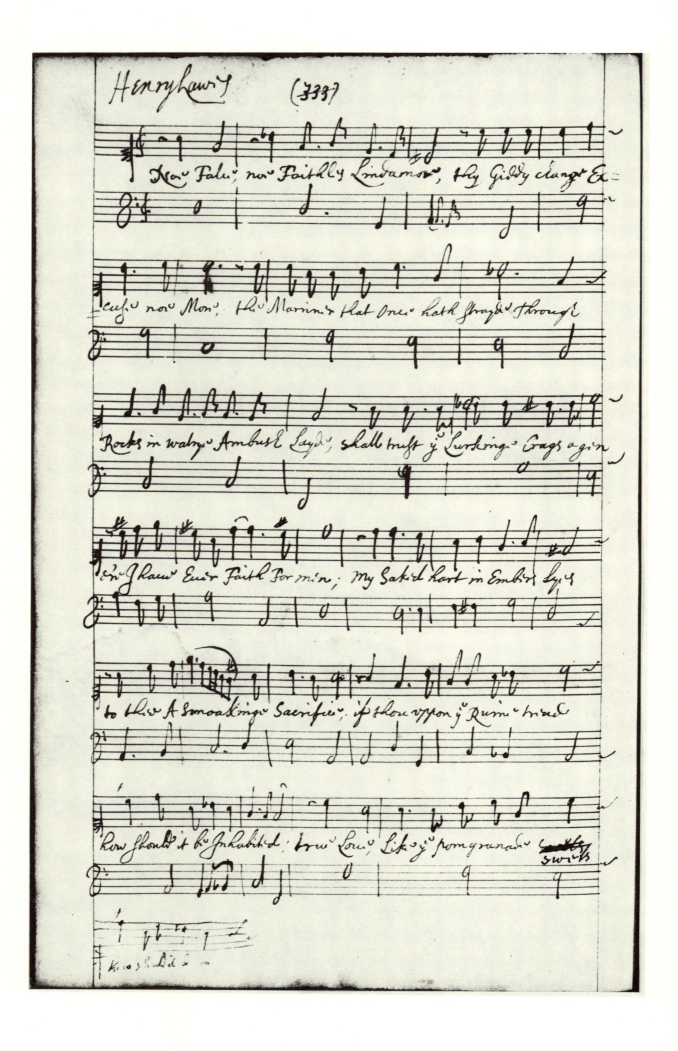

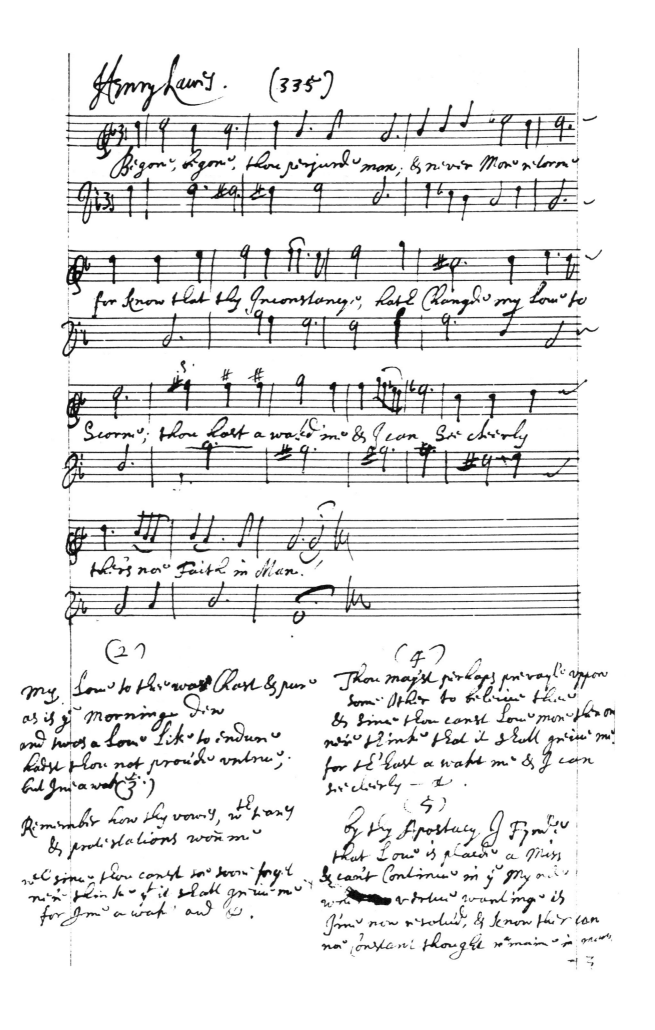

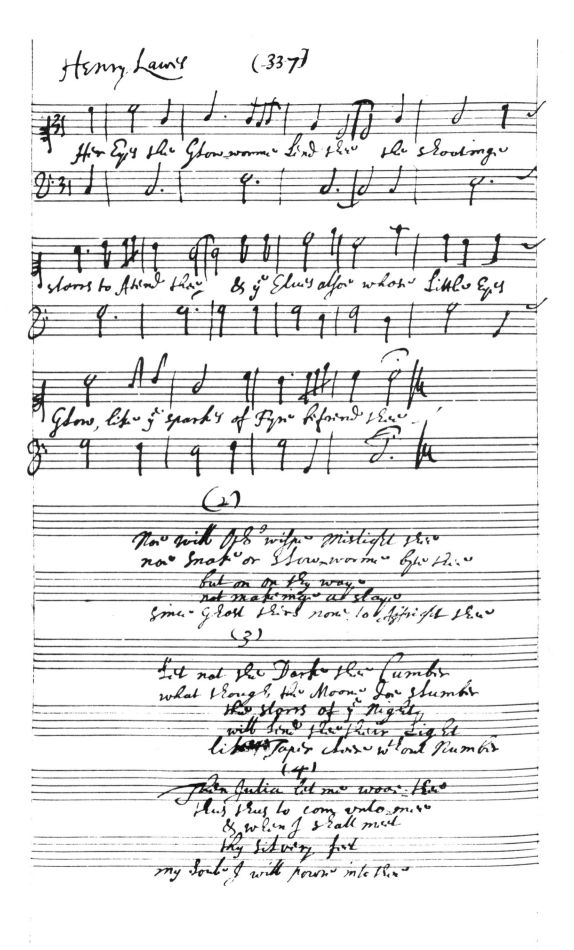

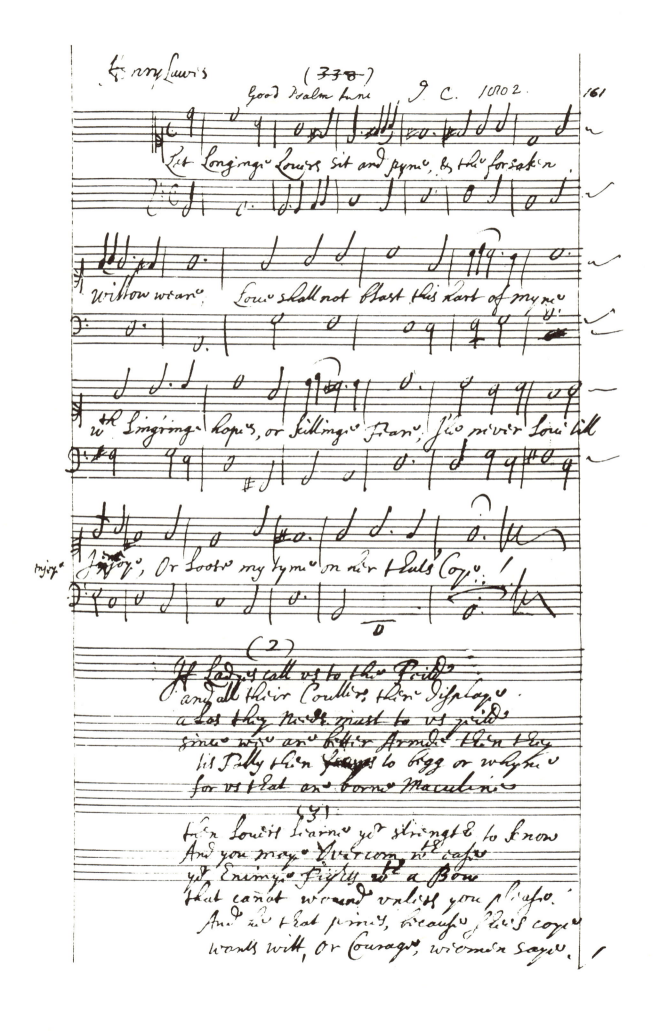

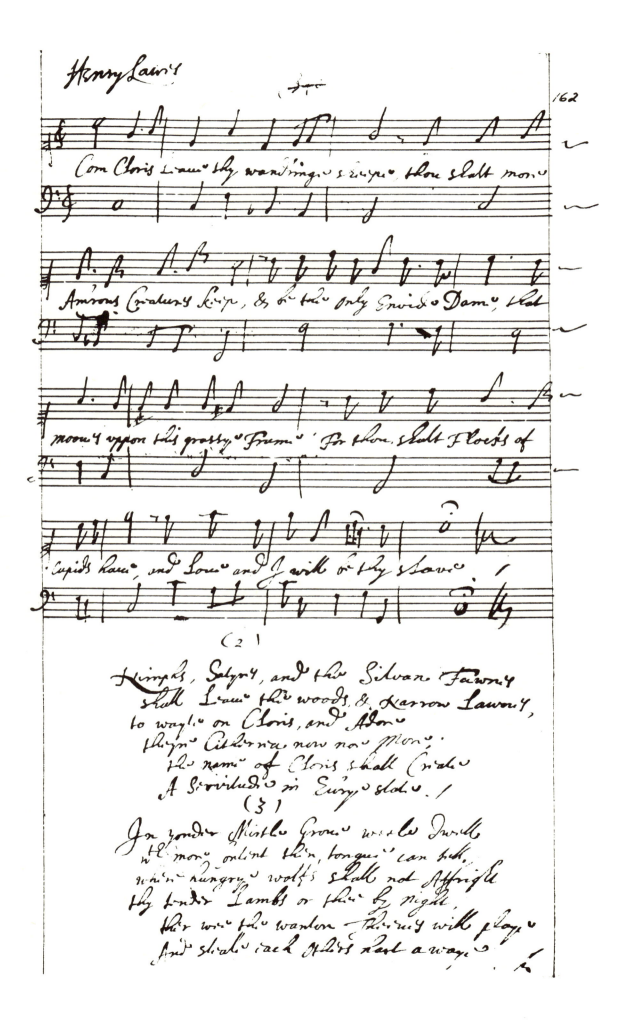

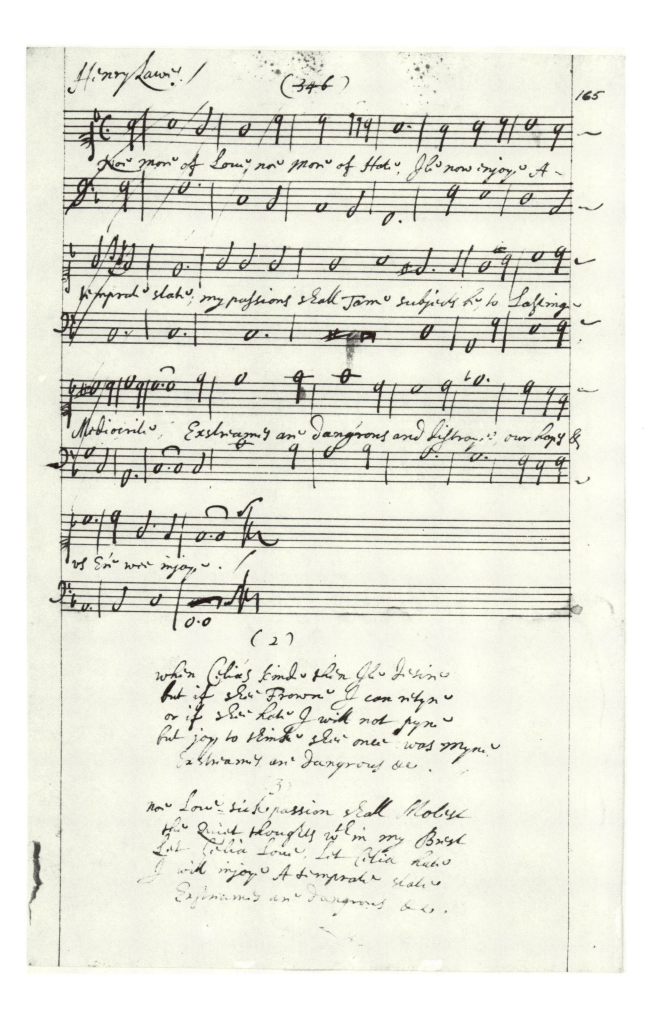

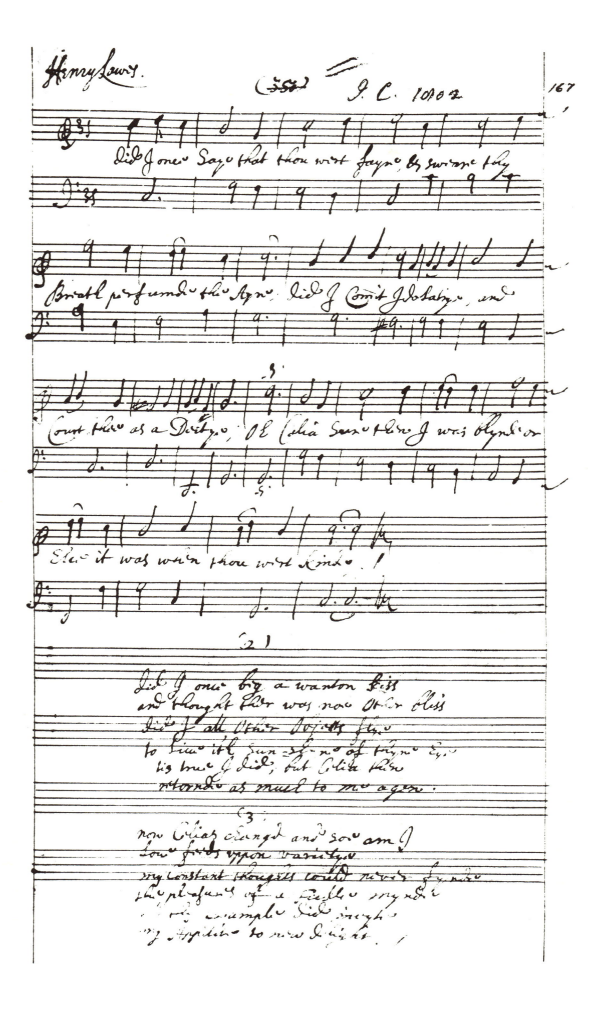

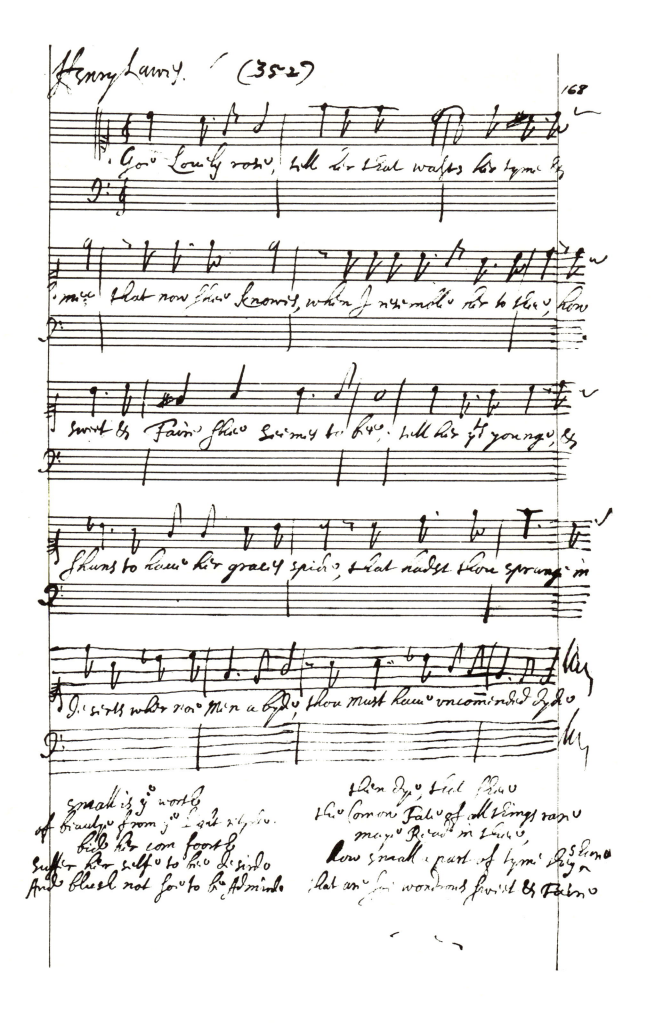

Henry Lawes.

Let not thy Beauty make thee proud
though Princes doe Adore thee; Since tyme and
Sickness win A Lowde to Mow Such Flowrs
For thee.

(2)
nor bee not Shy to that Degree
thy prayd may hardly know thee
nor yet Soe comeinge or soe free
that Every fly may blow thee

(3)
A state in Every princely brow
as decent is required
much more in thyne to whom they Bow
by beauty & Lightninge Fyred.

(4)
And yet a state soe sweetly Mixde
with an Attractive Mildness
it may Like vertue Sit betwixt
th' Extreamity of pryde & wildness

(5)
then Every Eye that sees thy face
will on thy beauty doate
and Every tongue that wags, will grace
thy vertue with a story.

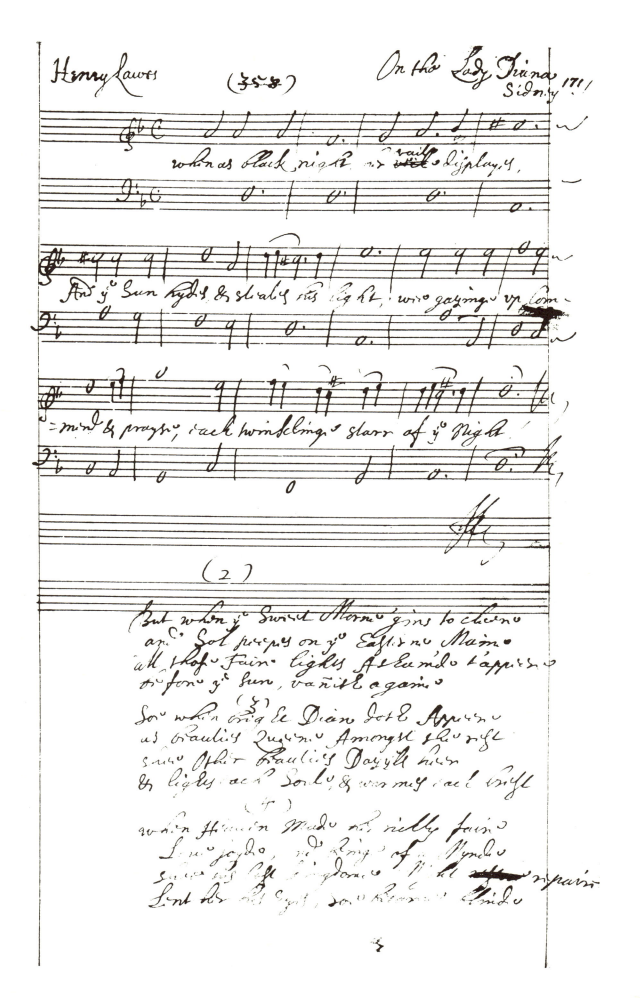

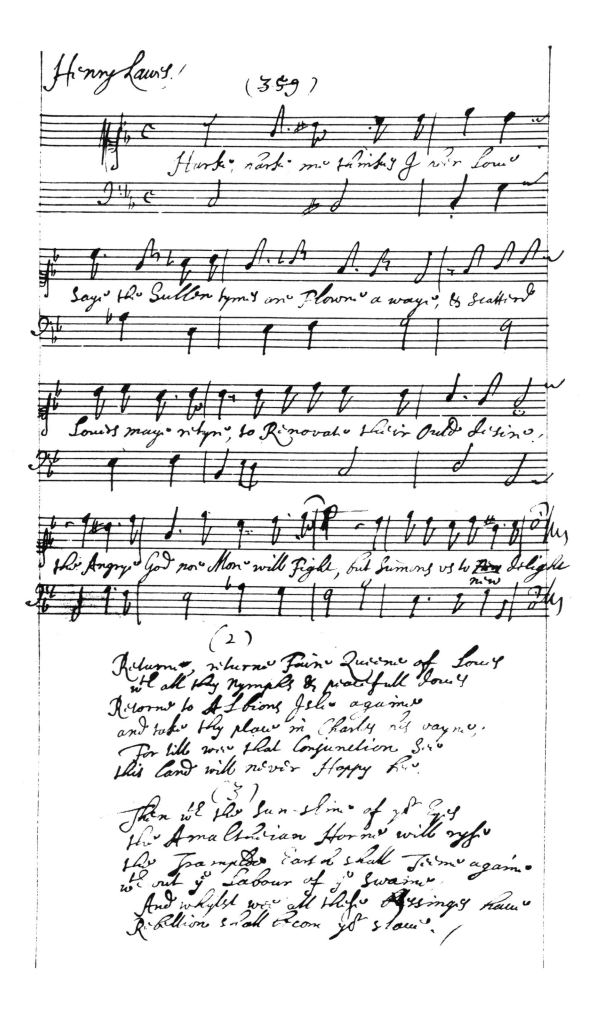

Henry Lawes. (762)

Henry Lawes. (364)

*Goe younge man let my hart alone, 'twill be a prisner
unto none, nor will I Cupids shackels ware, since Lovers
Lawes are for sivirer, Love is my slave, whych I despise
but One I cannot, whilst Tirranizes.*

'Tis Only beauty you Admire
& that's the Object of desyre
wch by degrees turnes to a Flame
& hence Love first receivd its name.
Then younge Man give me leave to dwell
Since Love's a Fyre, and Fyre will —

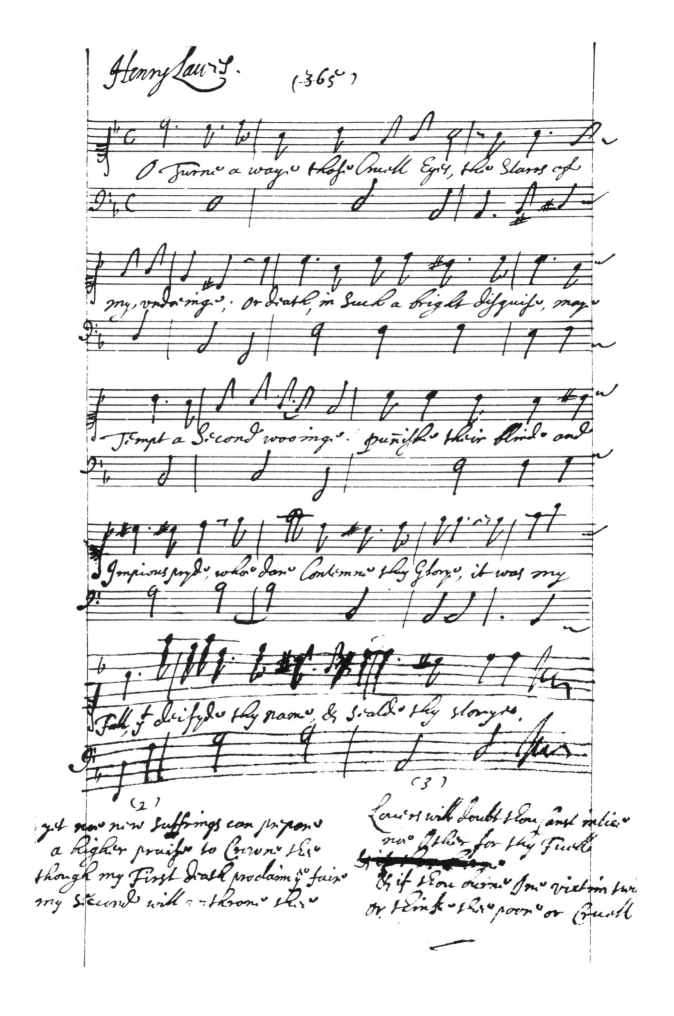

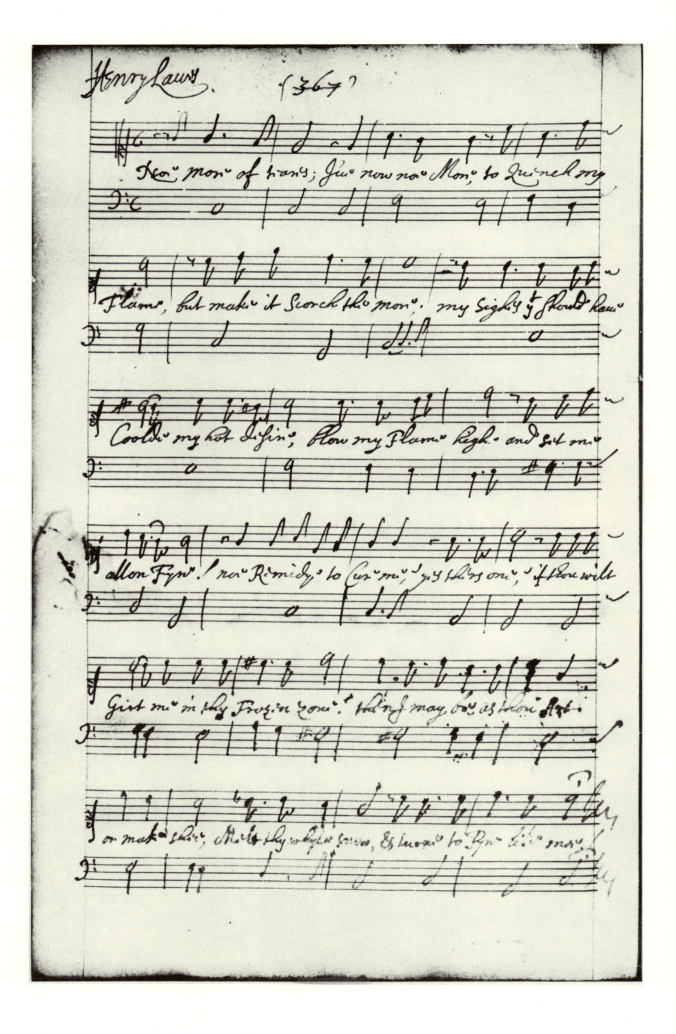

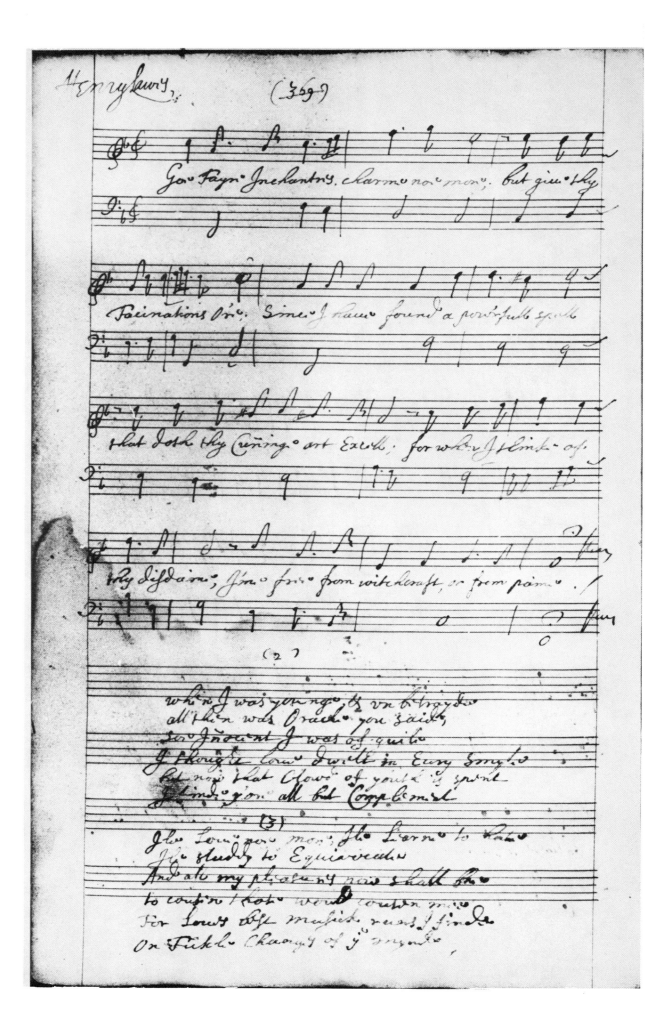

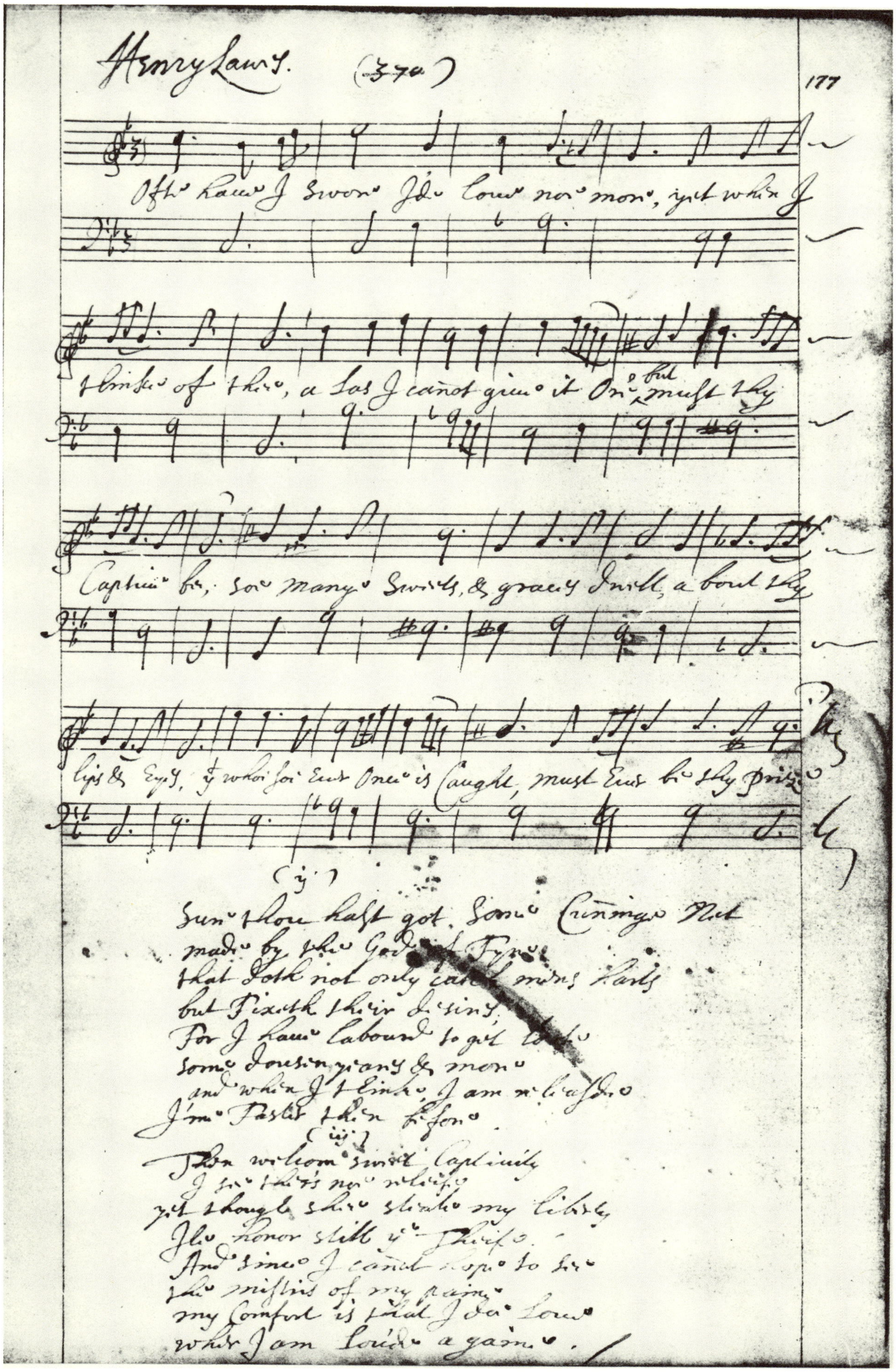

Henry Lawes

Oft have I sworne I'de love noe more, yet when I
thinke of thee, alas I canot give it Ore, but must thy
Captive bee, soe many Sweets, & graces dwell, about thy
lips & Eyes, y't whoe for ever Once is caught, must ever be thy prize.

(ij)
Sure thou hast got some Cuninge Net
made by the Gods of Fyre,
that doth not only catch mens harts
but fixeth their desire,
For I have labour'd to get loose
some douzen years & more
and when I thinke I am releas'd
I'me faster then before.

(iij)
Then wellcome sweet Captivity
I see there's noe releife,
yet though shee steale my liberty
I'le honor still ye theife.
And since I canot hope to be
the mistris of my paine,
my Comfort is that I doe love
where I am lov'd againe.

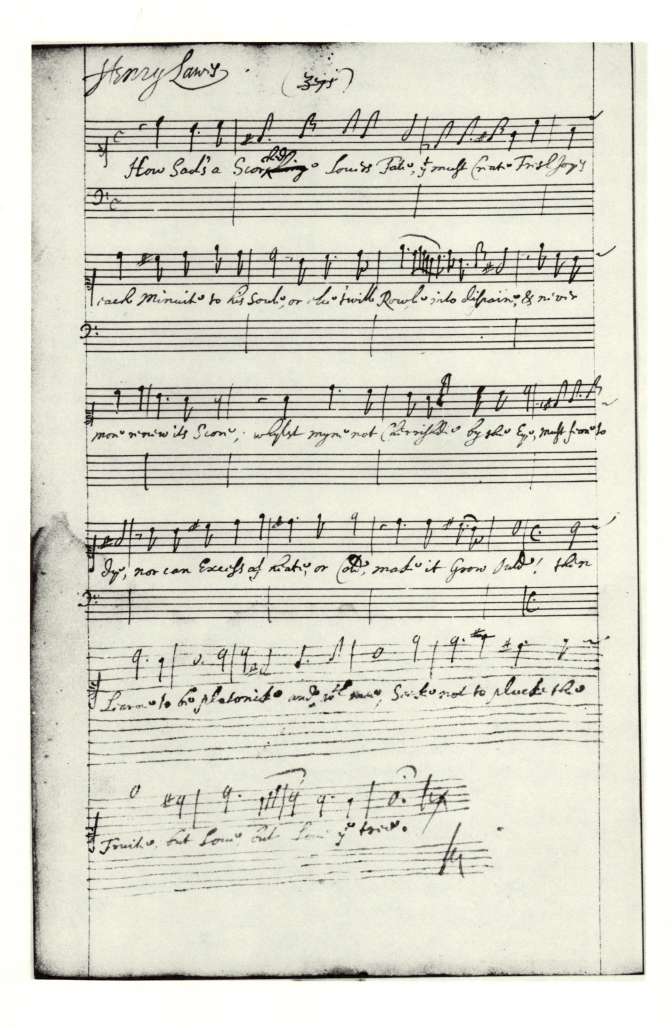

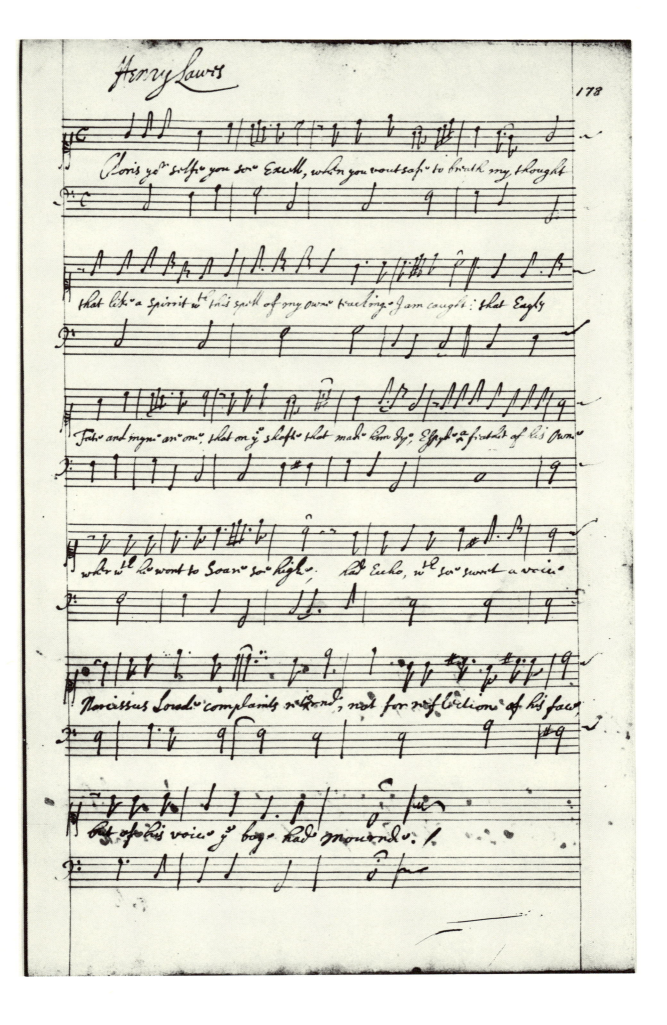

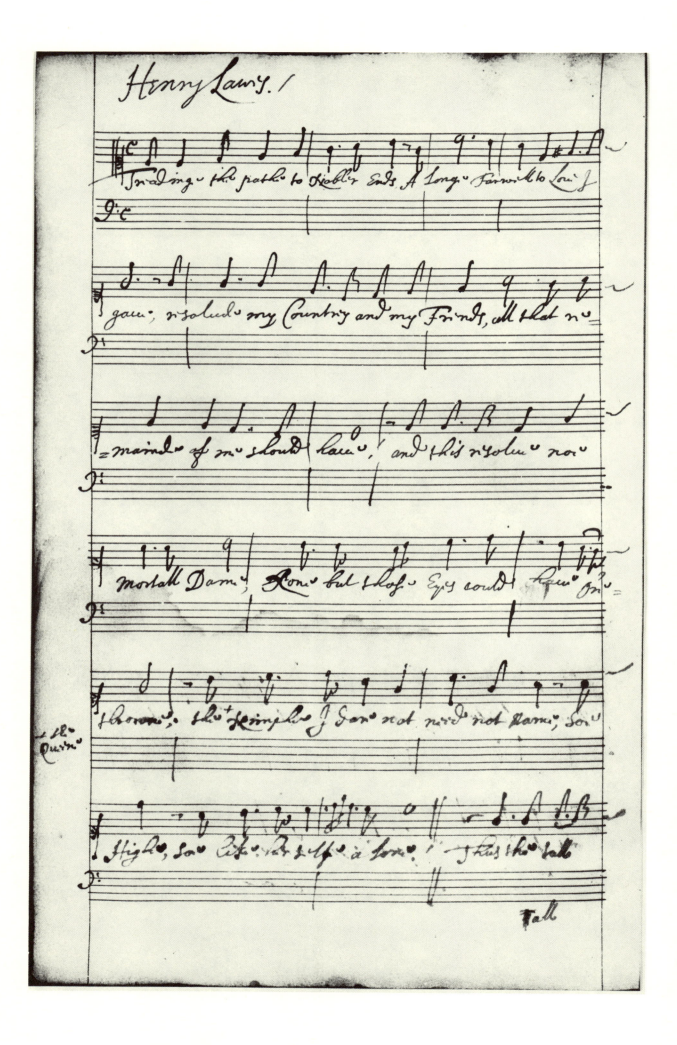

Oke wch now Assyria, a bove ye Fear of private fyres
Growne and designed for Nobler use, not to make
warme; but Build the House, though from our
meane Flames secure, must that wch Falls from
Heavn Endure.

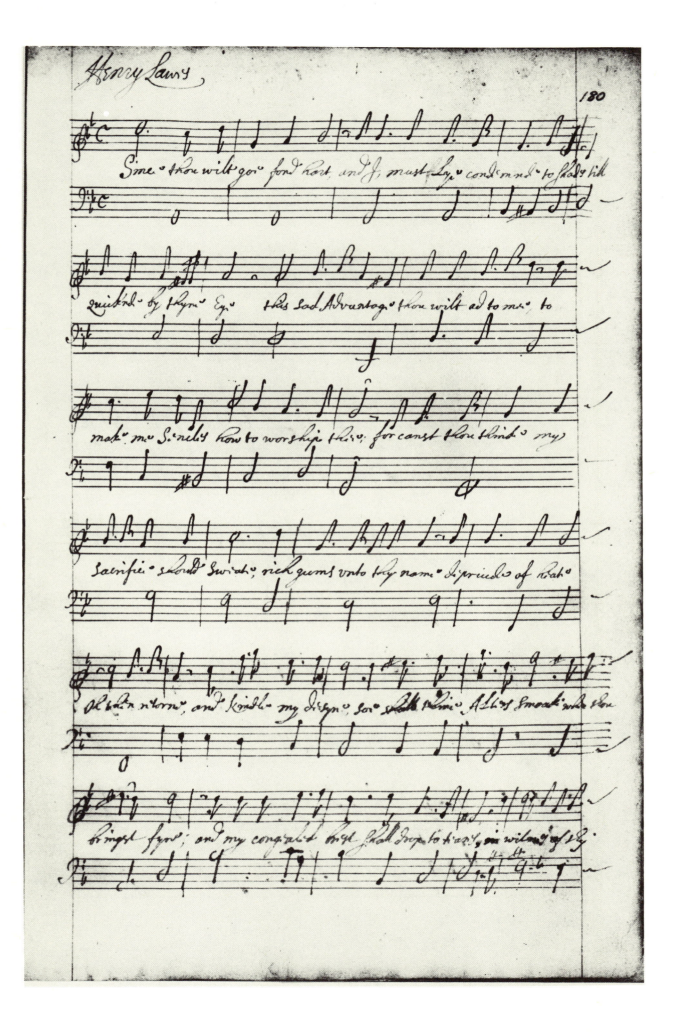

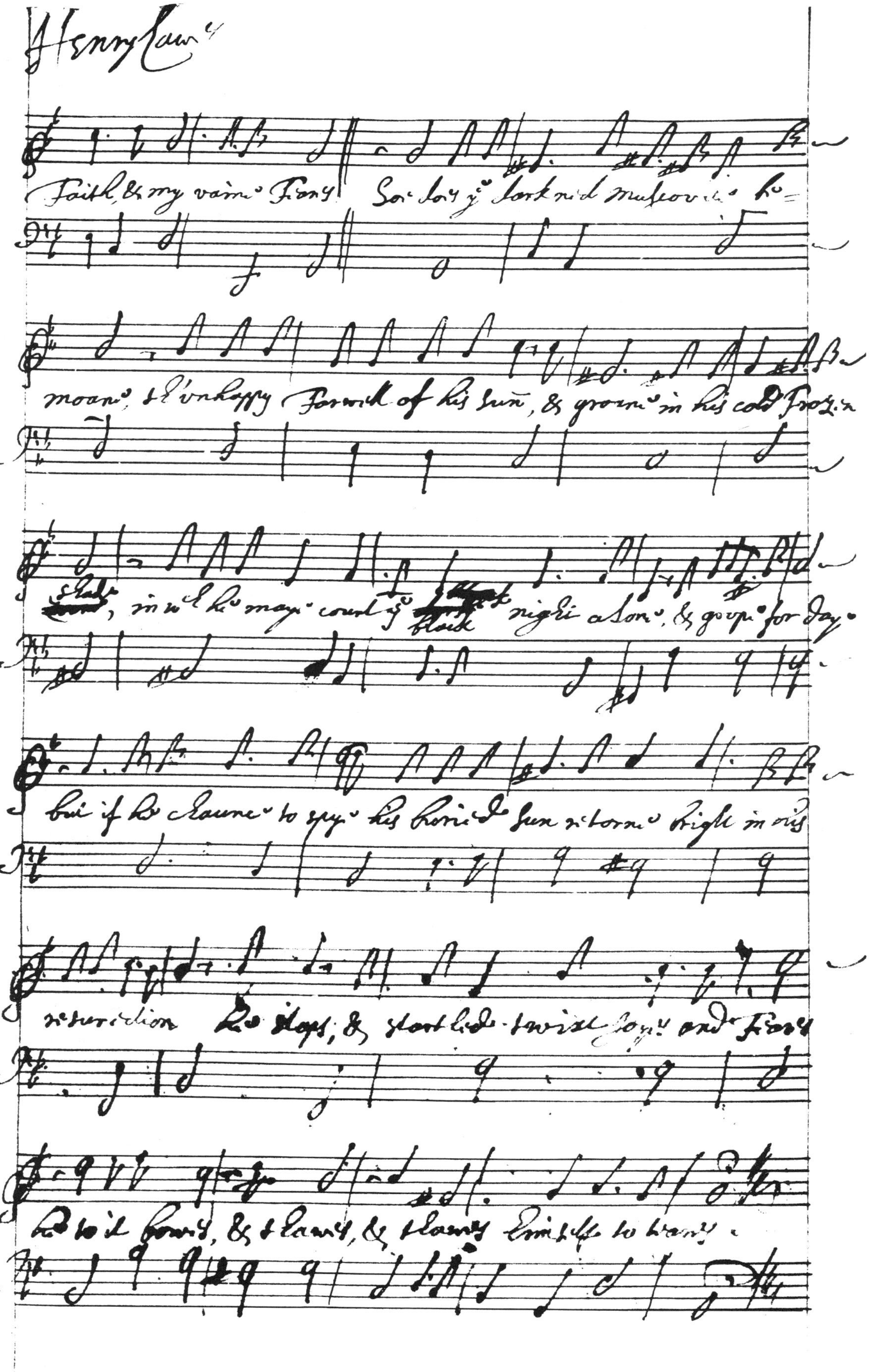

Henry Lawes

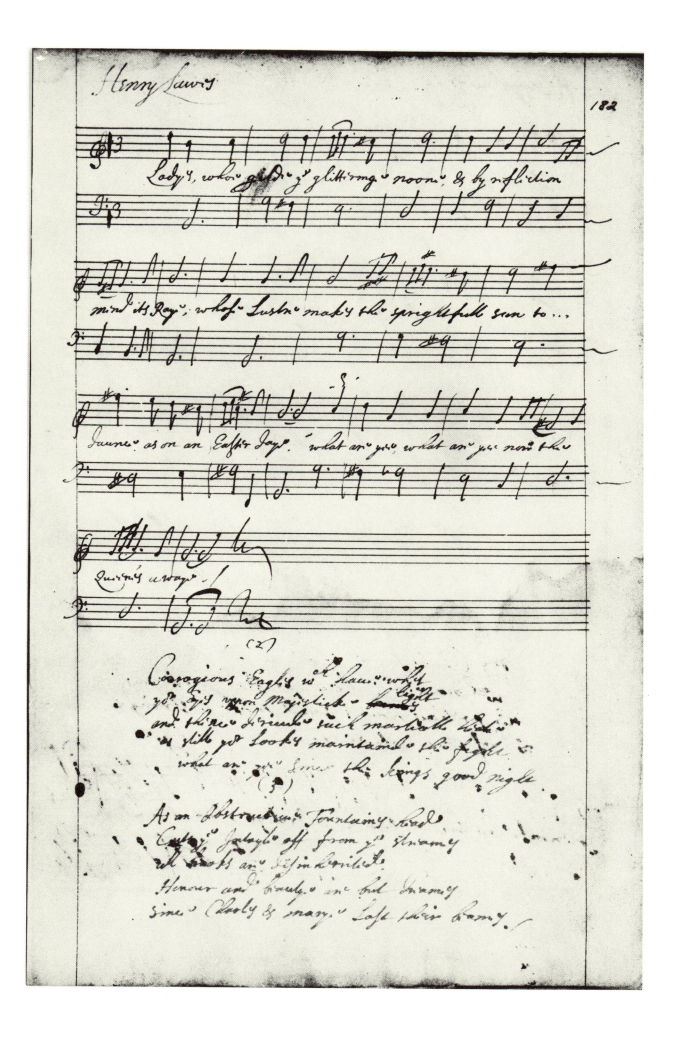

Henry Lawes.

Alas poor Cupid art thou blynd; canst not thy
bow & arrows finde. thy Mother Sure the wanton
playes, & Layes em up for hollidayes.

(2)
Then Cupid harke how kinde I'le bee
because thou once wert soe to mee
I'le Arme thee wth such powerfull darts
shall make thee once more God of harts.

(3)
My Cloris Armes shall be thy bow
wch none but Love can bend you know
her pretious Eyes shall make yt stringe
wch of themselves wound Every thinge

then take but arrows from her Eyes, & altyd's Lord at surely dyes

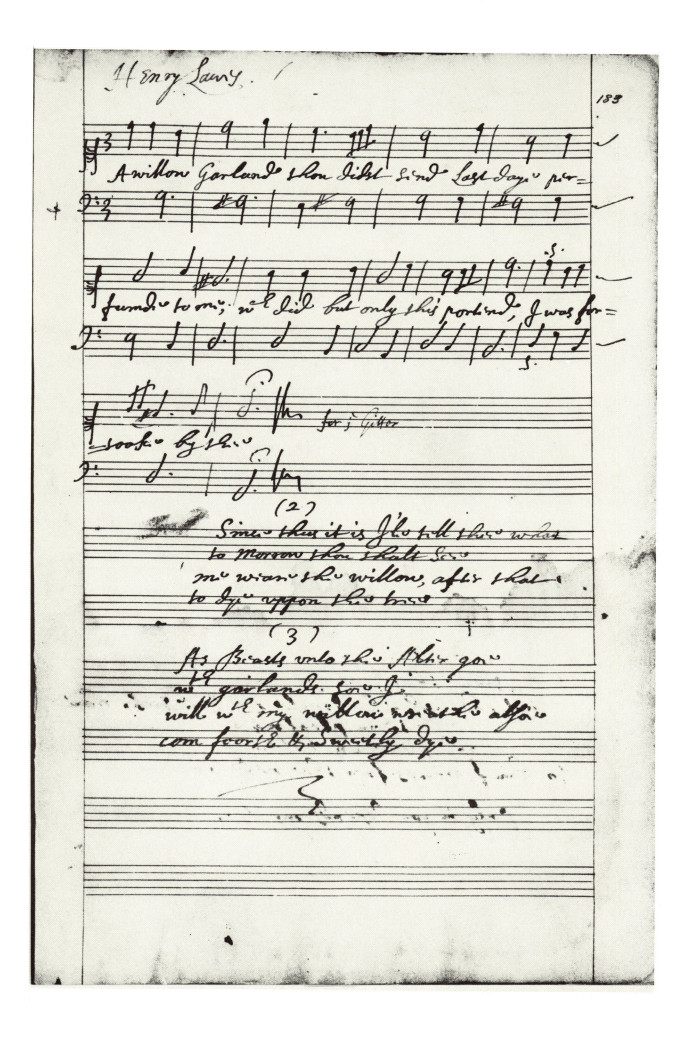

Henry Lawes.

for the
Gitter

when I adore thee, sweet, & I implore thee
would'st thou but prove me, how much I love thee

why then unkindly look'st thou frown on me
o then I know thou soon would'st pitty me

Only in you depends my lifes sustaining, nor fear I

Ought death then your disdain.

(2)
Do not despise me
since thus I prize thee
but cherish with a smyle my love sick hart
O how th'wou't pleasing
and give an easing
to him who vows from thee nere to depart

Only in you depends my &c.

If I seek t'enjoy ye fruit of my pain
Sce careles slights mee wth endless disdain
yet soe much I love her
that nothing can either remove mee or moove her

'tis not Love, but fate, whose powr I abyd
                    doome
you powr an' you plannets that destiny guide
change yor opposition
It fits heavenly powrs to be mylde of condition,

you only can alter her scorne & her pryde
who mee now disdaineth
for women will yeild
when ye right planett reigneth

A Swaine pursueing a Nimph that flyes him &c.

Swaine: 
Art thou gon in hast &c: not forsake this &c. Oh ye only one ye downes, through ye dimne shades
Runst thou not so fast, fle—— on take this) to ye fields to ye townes, through ye green glad downes

All a long ye playnes to ye highe mountains,
on and downe againe to ye low fountains.
Ecko then speak agen, till thee I follow
And ye floods, to the woods, carry my ladne

Nymph:
Runst show thee ne're so swift, thou shalt not catch me) from thyne Eyes will I fly forever
Let this speedie a shift, to On' matche this) leaving Ayre only seene, mocking thy

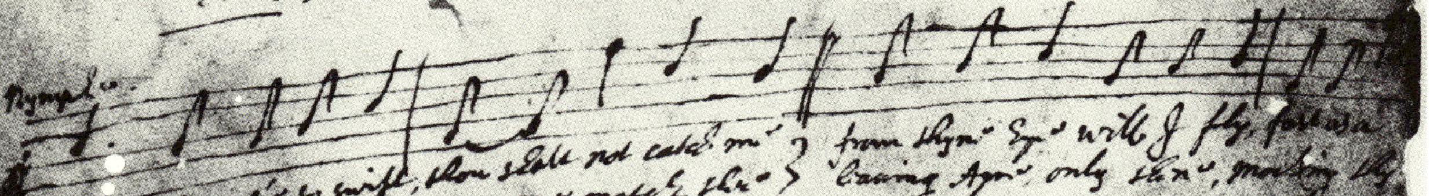

swallow
hallow
——— flies from place to place
if thou pursue mee,
shall thow never
            runne a race
but never view mee,
I will run like ye Nun
chac'd by Apollo
& my words into reed,
turn if thou follow